I'M GRATEFUL TO THE FOLLOWING INDIVIDUALS THAT READ THE EARLY MANUSCRIPT.

I've been fortunate enough to get to know Bill over the years. I love startup entrepreneurs, particularly British ones, who build companies from scratch. Bill has learnt a lot from this experience and many of his pearls of wisdom I agree with and would find useful were I starting a business.

—SIR RICHARD BRANSON
Founder, Virgin Group

Any man who has a Star Wars bar at his head office and a hugely successful business is worth listening to. The good thing is, this book is instantly interesting and readable, it's full of sensible, practical advice from a guy who's been there right from the start and is still there now putting it into practice.

—MARTIN JOHNSON CBE
Captain of England's 2003 Rugby World Cup winning team

Bill's story is extraordinary. His is a brilliant tale for anyone who wants to make a dream a reality.

—DERMOT O'LEARY
Host of *The X Factor*, broadcaster, children's book author

Bill's insights are the most valuable sort, not from theory or a consultant, but from real-world, hard-earned experience. There are lessons in here I can easily apply to sport (and life!), so whatever your team—big, small, business, personal—I can guarantee there's something here to elevate your performance.

—KATHERINE COPELAND MBE
Olympic gold medalist, London 2012, rowing

I have known Bill for over thirty-five years. Our first meeting was back in 1990. With his impressive approach to business and his focus and ambition clear to see, we agreed to become part of the new UK Fuels network.

The company has rapidly expanded since those days and diversified into other areas along with company acquisitions and joint ventures over the years. Nothing was going to stop Bill from achieving his goals in life and growing the company. With Bill's vast knowledge of the fuel industry, he has led from the front, making bold decisions along the way. He has consistently demonstrated an instinct for success, and this book captures those principles with refreshing honesty.

Across the following chapters, you'll find practical lessons shaped by real experience. These are insights forged during decades of building Radius into one of the most respected and innovative global companies. All this comes from someone who understands exactly what it takes to grow a successful business: a true entrepreneur.

—ANDY SHERWOOD
Radius's first customer

IT'S NOT ROCKET SCIENCE

IT'S NOT ROCKET SCIENCE

25 Real-Life Lessons to Help Entrepreneurs Start, Grow, and Lead a Successful Business

BILL HOLMES

Forbes | Books

Published by Forbes Books, Charleston, South Carolina.
An imprint of Advantage Media Group.

Forbes Books is a registered trademark, and the Forbes Books colophon is a trademark of Forbes Media, LLC.

Printed in the United States of America.

10 9 8 7 6 5 4 3 2 1

ISBN: 979-8-90180-018-8 (Paperback)
ISBN: 979-8-90180-019-5 (eBook)

Library of Congress Control Number: 2026901168

Cover design by David Taylor.
Layout design by Matthew Morse.

This custom publication is intended to provide accurate information and the opinions of the author in regard to the subject matter covered. It is sold with the understanding that the publisher, Forbes Books, is not engaged in rendering legal, financial, or professional services of any kind. If legal advice or other expert assistance is required, the reader is advised to seek the services of a competent professional.

Since 1917, Forbes has remained steadfast in its mission to serve as the defining voice of entrepreneurial capitalism. Forbes Books, launched in 2016 through a partnership with Advantage Media, furthers that aim by helping business and thought leaders bring their stories, passion, and knowledge to the forefront in custom books. Opinions expressed by Forbes Books authors are their own. To be considered for publication, please visit **books.Forbes.com**.

01-23-2026 12:59

This book is dedicated to John, without whom I would never have started Radius or probably ever become an entrepreneur. He always cared for the companies he owned and inspired this way of thinking in the people who worked for him. He was also the most generous person I have ever known, and he got pleasure from the people who worked for him doing well. Thank you, John, for your inspiration.

CONTENTS

LIFE BEFORE RADIUS

THE RADIUS STORY

ABOUT THE AUTHOR

Bill Holmes is one of the UK's lesser-known entrepreneurs, who has built his business, Radius, from a small office above a hairdressing salon in the town of Holmes Chapel near Manchester, to a £5 billion global empire straddling five continents. Bill reflects on his forty-year career with wit and wisdom, sharing deep insights into the important lessons he has had to learn along his journey.

Bill covers a range of topics across business, communication, and culture, all elaborated with witty anecdotes as well as real-life examples. These learnings are discussed in a series of twenty-five lessons that prelude each chapter of the book as it twists and turns from the early years before the internet through to the superdigital AI world of today.

It's Not Rocket Science will appeal not only to young people just starting out in their careers but also to older business heads looking for a few tips to help them take on the constant challenges they face as they make the difficult but exciting journey of building a business.

Learn more about Bill and Radius, and see lots of photographs, at https://www.billholmes.me/.

ACKNOWLEDGMENTS

This book would not have happened if Radius had never existed, and Radius only became the global company it now is because of the immense amount of effort put in by my many employees and partners over the last thirty-five years. I can't mention everyone, so I have tried to pick out a few whom I still have vivid memories of because of the fun times we had while working to build the business.

Ron for igniting my passion for sales as well as making sure the team always had some fun alongside the hard work in my early years at Esso, Joe for those Friday afternoons feeding the OKI printers with triplicate NCR paper, Karen for thirty-three years of fantastic work doing nearly every job in the company, Elaine for balancing all the site and customer stocks in the bunker network for nearly twenty years, Steve for all those early mornings at Café Nero in Manchester airport before our visits to Belgium followed by the cold beers at the Moroccan bar by De Pinte Station on our way home, Tom for all the trips to Copenhagen and Stockholm in the critical years for MCS before then helping to start the Telematics division many years later, Mike for saving us from the forty un-networked PCs and all the disks we had to copy every evening at the Sandbach office before we could go home, Malcolm for all the weekly trips to Dublin to see all our suppliers and battle with them on price with the odd fun night at Café on Seine, Colin and Ian for being the great early partners that got our unique JV model up and running with those many Little Chef break-fasts near the Penrith motorway junction, Hugh for all his introductions to the Texaco Distributors when we were just starting out and Gary for all those visits to the Irish border in the late 1990s where we established a market leading diesel network of bunded tanks, pumps, and card readers, Roy for constantly reminding the rest of the team "that you can have volume and margin," Nick for then creating all the spreadsheets that made this possible, Emma for dealing with the ever increasing number of HR issues you get as you scale an operation, Lee who has really helped transform the business in the last decade by doing most things better than I used to do and thus allowing me to begin a new, and hopefully less pressured, stage of my life and finally all my family for the immense support they have given me over many, many years during the ups and downs as well as the sometimes intense strains and pressures that are regular companions on the journey of building a business.

The good news is that we have the strongest ever group of young people coming through the divisions, who will make great leaders as well as great characters in the years ahead. They will be the ones who will really have to transform the company from selling diesel on fuel cards to one that will help customers across the globe embrace the energy transition, as well as the many other advantages that the world's rapidly evolving technology can bring. Hopefully, Radius will be able to play a part in this exciting change.

FOREWORD

7th January 1991—the day that changed my life!

I didn't realize it at the time, but this was my first encounter with Bill Holmes, when I arrived for an interview for the role of Office Administrator at the age of seventeen years old. Back then, the company "UK Fuels Limited" had been trading for 1 year and was made up of just five distributors and twelve sites on the network.

This book brilliantly captures the trials and tribulations of how a small business, based above a hairdresser's, grew to become a recognized one-stop technology solution, with a global presence across five continents.

If you're interested in setting up your own business, or just curious to know what success looks like, then turn the page. You'll be treated to a special privilege: the insight of a brilliant business mind who grew his own empire.

Bill's story shares what works, what doesn't, failures, and successes along the way, tips on getting the very best out of people, systems, processes, plus heart-warming stories of Bill's own personal life. It's interesting, creative, funny, and most of all real.

This isn't just about the development of a business, it's so much more. Bill also provides a great insight into the rewards achieved through hard work, focus, integrity, and commitment. His success is immeasurable when you look at how many people's lives have also been changed, again demonstrating his ambition to see others succeed too.

I will be forever grateful for the day that I entered the world of Bill Holmes, and feel proud to call him my friend.

Read the book and share his journey.

—KAREN SHONE
Second employee who became Group Operations Director–
Telematics before retiring in summer 2022

AUTHOR'S NOTE

WHO AM I, WHAT DOES RADIUS DO, AND WHY THIS BOOK?

Hello, reader, good to meet you. I'm Bill. Let's do the basics and then dive in. I was born in the village of Chislehurst, South East London, on 16th March 1964, and went to school at St Dunstan's College in Catford. I studied mathematics, physics, and chemistry at A level before going to the University of Leeds to learn biochemistry. In my first year at Leeds, I won the Crabtree prize for outstanding academic performance before going on to achieve a first-class honors degree in 1985. After finishing at Leeds, I went on to join Esso Petroleum, a subsidiary of Exxon, on their sales and marketing graduate scheme, where my first job was as an area manager selling bulk fuels, including diesel, gas oil, kerosene, and fuel oil, to commercial customers in the North West of England. Following a move to London, where I worked for two years in corporate planning, I left Esso at the end of 1989 to found Radius.

Radius started its journey on 8th January 1990, in a small flat above a hairdresser's shop in Holmes Chapel, Cheshire. I was backed by two financial partners who invested a total of £58,000 of capital into the original business, UK Fuels. Radius is now one of the largest private companies in the UK, with a turnover approaching £5 billion and employing nearly three thousand people. It operates in over twenty countries across five continents and has more than fifty offices, including a state-of-the-art global telematics hub at Arden Square in Crewe. Revenue has grown every year since inception, even during the difficult years of the COVID-19 pandemic. Profit has also grown relentlessly during this period, without a single blip in the financial results, and EBITDA now exceeds £130 million per annum. After twenty-five years in the fuel card business, driven nearly entirely by organic growth, Radius has now expanded to include six divisions across telematics, telecoms, insurance, vehicle leasing, EVs, and energy. These divisions provide mobility and connectivity solutions across the globe to more than four hundred thousand customers with over two million vehicles. This rapid expansion was helped by a period of M&A, when we acquired more than twenty-five companies in less than three years. The telematics business is now one of the fastest-growing industries in the world and offers a full range of solutions, including vehicle tracking, asset tracking, and dashcams.

I've won several industry awards since founding the business, including the 2014 EY Entrepreneur of the Year for business products and services and the Lloyds Bank 2017 Entrepreneur of the Year. Radius is still majority owned by my family and has regularly featured in *The Sunday Times* HSBC Top Track 100 league table.

I've created more than sixty millionaires while building Radius, with many of these partners and employees receiving £5 million, £10 million, or much more as a result of the unique long-term share incentive scheme I introduced. My family and I, who own more than 60 percent of the group, also regularly feature in *The Sunday Times* Rich List, in which, according to the 2024 edition, I'm "richer than the king." That got a few jokes from my friends! My family was also on the UK Giving List in 2024 because of the many conservation projects my two daughters and I fund through our charity, The Helvellyn Foundation, founded during COVID-19.

In my downtime, I enjoy walking, sailing, skiing, drumming, and spending time with the family. Alongside many trips to Wales, Scotland, and the Lake District, I've walked several of Europe's GR treks and further afield, I've done the Milford Trek in New Zealand, the W Trek in Patagonia, the Inca Trail in Peru ascended Mt Toubkal and Mt Kilimanjaro in Africa, and been on the highest via ferrata in the world on Mt Kinabalu. I also enjoy playing chess, and a quirky claim to fame is that I beat Leonard Barden, the former British Chess Champion, when I was twelve.

My aim in this book is to pass on some of the experience I've gained over nearly forty years of work to those of you who are students or just starting your working lives and to more experienced business-people who still have the zest for work that continues to excite me. I don't expect you to agree with every one of the twenty-five lessons, but I do hope that some will strike a chord and save you the many years of hard work it's taken me to learn them!

The lessons are woven into the story of the business, preluding each chapter as I weave through time, from the starting of the business in 1990 to building it into the nearly £5 billion turnover company it is today. I hope you enjoy the story.

—BILL HOLMES

THE TWENTY-FIVE LESSONS I'VE LEARNED

1. Care for every pound as if it's your own.

2. Start before you're ready.

3. Sell what you've got.

4. Compartmentalize.

5. Do more of what's going well and stop when it isn't.

6. Don't spend too much time and effort hunting whales.

7. Make lots of small improvements.

8. Relentless performance management.

9. Do things in the right order.

10. Tell your boss.

11. Ask your boss.

12. Don't believe anyone; test everything.

13. You can have volume and margin.

14. Think everything's going badly.

15. Never blame the market.

16. Don't wear rose-tinted spectacles.

17. Organic growth is best.

18. Bide your time.

19. Own your own customers.

20. Reward over the long term.

21. Don't let software projects grow legs.

22. Work from the office.

23. Keep moving your people.

24. Get your reporting structure right.

25. Never stop learning.

INTRODUCTION

I WISH I HAD KNOWN THEN
WHAT I KNOW NOW

I'm not sure what happened on the night of 28th January 2021, but I woke up that morning and started thinking about chapters for a book, so here we are. Not having written before and having been especially bad at English at school (I got a C at O level), I don't have high expectations of creating a literary masterpiece, but I hope that if you can give me a chance by making it through to the end, you will pick up something useful along the way. (If you're not familiar with the UK's education system, O levels were the national exams that used to be taken at about age sixteen. Think of them as our equivalent of final exams during high school in other countries, just with more tea breaks.)

Good businesses can be started and run in different ways, with vastly differing cultures and principles, so this is not meant to be the perfect or only blueprint for what to do, but more my story and the things that have worked for me.

So, first things first: What's with the title *It's Not Rocket Science*? Well, it's a phrase that I've used frequently over the years, often when explaining to managers that what I am asking them to do is not as complicated as it might first appear. In their defense, many common-sense business concepts can only be seen that way after you've actually tried them. Helping others get comfortable with that is a key aim of this book.

The phrase *it's not rocket science* became an idiom around the time I was entering the world of work, with the first recorded printed use being in 1985 by a football hack on the Pennsylvania newspaper *The Daily Intelligencer*. By 1990, the year Radius began, it was a popular saying across the world. So I can't claim to have coined the phrase; I'll just have to lay claim to being the first person using it regularly in a small office above a hairdressing salon in Holmes Chapel, twenty-five miles south of Manchester.

So, how is the book going to work? Well, I have cooked together some of my business experiences and learnings, alongside telling the thirty-five-year story of Radius, throwing in a handful of stories I hope you'll find amusing and then baking it all into something that's both easy to read and a little educational.

So, back to the title of this chapter, "I Wish I Had Known Then What I Know Now." You probably have heard older people say this when referring to how they might have done things better or faster in the past with the knowledge they have now accumulated. Well, this is the driving force behind my aim to fast-track you with this book in just a few short hours, something which has taken a lifetime for me to learn.

Let's begin with a little personal history from my early years before we start talking business.

LIFE
BEFORE
RADIUS

MY NORTHERN ROOTS

Let's go back to the very beginning and give you a bit of background about my parents and family. My father, Edward Stanley Holmes (Stan), was born in Newcastle on 27th May 1930, which is why I still keep an eye on the football results even though it's never been my sport. Dad always talked about the good old days of the 1940s and 1950s, when Newcastle United was regularly near the top of the division and Jackie Milburn was playing, which is what they need a little of now, given their form during the last few years! The good news is that there have been some big changes for the Magpies, and they now have new Saudi owners, so hopefully some better times lie ahead. I had to go back to this page before I signed off the final edit, as they have now won their first title in seventy years. "Howay the lads!" as they say in Newcastle.

His father (my grandfather), another Stanley Holmes, was born just before the turn of the century and fought at many of the famous World War I battles, including Ypres and the Somme. When Dad used to show us old photos of Grandad, he always pointed out the wound stripes on Grandad's uniform that signaled how many times he had been shot during his various encounters on the front line. Twenty years later, during World War II, when he was too old for action on the battlefield, he still did his thing back home by becoming head of the local Home Guard in Tynemouth. Given what Dad used to say about him, I'm sure that he kept more discipline and professionalism than Captain Mainwaring did in the famous BBC TV sitcom *Dad's Army*!

When I am up in the area, I still go and visit my grandparents' old terraced house in Hawkeys Lane, North Shields, as it brings back great memories of numerous childhood visits there for Christmas and Easter. One story frequently recounted during these visits was of a bomb dropped on their street by a German plane. This resulted in a large piece of the road being blown into the air and then coming through my grandparents' roof into the bedroom, landing in the middle of their bed. Luckily, they were safely underground in their garden air raid shelter, as bombing was a common occurrence, given that the harbor in Tynemouth was the last bit of land before the bombers headed back home across the North Sea to Germany.

Grandad ended his career running a small café for fishermen down by the harbor at Tynemouth, and I can still remember visiting him there with my sister on occasion when I must have only been about five or six. He'd always slip us a few sweets without Mum knowing. He and Grandma also always pushed a few coins into our hands as we headed home after visits, which definitely helped their position as favorite grandparents! In later years, they became mayor and mayoress of Tynemouth, and I still have Grandad's gold mayor medal and chain tucked safely away in the loft as a special memento.

Family car journeys north to the Lake District from London were always full of stories about Grandad's many achievements, mixed in with singing old wartime and football songs that always included "Pack Up Your Troubles," "It's a Long Way to Tipperary," and "Blaydon Races." These songs have stuck with me all my life and have often been sung (very badly) in pubs and on coaches after quite a few beers on a night out.

Before I move on, I need to tell you one final piece of history about Grandad's life, which I only came across by pure chance in the last year or so when we bought a small telecoms business in North Shields called Frontier Group. When I went up to visit the business during the due diligence process, I decided I would see if I could find Grandad's café down in the docks where he had worked in his later years. Although I drew a blank on the café, which looked as if it had probably been demolished, I did come across an article on Google that mentioned how Grandad had helped some Jewish families escape Nazi Germany just before the onset of World War II. Curiosity led me to send a message via LinkedIn to the author, Walter Knoblauch. I was surprised to get an almost instantaneous response of heartfelt thanks for what Grandad had done for him and his family all those years ago, and he said that I must come and see them in Gosforth on my next visit north, and so I did.

Walter and his wife made me feel so welcome and told me that they were just one of many families that Grandad had helped settle in Tyneside during those years when he worked as a business representative on the local council. Their particular story was one of a last-minute dash to the border on the day before war broke out, when Walter was only three years old. They've never forgotten the amazing generosity and kindness that was shown to them in this unknown city and country and the part Grandad played in making it happen. Given some of the things I now know about Stanley Holmes, I think he would be worthy of his own book or maybe even a film! I feel very proud of his achievements and wish I had taken a little more time over the years to talk more to my father about him.

So, back to Dad and a little more about his life. I can't remember having ever heard anything about his very early years, except for the fact that he went to boarding school at St Bees, a small village on the

Cumbrian coast just next to the Lake District. The Lakes, as the district is known, would subsequently prove to be an important influence not only on my life but on our whole family, who have all ended up becoming keen walkers and trekkers. My partner Eleanor and I actually climbed Helvellyn, my favorite mountain, the day before I wrote this paragraph. I did make sure we weren't overtaken by other walkers on the ascent, much to her annoyance, as this was something Dad never liked to have happen whenever we were out on the fells! I did suffer, though, as the following day, I was hobbling around, beginning to realize that I am not as young as I used to be. Following his time at St Bees, Dad then headed for Durham University, where, luckily for me, he would eventually meet Mum, Rosemary Ward. If he hadn't met her, all these words would vanish, and you'd be looking at a blank page.

So now to Mum and her family history. My mother's father, William Ward, was born near Covent Garden in 1902. At that time, there were stables underneath the market. From there, his family moved out to Saffron Walden, where William got his early education and eventually won a place at the local grammar school. After passing his Highers (the old A levels), he headed to Cambridge University to study chemistry, eventually graduating with a first in the early 1920s. Following a postgrad year at Imperial College in London, where he studied chemical engineering, he went on to join Imperial Chemical Industries. His first job was in the research department of Billingham refinery at Teesside in the North East of England.

There he would meet his future wife (my nanna), who also started her first job as a records clerk in the same department as him just a few years later. Nanna was from Longridge in Lancashire, where both her parents worked in the cotton mills. Born in 1907, she was the first girl from her village to go to university, where she studied chemistry and maths at Royal Holloway College in London. She also got a first, which is one of the reasons there was always a family joke about the brains coming from Mum's side of the family.

After a couple of years together, they decided to get married, although not before Nanna had paid back her college fees so her sister could have the money for her studies. They had their first child, Daphne, just a year later, and then two years after that, Mum was born on 2nd April 1936, not very long before the outbreak of World War II.

In 1939, when Mum was just three, Grandad was asked to help design and build a new specialist oil refinery in Heysham Harbour to make high-octane fuel for the new Spitfire and Hurricane fighter planes. Although this was on the other side of the country, my grandparents still experienced regular air raids, as the Germans would frequently empty what was left in their bomb racks over the town after they had attacked the important shipyards just up the coast at Barrow. In a similar situation to the one with my other grandparents in North Shields, they also had a close call when a bomb dropped by a German plane landed next to their back hedge and caused a lot of damage, including the destruction of Grandad's beloved greenhouse.

After the war finished and their time here came to an end, William was posted back to Billingham, where he became technical director and later refinery chairman. Outside work, he was a keen naturalist who studied butterflies, birds, plants, and more. Holidays were full of exploring the countryside, and he was planning to spend much more time on these hobbies after his retirement. Sadly, shortly after a trip to North Berwick to visit the famous Bass Rock, he suffered a stroke and passed away within a few days of his fifty-ninth birthday. This was in 1961, so unfortunately, neither my sister nor I had the chance to meet him.

After the family had returned to Stockton-on-Tees and Mum had completed her eleven-plus, which she apparently failed, Mum was sent to boarding school at Abbots Bromley in Staffordshire. There, she studied the sciences like her older sister, which I don't think she had much choice over. Following school, she went to Durham University to read botany and zoology. These are subjects that would form some of her favorite interests throughout her life and ones that would also percolate down to me in various ways.

Durham University was the place where Mum and Dad met, although their experiences there were very different. Dad arrived there in 1950 to read chemistry; however, sport was top of his agenda. He played rugby, fives, and cricket and even took up rowing. After failing his second-year exams, he left to do his national service in the Signals for two years, where he was posted to Oznerbrook in Germany. I think I got my poor language skills from Dad, as I don't think he learned more than "ein groß Bier, bitte" during the whole time of his posting there! After returning to Durham to retake his second year, he would meet Mum in the botany lecture theater, although I think he was still not working very hard on his studies, as he was now captain of the university rugby team and playing more than ever.

A typical Holmes, Dad persuaded Mum to join the climbing club on their first date, which reminds me of my second date with Eleanor, when I suggested Striding Edge on Helvellyn as a nice, easy Lake District walk. (It is, in fact, anything but nice and easy.) Somehow, Edward managed to scrape out a general degree and left Durham to head back to Newcastle to begin his working life as a sales representative for Esso, selling heating oil to businesses and marine fuel to the many trawlers based in the bustling port of Tynemouth. He lost touch with Mum at that point and got straight into playing rugby for Percy Park RFC and enjoying the start of his working life. He would eventually go on to captain the club, which became one of the cornerstones in his life and a place we would frequently visit on our trips north as children. It also helped him get access to tickets to the rugby internationals for many years to come. He always passed on some of these to me and my siblings when it was virtually impossible to get them, at a time well before today's online marketplaces. Although my brother and I never played rugby to a very high standard, all three of us siblings enjoyed watching and still regularly go to the Six Nations matches.

Mum followed north to Newcastle from Durham a year later, when she started work at the Hancock Museum as a trainee curator. It wasn't until two years after that that she would meet Stan again at a mutual university friend's wedding. Dad was the best man to a rugby pal, Ken Beresford, and Mum was Ken's fiancée's roommate. This time, their meeting wouldn't end after just a year but would last a lifetime. Little did Mum know at the time but her daughter Elizabeth would follow in her footsteps and go on to become the curator of the Mansfield Museum where she would receive an MBE for her "Outstanding Contribution" to the local region.

Within a year of the Beresford wedding, Mum and Dad followed suit on 16th July 1960. The engagement had only been five months long, after a proposal in which Dad had apparently said, "He would carry Mum's rucksack anywhere!" Their honeymoon location, which was mentioned to us many, many times over the years, was Ennerdale in the Lake District at the wonderful Anglers Hotel. The reason for the oft-told story was that Mum was forced to wade across the freezing-cold River Liza, which always sounded like a very believable story, knowing Dad.

Once back from the honeymoon, it was only six months before Dad was offered a job move, promotion, and relocation to London to become sales manager at the Beckenham office. After a week looking round various villages, Mum settled on a small semidetached house in Chislehurst, close to three bus routes and only five minutes' walk from the local shops. Mum set about decorating and gardening to turn the house into a home and ready it for the arrival of their first child, Elizabeth, who was born on 16th February 1962. Not much more than a year later, Mum was pregnant again, so she enlisted Nanna to come down as an extra pair of hands to look after toddler Liz.

THE EARLY YEARS

So my story begins at number 82 Green Lane, Chislehurst, Kent, in South East London, where Nanna reputedly delivered me at home single-handedly before the ambulance had time to arrive, on the morning of 16th March 1964. The clues to my two forenames were mentioned earlier in the book: William and Stanley are my two grandfathers' first names. Before I go on, I must mention another coincidence that happened recently (sixty years later) at my CEO Lee's fiftieth birthday party. I got chatting to a couple who were friends of Lee and Claire, who lived in Chester. I had never met them before, and they had also lived at 82 Green Lane about fifteen years earlier. What a small world!

My education started at a local nursery school, followed by Willow Grove Primary, then on to the local junior school, Red Hill. Red Hill wasn't the best of schools academically, and as my parents were really keen for their children to get the best education possible, they put me in for several entrance exams to local fee-paying schools. I was fortunate to pass one of them and get a place at St Dunstan's College in Catford, where I moved at age eight in 1972. This was the start of a daily commute over the next ten years that would take well over an hour each way, either by bus and train or by two different buses. Bickley station and the number 227 bus became regular fixtures in my life, and this daily journey probably contributes to my being scornful when employees complain if they have to make a fifteen-minute walk in the morning because we can't fit every single person's vehicle into our office car parks!

Many of my commuting hours were spent playing Top Trumps cards with my friends, with our three favorite games being Supercars, Battle Tanks, and Military Aircraft. A Ferrari V12 for its number of cylinders, a Chieftain tank for weight, or a Blackbird spy plane for speed were all winning cards to have in your hand. However, my favorite was the old Aston Martin V8 Vantage, good in nearly every category of the game as well as being fantastic looking. This car is one that I am now lucky enough to own in real life and take out on the occasional sunny day in Manchester.

As my parents have reminded me over the years, I was a slow starter. At the end of the first term in December 1972, I was bottom of the class (twenty-seventh); I still have my end-of-term reports to prove it. My form teacher's comment read, "A very poor term academically due to his not giving care and attention to his work. I shall be looking for great improvement next term. It is pleasing to note his enthusiasm for chess!" During the next couple of years, I improved slightly, but only just (twenty-fourth), and I didn't really show much aptitude for any particular subject. Mum was the one who used to help me with my evening homework at the kitchen table and with A2 charts and Latin translations on weekends, when I always needed a lot of cajoling to knuckle down and get them done.

Although I don't recall Dad helping me too much with schoolwork, he taught me chess, and we regularly played on the sitting room table. I was still only nine or ten at the time, but I began to play frequently at school and the local village club, competing in matches against the clock versus other clubs and also in the annual London championships.

That leads to the first really memorable date in my life: 20th October 1976, a Wednesday. On that day, I walked down to the village club as usual for a half past six start, but that particular evening, the club had a visiting professional player for a simultaneous exhibition match. In this format, one very good player can take on many amateurs at the same time. If you saw *The Queen's Gambit*, one of the episodes had Beth Harmon playing this way at a local school, moving from game to game inside a square of tables and subsequently beating all her male opponents. Our special guest that evening was none other than Leonard Bardon, the former British champion and a chess master who would take on the twenty lucky players chosen by the club. We all sat down, and the games commenced, with Leonard racing round making his same first move as white on all the boards, P–K4. The next thing I remember was running all the way home, knocking madly on the front door and shouting to my parents, "I beat him, I beat him!" Leonard kindly signed one of his books for me after the game, and it still has pride of place on my bookcase even though I retired from playing the following year and have really only ever played a few times since. I was also on the front page of the local *Kentish Times* that week, which Mum bought multiple copies of, and I still have a framed copy in the house, hanging next to a framed old school report in the downstairs cloakroom. The family has nicknamed this room "The Shrine," as it has a growing number of photos and news cuttings covering its walls. A final corollary to this story, "which is actually going to be one of the very last edits," is that my nearly four-year-old boy, Finn, has recently shown an interest in chess and has now played every day for the last month. At the speed he is picking it up, it won't be long before he starts to give me a good game, which I am sure will be followed at some point thereafter by a win at a lot younger age than I first beat my dad!

Back to school and O levels, where I got A's in art, chemistry, geography, and history; a B in physics; and C's in English language, English literature, French, maths, and general studies. If I had been able to choose my own subjects for A levels, I would have chosen chemistry, art, and history. Back in those days, however, you got told what you had to take by your parents or the school, and if I wanted to take chemistry (my favorite subject), then I had to do maths and physics alongside it. I had not shown much promise at these and only scraped through my O levels, so it was going to be a difficult couple of years ahead. On reflection and having gone through the same process with my two daughters, I do actually think there was a lot of merit to the old system, although I have to keep that to myself for fear of being called a dinosaur! The only other choice if you were doing the sciences was A-level biology, but because I was in the bottom set, this was not an option for me, so I had to settle for the classic three.

There was one difference in the old days that made things a little easier, which was that for A-level maths, you could choose between mechanics and statistics as your specialism (you have to do both now). Hence, at least I got off a little more lightly, as I hated all the equations in mechanics. Looking back at my education, this solid maths and statistics grounding has been very important throughout my working life, as nearly every business decision is driven by numbers and the ability to interpret them quickly. This was a good choice and has stood me in good stead. You would be surprised by how many financial people don't have very good number skills—more about that later!

Chemistry, however, was the subject I had become much more interested in, and I can definitely thank my teacher for that. Mr. Ellis always tried to add a little excitement to our two-hour practical classes and often talked about some of the things he got up to when he was growing up. Therefore, there were always a few bangs or nasty smells in the laboratory before the afternoons were done. Some reactions sparked a particular excitement in him. One of these was the thermite reaction, which demonstrates very dramatically that aluminum sits above iron in the metals reactivity series of the periodic table. He explained very animatedly in one lesson that the thermite reaction is extremely exothermic (giving off heat) and was historically used to weld railway lines together, as the reaction's main product was molten iron. What made this reaction even more interesting was that the two reactants were very safe to handle and could be mixed together without anything happening, as the reaction required a high activation energy to get it going. However, once started, there was no way of stopping it!

Anyway, you probably already know where this story is going. My friend Richard and I ordered the two main components, iron (III) oxide and aluminum pellets, to be delivered at home, and we probably pinched some magnesium ribbon from the lab to create the initial heat to get it going. Then one Saturday afternoon, we set about doing some home experimenting in Richard's back garden, without telling his parents. We built a small brick structure, which we filled with the correct mix of products, and found a concrete paving slab to put on top of the structure once the reaction was underway. We then broke up some magnesium ribbon, put this on top of our mixture, lit it with a match, put the slab on top, and retreated rapidly to a decent distance. We didn't have to wait long for some action …

BOOM!

Almost immediately, the whole slab lifted up as flames shot out from the sides, combined with hundreds of pieces of molten iron spitting across the patio! The upshot was that we burned a huge hole in the stonework, which didn't go down too well with Richard's parents, and we thought that we should probably keep our experimenting to things a little less industrial after that.

Mr. Ellis can also be thanked for instilling a way of learning in me that involved both continually writing while revising and repetitively answering old exam questions. This methodology proved very effective for me and was probably the most important reason behind my significant improvement in academic performance in my last three years of school.

A fun example of this is the order of reactivity of metals in the periodic table, where I made up a very strange sentence to help me remember the sequence. It also shows how bad my English was!

"K, Na, Ca, Mg, Al, Zn, Fe, Pb 'H' Cu, Ag" became the "kniving narcotic carried Maggie, although the zoo felt particularly horrified, curious, and aghast." My sporting achievements weren't anything special, much to the disappointment of Dad, although I did enjoy playing rugby for the school, but only for the second team. I think he hoped I would follow in his footsteps on the rugby field, but that was not to be. I was, however, better at cross-country, winning the school's annual race one year and also competing in the London championships. Although I didn't continue competitively with running, when I left school, it was the start of a regular exercise regime that still sees me try to do something five or six days a week, which I find important for my work-life balance.

My musical prowess was a little like my aptitude for sports. I liked listening to music, but that didn't progress to actually playing an instrument very well. I listened to Asia, Santana, Meat Loaf, Dire Straits, The Stranglers, and Pink Floyd, as well as a wide selection of heavy metal, including Deep Purple and Rainbow, but I failed to even get past my Grade 1 piano exam, as I wasn't good at practicing. I also went to quite a few Motörhead and Status Quo concerts, even though Mum's kitchen stool haircut meant I never looked much like a rocker. I have always regretted not persisting with music lessons, so I finally decided, at the age of fifty-nine, to give myself a second chance and started playing the drums. Instead of struggling to put in the required effort between lessons, I now have Eleanor complaining if I spend too much time playing and not enough time looking after Finn, my new little boy, who arrived just as the COVID-19 crisis was calming down. I'm improving slowly and now on Grade 3 where my latest pieces are "Sweet Child of Mine" and "Play that Funky Music," which I have to try and learn over the next couple of weeks before my next lesson!

At home, like most young kids of my time, I had a big radio cassette player. The trend was for radio cassette players to get bigger and bigger, with more functions and more highly powered speakers, every year. I then progressed to a mixed hi-fi setup in my room, with a Marantz amp, Celestion Ditton speakers, Hitachi tape deck, and Sony record deck and tuner. This was wired via a coax cable to a large aerial that I put in the loft, which allowed me to listen to a huge array of music channels. I had hours of fun in my room, recording tracks from the radio onto the stacks of BASF and TDK blank tapes I used to buy.

If my music tastes were rock and heavy metal, my movie favourites were Old War films, Bond and Star Wars. I was brought up on *Where Eagles Dare*, *The Guns of Navarone*, *The Eagle Has Landed*, and *Bridge over the River Kwai*, alongside *Goldfinger*, *The Spy Who Loved Me*, and *From Russia with Love*. I think my favorite Bond was *Live and Let Die*, so when my partner Eleanor treated me to a trip to New Orleans for my sixtieth birthday, the first thing we did at six in the morning on day one was go to Chartres Street where the famous assassination scene had been filmed in the French Quarter. We had a fabulous day on Mardi Gras too, where we started at Tipitina's for the dawn music session followed by a day collecting beads at the many parades, eating beignets, having a few beers, and finally finishing in the 21st Amendment Bar off Bourbon Street. I would highly recommend a trip if you haven't been yet!

This was also about the time I got my first job as a "pools boy," collecting football coupons from people who lived in the local area and liked a flutter on the Saturday game results. This involved three hours on a Thursday evening, visiting flats and houses in the local area in all weathers and then coming home and totting up the cash before deducting 12.5 percent of the money as payment for my efforts. It was a great start to the experience of work, especially at Christmas, when all the customers were very generous with their tips. It also gave me an insight into what it must be like to be a postal worker because of the many crazy dogs I would encounter on my weekly circuit. They would often throw themselves at the glass doors and windows in an attempt to get at me, or at the very least, tear the pools coupons to pieces when I put them through the letter box of someone who wasn't home!

When I was seventeen, I also started going out with my first serious girlfriend, Kim, whom I'd gotten to know on my daily school commute, as she caught the same train. Once I learned to drive, not long after my seventeenth birthday, I made regular trips over to Kim's house in Orpington to take her out to the cinema, country pubs, and the Sevenoaks forest.

Mum had done most of the driving with me before my test. I don't think Dad had the patience, as on the odd occasion we did go out together, we would always come back very quickly after having fallen out. Mum's green Hillman Avenger estate was therefore the first car I drove, which did have the added advantage of a large boot capable of holding a few extra friends on a trip out. Driving in the old car, which Mum had nicknamed Veronica, all changed one day when I came home and a brand-new two-tone blue Ford Capri sat on the drive. I apparently said, "Mum's got a sports car!" It was only a 1.6-liter special edition and not the 2.8-liter injection beast that was the top of the range, so it was a bit of a sheep in wolf's clothing. However, it was still a big upgrade from the Avenger.

Orpington was also home to my best mate, Duncan, who was one of a group of friends from school that we later nicknamed "The Bromley Boys." One of them, Justin, who lived in Blackheath, became my best man and later godfather to my eldest daughter, Lauren. The Avenger was the perfect vehicle on a Friday night, as we could squeeze the whole gang in when we went on one of our regular trips to the Fox & Firkin pub in Lewisham. This was one of the original pubs that brewed its own beer, where instead of drinking the classic Bruces Best bitter, we usually opted for the stronger pint of Dogbolter that was like rocket fuel and great for getting the night going. A typical bar order was, "Can you give us five dogs, please, mate?" in a Cockney accent!

The Fox & Firkin had a Chas & Dave pop/rock–style band on Friday nights, who sang old wartime songs. Paper song sheets were handed out for all the newbies. We had some great nights there, and they helped add a few more songs to the repertoire Dad had taught me on our car journeys north to the Lakes. We used to rotate the designated driver duties, as getting home from Lewisham at midnight was not that easy without your own transport. It was always difficult for the driver. With five drunken mates on board, the drive usually involved a stop at a late-night kebab house for a large doner with extra chili sauce. I did return recently to the Fox & Firkin for the first time in probably forty years, and it has definitely changed. It is now better known for funk and soul nights and has stopped brewing the old Dogbolter beer, but I'm sure it's still fun on a Friday.

As I moved into my final A level year, it was time to think about what I wanted to do at university, and chemistry was the obvious starting point. I also realized from the entry requirements that bio-chemistry was an option despite the fact that I hadn't studied biology at either O or A level. However, while I was looking through the enormous number of courses, I found a very obscure one at Glasgow's Heriot-Watt University that interested me: a BSc in brewing.

I had always enjoyed brewing beer at home in the airing cupboard and fermenting wine from the grapes that I grew on the front of the house. So why not get a degree in alcohol and learn about making it on a much bigger scale? However, I eventually settled for the more sensible choice of biochemistry and applied on the old university entrance system to Bristol, Leeds, Warwick, York, and Southampton. After a series of interviews, I actually only got two offers from Leeds and Warwick, mainly because of the low predicted results my teachers had put on my application forms. In the end, I proved them wrong, as on one August morning in 1982, I opened the post to find I had gotten an A, A, and B in maths, chemistry, and physics, so it was off to Leeds for me.

A few boys' trips to the Lakes and Cornwall followed in the summer between school and university, alongside seeing The Rolling Stones at Wembley and spending plenty of Friday nights at the Fox & Firkin. Then, it was time to pack some things, including a few bits of my hi-fi, and head north to the University of Leeds and Devonshire Hall, the accommodation I had been allocated for my first year.

My start was a little bit tough, as all my fellow course mates had studied biology at both O and A levels. I didn't even know what a cell really was, let alone a nucleus or mitochondrion, so I had to do some rapid catching up during the first few months. With twenty-six hours of timetabled lectures and practicals a week, it was pretty full-on, including quite a few graveyard lecture slots at five to six in the afternoon. This was in stark contrast to some of my fellow Devonshire Hall students doing history and English on three to four hours a week of lectures (combined with reading the odd book). I think my positivity towards job applicants with science degrees when interviewing for roles at Radius stems back to what I thought was this early injustice!

I soon settled into the social life in Leeds and especially liked a regular pub crawl called the Otley Run. This involved drinking as many pints of Tetley's Bitter as you could while still being capable of walking another few hundred yards down the road to the next stop. Having been back in the last few years to visit both of my daughters (who also ended up at Leeds), I think most of the pubs we used to go to are still there, including Woodies, The Skyrack, The Original Oak, The Hyde Park, The Pack Horse, and The Eldon. There are also plenty of new additions that have been added, so I'm not sure it would be possible to do the whole run now and still drink a full pint in every pub. Not that many students actually drink pints of Tetley's anymore anyway!

It wasn't long before I really started to get into my course. At the end of the first year, I got four firsts and a 2:1 in my five subjects and was awarded the Crabtree prize for outstanding academic achievement—a far cry from the early days of being bottom of the class at St Dunstan's.

I had still been seeing Kim from school during that first year, but once my second year came round and Kim left home for the University of Nottingham, the relationship came to an end quite quickly, and it was time to move on. I moved out of Devonshire Hall and into a typical student house of the time, with five bedrooms and one bathroom, not like the luxury ensuite accommodation students enjoy today. This meant more fending for yourself, and there was a regular weekly shopping trip to Morrisons supermarket with my housemate Andy and alternate nights cooking during the week. Our diet consisted of Fray Bentos tinned pies, fried liver, and sausages and spaghetti on toast! Wednesday night's treat was a whole chicken cooked in a Heinz soup with onions and mushrooms, which is still one of my specialties at home, aptly named "Chicken à la Bill." An added extra was when Andy had gone home to see his girlfriend Adele in Worksop at the weekend, as he would always bring back a large M&S Lasagne his mother had given him. The simple cooking I had learned under my mother's tutelage proved useful, even if everything I cooked ended up very well done and often with chips. Meals during the holidays at home started to become less healthy, too, and involved a lot of takeaway food when I was out with my mates. I remember one particular holiday when we realized after four weeks that we had eaten at McDonald's every day, so not wanting to break this great run, we sometimes ended up doing a late ten-thirty-in-the-evening dash to get a burger and fries!

As I wasn't on a sandwich course, I started to think about trying to get some relevant experience for my degree in the summer holidays after my second year. I applied for several different things, and eventually, I was lucky enough to get a ten-week placement in the biochemistry department of Aarhus University in Denmark. A small biotech start-up, Senetek, was paying a research group to do some genetic engineering aimed at understanding more about the causes of aging. Aarhus is a really vibrant city with lots of students and a great summer climate, located on the east coast of Jutland. I had a fabulous time there, where a day normally started with getting to the lab early and setting all the experiments running before a two-hour windsurfing break at lunchtime, followed by a few more hours in the lab and a finish at about half past six. I had a great couple of months there, learning to windsurf and to speak a little Danish and doing some exploring of the mostly flat countryside and coast.

At the end of the summer, I was back in Leeds for my final year to see if I could get the good degree that my first- and second-year results had pointed to. Back in those days, all my degree marks were based on my final-year studies, with most of the score allocated to the end-of-year exams and only 15 percent allocated to my final-year project. I am not sure the words *continuous assessment* even existed back then. Schools also didn't give firsts away like jelly beans (which is a joke some of us oldies make about the education system today). In my year, this grade only eventually went to two of the thirty-seven students on the course, including me.

After getting back from Denmark, I chose my final-year project and joined one of the internal research teams at Leeds to work on the effect of testosterone on rat seminal vesicles. For the scientists among you, this was a project that involved using radioactive isotopes to label polyclonal antibodies. In layman's terms, this means making a chemical bond between an antibody and a radioactive atom and then using this label to see what the antibody binds to. Much of this identification involved using large sheets of photographic paper to record the radioactivity, which then had to be put in deep freezers alongside the samples. I think the cold was needed to maximize the transmission.

It's difficult to believe now, but I had never used a typewriter, and it was the year before PCs and word processors started to make more of a serious appearance at universities. So, I had to find an alternative solution for putting together my final-year project thesis. Luckily, my girlfriend at the time, Karen, who was at Leeds Polytechnic doing a business course, was a very capable typist, so she kindly helped me put my thesis together with the aid of more than one bottle of correction fluid.

One funny story from my many hours in the biochemistry labs was about one of the less-capable students in my course, who normally found a way to muck up most of his experiments. I think he had the nickname "Roger the Bodger" for obvious reasons. Anyway, whenever you use isotopes like the ones we were using, you always have to carry a Geiger counter with you to make sure you don't get close to too high a dosage of radioactivity. Normally, the instrument just clicks away slowly in the background, picking up the gamma rays that are common in the normal atmosphere. Well, on this day, Roger was working away in a room on his own, doing some experiments on his project. I opened the door to go in, and my counter went off the scale. There was a crazy loud static noise that sounded like something you would hear in a James Bond movie. Needless to say, Roger was rushed out to take all his lab clothes off and have a very good wash and shower to get rid of whatever he had spilled. I think the research scientists kept a much closer watch on him after that.

My taste in music became a bit more varied and now included Sade, The Pointer Sisters, Frankie Goes to Hollywood, and others, as well as the traditional metal bands. I went to quite a varied mix of concerts in the university refectory, including shows by Orange Juice, The Flying Pickets, and U2. However, my best music night during university was when Thin Lizzy played a gig at the car sales warehouse in downtown Leeds. It was one of the last times that lead vocalist Phil Lynott was on stage before he died a year later in January of 1986. The band's track "Still in Love with You" is still my favorite today, and it always takes me back to Phil's guitar solo on that memorable night in the warehouse. Those nights out in town were always followed by a walk back up the hill towards Headingley, with an inevitable late-night curry stop before heading back home to the student house.

Early in 1985, I was busy finishing off my research project, revising for my finals, and also starting to think about what I was going to do after I finished my degree. The company Senetek, which I had worked for in Denmark, offered to have me return full-time and to sponsor me through a PhD. That initially felt like the right direction, especially since I had liked Aarhus so much. I also got a second PhD offer from the Leeds laboratory group, where I had done my final-year project, thus giving me the possibility of working in two different research areas. However, like a lot of my course mates, I also started to apply for some jobs on the milk round, where the big blue-chip companies recruit their annual intake of graduates. I can't remember how many applications I filled in, but they definitely included Unilever, Procter & Gamble, Amersham International, Shell, BP, and the company where my dad had spent his whole career, Esso Petroleum.

At some point before finals, I got a job offer from Esso to be one of their sales and marketing graduates in their industrial and wholesale division. Therefore, I was forced into a decision between science and business before I even got the results for my degree. I'm not really sure what swayed my final choice, but maybe I felt that I had done enough equations, Krebs cycles, reactions, and experiments, and it was time for something a bit different, so I accepted the offer from Esso. Thankfully, Dad was working in Bahrain at the time and was only a couple of years from retirement, so we wouldn't have to cross paths when I started out.

At this point, I had very little idea about the world of work and anything outside school and university. I also had no idea about what I wanted to do with my life or what, if anything, I would be good at, which I think is still the same for a lot of young people. I do think the greater number of sandwich courses and internships today helps a little with gaining proper experience. At the time, my world of work had consisted only of a football pools round and making breakfasts on a building site.

Before I go on, let me tell you a little more about what I used to do in the holidays during those early school years.

THE LAKE DISTRICT

Dad's passion for walking and rock climbing, combined with his exploring of the Lake District fells when he was at school, meant that there was only one obvious place to head for holiday breaks with his new family. I'm not sure the fact that Nanna was living in Windermere was a wholly positive thing for him, but when she kindly offered to lend them a thousand pounds to help towards buying a small holiday cottage, Mum and Dad started a search for a place in earnest. After several months of looking through *The Westmorland Gazette* and local auctions, they found an idyllic old miner's cottage in a village called Glenridding at the end of Ullswater lake. It wasn't in the village proper but at the top of a very rough, unmade road on the slopes of Helvellyn, tucked away in a copse of trees, with no water or sewerage mains. The cottage would be the start of a new walking holiday custom that would eventually become one of my passions, both within the Lakes and the wider UK, and then later on to exciting places much further afield.

Liz was four, and I was two, and it wasn't long before we were being sent down the hill to the farm to fetch milk in the morning before setting off on our ever-lengthening daily walks. There were not many rest days during our typical two-week stay, so we always looked forward to our midweek trips on the Ullswater Steamer, where we were allowed a Crunchie chocolate bar before a relatively flat walk back along the side of the lake. Helvellyn was also always on the agenda, as we could literally walk up the stream at the back of the cottage and follow a sheep track until we got onto the main route much higher up. Walking up this mountain (the third highest in England) was always very hard work in the early days, but I do think the repetition finally won us over. I can now say it is definitely my favorite mountain and one I have probably summited nearly a hundred times over the years.

The stream that ran by the cottage was a source of hours of fun most days, with regular dam-building challenges to make the deepest pond possible. It was also the place where I had a nasty fall one year, which resulted in a large gash down the front of my leg. It never got stitched, and I still have a nasty scar nearly fifty years later. As Dad closed in on his retirement and my parents were thinking of where to base themselves for the next part of their lives, there was really only ever one choice: the Lakes. The cottage was going to be too small, so with great sadness, they sold number 4 Birkside Cottages and bought Nanna's house in Windermere. At the same time, Nanna moved into a small bungalow that had come up for sale next door.

Before I get back to the start of my working life at Esso, let me give you a few thoughts about the label *entrepreneur*.

I WASN'T AN ENTREPRENEUR

While I was at Leeds, and then later during my first few years at Esso, the word *entrepreneur* wasn't one that was used very often, and it certainly wasn't something that very many young people in their early twenties talked about as a career option. Back then, you were either planning to be a doctor, vet, teacher, pharmacist, or accountant; doing some form of postgrad education; or applying to big blue-chip companies. Anything different from those options was seen as extremely alternative, and not many students even took the choice to travel, like so many young grads do today.

If the word *entrepreneur* was actually used back then, I would say it was reserved for a handful of globally famous individuals, such as Bill Gates, Steve Jobs, and Richard Branson. Little did I know that in forty years' time, I would be lucky enough to regularly take my family and friends to the little slice of paradise that is Necker Island in the BVI. An entrepreneur certainly wasn't anything you could become by leaving university and just setting up in your bedroom at home with an idea.

I definitely never saw myself as an entrepreneur when I was young, and for most of Radius's history, I just considered it work. It was a shock when, nearly thirty years later, Ernst & Young (now known as EY) asked me to take part in their annual Entrepreneur Of

The Year competition. After spending so many years with my head down in the diesel business, it felt surreal to be competing against "real entrepreneurs," many of whom had only taken two to five years to build their businesses.

If I am now classed as an entrepreneur (as Wikipedia defines me), then I became one over a period of many, many years, and it is something I learned to be rather than being born that way, hence the title of this chapter. In biochemical terms, you could say that, for me, it was an environmental evolution rather than an original genetic feature. This might not be the same for everyone, but it definitely was for me. So, for those of you who think that you're not an entrepreneur already, there is plenty of time for you to become one. Plenty. To emphasize this even further, I believe I have been at my most effective, business-wise, since I turned fifty. So please, reader, never think it's too late.

At this stage, let's go on to the things that happened in the four and a half years after I left university in June of 1985 until the day I took my big leap into the unknown on 8th January 1990.

FINDING MY PASSION

My first day of work at Esso was in early September 1985, when I started on the initial six-week sales and marketing graduate training program at Victoria Street, London. All the grads had to go through this before we were split up and given our first full-time roles out and about in the business.

Living in one of the St. Ermins, The Rubens, or the Royal Westminster hotels located near Victoria was a real change of lifestyle from the terraced house in Leeds. An added advantage of being a relatively long-term business guest at one of these hotels was that they nearly always upgraded us to a suite. This proved perfect for having my mates up to stay on Friday nights, when I proceeded to tick every box on the breakfast-in-room menu before hanging it on the door and finally getting into bed. This resulted in a huge trolley of food being delivered the next morning: orange juice, apple juice, coffee, tea, toast, croissants, yogurt, etc. This always caused much amusement when the waiter opened the door and I pretended that I was the only one in the room!

Another big change was having to learn to type, which must seem alien nowadays, but I had really never used a PC before joining Esso, other than just a few taps of the typewriter to help Karen with my thesis. It's funny how much technology has changed when I see my Finn prodding at my iPhone at only seven months old. Who knows what it will be like in another thirty years? But one thing is for sure: Finn will be typing at an age before I ever did.

My next step was a move from London to Esso's northern regional office in Wilmslow, where I was put in the customer services group, selling lubricants and antifreeze over the phone while waiting for my first designated long-term role to become available. This job was the first time I had ever had to call someone I didn't know. It was also the first time I had to try to sell something over the phone, so it was a daunting first few weeks. It was made easier by a friendly team, in which Steve Howarth, the manager, and Mike Hart, a colleague, helped me get into the groove. It wasn't long before, in January 1986, a role was found and I was appointed area manager for industrial fuels. My patch would cover North Wales, Liverpool, Manchester, and the Peak District down to just north of Birmingham and east over to Derby and Loughborough.

After having been on the company's expenses staying at The De Trafford Arms hotel in Alderley Edge for nearly three months, I now had to find somewhere to live and fend for myself. As the existing customers I was inheriting were spread all across my patch, I had a few towns and cities to choose from. I eventually settled on Chester, which was fairly central with a maximum two-hour drive to the edge of my patch, no matter which direction I went. It was also very close to the M56 motorway, with easy access to the M6, which was soon to become a road I would know very well. We're a truly global business now, but there was a point in my life when, if you had cut me open, you'd see the M6 running through me. Within a few weeks, I found a small three-bed semidetached house at 18 Thackeray Drive, Vicars Cross, for £31,500, and with Mum and Dad helping with £2,500, I was on the property ladder in January 1986.

As Esso was in the process of rationalizing its regions, my handover involved visiting customers with several different colleagues who were either retiring or having their sales areas altered. This process was basically me running my colleagues round in my new white Vauxhall Astra GTE for a series of very boozy lunches before dropping them home or at a handy railway station.

One of these early visits was to a haulage customer, Sherwood's Transport near Derby, right at the southeast corner of my patch. Trevor Clough, the current area manager, pulled me to one side before we went in to meet John Cartilage, the buyer, and said, "Bill, I always like to write my best price down on the palm of my hand so I can remember it when I'm in the meeting." He proceeded to get a biro out and wrote 18.70 ppl (meaning "pence per liter") on his hand before showing me his almost comical negotiation technique, which I'm sure John picked up on. This was the start of my sales training in the industrial and wholesale northern region group.

I was the new youngster as part of a seven-person team covering from the Midlands right up to the Scottish border. I was working for Ron Cook, a veteran sales manager with over thirty years' service. The existing youngest member of the team, Richard Barton (nicknamed "Special Agent Dick Barton"), was forty, and the remaining team members averaged well over fifty. I look back on the next couple of years, when I started to learn about the world of sales, with very fond memories. That's when I got my love for an early start, regularly leaving the house before six in the morning to go and explore my patch. Ron also ensured that we had some fun along the way, and a regular fixture for the team was the quarterly sales meetings, usually held at Crosland Heath, Ron's local golf course. These involved an early train journey to Huddersfield, and a taxi ride up to the club, followed by our individual presentations, then a boozy lunch at the local pub that lasted well into the afternoon. Getting back home on the train afterwards was often a little tricky, and Ron always joked that we should have brought signs with our home addresses to hang around our necks to make sure we all got back safely.

Ron was the only person I have ever met who actually talked about gallons when we were out drinking. If he said he had been out for a half, that meant he'd had four pints, and if he had been out for a couple, that was sixteen pints! When he held court at the bar during our infamous sales meetings, he used to casually drink a whole pint of Tetley's while ordering a round and then get a second for himself before sitting down. Two or three of Ron's sips, and the next pint would soon be gone too.

At Esso, everyone who got to the age of fifty had to undergo annual medicals at the company's in-house medical facility at the head office on Victoria Street. This seemed to provide a regular annual stimulus for my more experienced colleagues in the sales team to reduce their beer consumption and, in some cases, cease completely for the few weeks leading up to the checkup.

I think they thought that a couple of weeks off the beer would make a big difference to their cholesterol and other important blood test checks, but I'm not sure they did. I remember one team meeting shortly after Frank Kershaw had had his annual checkup. He recalled a little of his conversation with the doctor, which put a smile on everyone's faces. To picture the following exchange, you must know that Frank was a rather portly five-foot, eight-inch Yorkshireman from Cleckheaton near Leeds, with a very broad Yorkshire accent and a penchant for mucky pork sandwiches. He recounted the conversation as …

Doctor: "So then, Frank, how much beer do you drink?"

Frank: "About seven or eight pints."

Doctor: "That's very good, Frank. A very normal amount for someone of your age."

Frank: "Aye, sir. And about double on weekend evenings."

I have so many good memories and stories from that time, but I do need to mention this one about another member of the team, John "Gribbo" Gribbin, who became a good friend and mentor to me and provided more useful help than Trevor's biro-price-on-the-palm-of-your-hand trick. John had a close resemblance to James Bolam from *The Likely Lads*, and Ron was always joking with him, especially as he didn't have the same capacity for drinking pints of Tetley's as the other team members, probably because of his much slimmer stature. This meant that his condition often used to deteriorate more quickly than the rest of the team when we were out trying to keep up with Ron's rather rapid drinking pace.

This story was from before the time I joined the team, but it was a favorite tale that Ron used to tell. It took place after another one of the famous sales meetings. Ron had put John back on the train at Huddersfield and then called Fay (John's wife) to make sure she was at the station to pick him up, given his rather happy state. When she got him home, she promptly put him in the spare bedroom and left him to his own devices so she could get a decent night's sleep.

In the morning, she heard him shouting for help, saying, "Fay, Fay, help me! I'm burning up! I can't move my legs!" She rushed in to find that, rather than a serious medical incident, what had actually happened was that he had gone to bed with both legs down the same pajama leg and the electric blanket set on maximum heat. Ron's regular recount of this story involved a great impersonation of John calling Fay for help, which always got a few good laughs from the team.

Besides the fun, there was a serious side, and I was busy trying to both maximize volumes from existing customers and work on the harder task of finding new ones. Esso had a very old reporting system, and it was more than two weeks after the month's end when you got a hard-copy report through the post, telling you what all your figures were. I always looked forward to getting the numbers, which was probably the start of my more volume-oriented leaning as well as my competitive nature. I grew the total product volume across my patch in the first year by more than 300 percent, earning me a pat-on-the-back letter from the divisional director. However, I was never given the margin figures, and I know I definitely didn't have the most profitable sales area, but I was happy anyway. I was really starting to enjoy the job and my first taste of the diesel industry as I traveled around, trying to sell as many tankers of fuel a month as possible to transport companies of various shapes and sizes. A new standard weekday diet also started to emerge, as the six-in-the-morning start usually necessitated a decent breakfast, which was where the big network of Little Chefs came in useful. I soon got to know all the ones on my patch, and I used to get the Early Starter full breakfast on the A41 near Heswall or the Chicken Platter lunch at Uttoxeter on my way back from visiting Sherwood's Transport in Long Whatton.

While living in Chester, I also started to windsurf again at the weekends, with regular trips to Bala Lake in North Wales. This was a far cry from the lovely warm beaches in Aarhus, where I had first learned, but it was still good fun, and I made a great new group of friends there. On these trips out to the Welsh countryside, there was often snow on the hills, which meant that, even with a decent wet suit and gloves, it was still bitterly cold most of the time.

During these first two years of living in Chester and working on the road, I met someone who would ultimately inspire me to take the leap that would change my life forever, but I was not quite ready to take that jump just yet.

THE FIRST SPARK

So let's get to the first spark of an idea that changed my life from working for Esso, once the world's biggest company, to working in the smallest business possible: a brand new start-up.

One of my customers in my new sales job was M6 Diesel Services, run by brothers John and Toby Atkinson and a third partner, John Dunning. M6 Diesel was a collection of truck stops from Carlisle, Tebay, and Crooklands in the north to Birmingham and Luton in the south. Instead of being like traditional motorway service areas that most of you have visited at some point in your life, these were garages where trucks could refuel. They were nearly always located close to motorway junctions rather than on the actual motorway itself. The sites would have multiple lanes where the trucks could refuel, with some able to fill ten trucks at once with high-speed pumps. They would often also have other facilities, such as a truckers' café, overnight parking, or even a truckwash. The Atkinson brothers and Dunning got their big break when the M6 motorway was originally extended north of Preston towards the Scottish border. New junctions were luckily located either where they owned an existing petrol station or, in Dunning's case, on large swathes of farmland. In the 1970s and 1980s, after the motorway opened, they started to develop the sites and expand their facilities. In addition to building new truck stops, John Atkinson set about driving up to Glasgow, Aberdeen, and Inverness to look for new customers.

These tended to be Scottish transport companies that wanted to refuel their trucks on the M6 as they moved fish, beef, and other cargo south to Manchester, Birmingham, London, and even the Continent.

The unique concept that M6 Diesel came up with, alongside another operator, Exelby Services (based on the east side of the country, near the A1), allowed their big customers to bunker their own diesel and simply pay the sites a handling charge of about 0.9 ppl. The transport companies would buy tanker-loads of diesel from major suppliers, such as BP, Texaco, Conoco, Phillips, and Esso, and arrange for them to be delivered into one of their truck stops. Then, as the individual vehicles from these transport companies refueled at the different locations, they would draw down on this stock until another tanker-load was needed. Some of the trucks used 250, 500, or even more than 1,000 liters every time they filled, so they used to go through the stock fairly quickly. In those days, everything was done on paper sheets that the drivers signed as they fueled, and at the end of the week, the closing stock position was calculated manually.

The big advantage of bunkering was that there was no credit risk, as the customers were buying their fuel from the oil companies, which ultimately held this risk. However, the big disadvantage was the very slim handling-charge margin, which meant the sites had to do a lot of volume to be profitable from bunkering alone. Other products, such as lubricants for the truck engines and gas oil for the refrigerated trailers, helped boost this margin. M6 Diesel also bought its own product to sell to smaller transport companies and owner-drivers. They called this type of user a credit customer, and the margins here were much bigger, but they also had an associated risk. This was how my relationship with John Atkinson began. I started to sell him more and more tanker-loads of diesel for these credit customers as I worked hard to build volume on my patch. Over the two and a half years I was on the road in the northwest, not only did John become an important customer of mine, but we also became good friends. He started to explain more about the bunker business and how it had developed since the initial concept was thought up by John and his good friend from over the Pennines, Ron Exelby.

Since M6 Diesel did not have the only truck stops in the UK—remember the aforementioned Exelby Services, plus there were individually owned stops—the big trucking companies had to hold stocks with all these different suppliers, which tied up increasingly large amounts of their cash. This was further exacerbated as the price of diesel continued to rise, helped along by the relentless increase in excise duties and crude oil prices. Not only was there a growing financial cost for the transport company, but every supplier had a different manual paperwork system, which meant that keeping tight control over how much fuel any one truck was using became almost impossible to calculate.

These two factors were probably the important drivers as to why a new company, Keyfuels, emerged in the mid-1980s and started to change the truck stop dynamics with a great new concept that solved both of these problems for the trucking companies. First, Keyfuels established its own stock with all the groups, including M6 Diesel, as well as all the individually owned truck stops. In its model, the customer only had to hold a single stock in its virtual system rather than one at each site. The customer still had to arrange for a delivery of fuel at a specific site from an oil company, but once the delivery took place, it had a global credit it could draw down at any of the sites on the network. The simplest analogy I often use is that it was like a bank for diesel, where the customer deposited money into one branch but could then draw it out in small amounts from any of the other branches around the country. Once the diesel was used up, it needed to be replenished, but this could also happen at various locations.

Keyfuels constantly balanced the system to keep all customers and locations positively stocked.

Having a single stock with Keyfuels also solved the second issue of multiple paperwork. It had one type of manual sheet that, instead of being sent back weekly or monthly, was sent daily by reply-paid envelope or even faster on the new, supermodern facsimile machines that were starting to become a mainstay of every office. To allow the sites to identify all the different customers and drivers in its growing system, Keyfuels introduced a third new feature—a plastic numbered key, hence the name *Keyfuels*. This key was given to all the drivers or was often just kept in the truck. When the key was presented at the site, the key number was noted, along with the date, amount of diesel, and site name, and then it was used to create a transaction each time a truck fueled up. Once the sheets arrived back at the Keyfuels office in Walsall, they were manually entered into a database to create weekly reports that showed the transport company customers exactly how much every truck had used. This was a big step forward, although the rapidly growing customer numbers meant an ever-growing amount of manual data. Lots of people were needed to punch in figures to keep up with the thousands of daily transactions that were now occurring on the network.

It wasn't long before Keyfuels realized it could take advantage of something else from the banking world—magnetic stripe card technology. The stripe on the back of a classic bank card that effectively holds the account number could be used similarly in the fuel card world and would allow Keyfuels to start transforming its manual transaction system into an electronic, automated one. So, in or around 1989, only a few years after it started, Keyfuels began to issue magnetic cards to its customers. This was the beginning of a new fuel card world in the UK.

At the same time, Keyfuels bought some Fortronic card readers, which it put on the counters at its busiest forecourts, allowing it to swipe these new cards and capture the transactions electronically rather than on the old-fashioned no-carbon-required (NCR) sheets. Keyfuels then polled each of the terminals via modem overnight to receive a nice, neat file of data, which could be imported directly into its main processing system within a few minutes of the start of the day. These files were even available on weekends if you wanted to run a seven-day-a-week service.

Keyfuels had a massive positive impact on the truck stops. With its new automated service and a growing network of more than seventy-five sites, it attracted more and more customers, accelerating the growth of volumes at all locations. There was a sting in the tail, though, that not everyone could see at the time, which was that the truck stops were losing control of all their direct customers and becoming overly reliant on one very large customer, Keyfuels. Keyfuels was also making sure that the handling charges it paid to the sites didn't go up but rather edged down so that it could make a larger margin.

This was all happening right at the time when I was selling tanker-loads of fuel to John Atkinson and the first spark of an idea for a new bunkering company owned by a truck stop business came into my mind. This was a simple idea that would eventually germinate and turn into a £5 billion global business. This would give the customers all the advantages that Keyfuels could offer while staying under the ownership of the truck stops.

Although this was an idea we started to talk about, it was still in the very early stages of gestation and wasn't a serious option I was considering as a career move just yet, especially as my next job on the Esso graduate scheme was just around the corner.

WHAT PUSHED ME OVER THE EDGE

I had been in Chester for more than two years when my boss Ron approached me to start talking about where I might move next in Esso as part of its typical graduate rotation program. During my time on the road, I had gotten to know nearly every transport and haulage company on my patch, as well as a lot of different businesses from a multiplicity of sectors. I had done a deal to sell a five-thousand-ton ship cargo of kerosene to a firefighter equipment manufacturer, sold fuel oil to one of the UK's largest manufacturers of fertilizer, and supplied gas oil to many of the local councils and schools, as well as numerous other combinations of products to many different users.

Having started on the Esso program with a sales job, I was now due to do something very different for my next move, and in early 1988, I was appointed as an analyst in the corporate planning group based at the Victoria Street head office in Central London. I was in a small group of four people, with my role specifically responsible for longer-term planning in the lubricants and bitumen business, something I knew absolutely nothing about.

My job changed from being very people oriented to much more analytical. I spent many hours in front of an early IBM PC doing lots of complex Lotus spreadsheets and using some of the very old Esso mainframe systems. I had a great new boss, Pete Szanto, who although very different from Ron, still thought it important to have some team fun every now and again, alongside the hard work.

One early recollection from not long after I had joined the group was at a send-off for Nick, a member of the team who was moving to a new role. A late lunch had been booked at a local Chinese restaurant in Victoria, and we all headed down in the lift from the seventh floor sometime after one o'clock. The first thing (and nearly the last thing) I remember was having a few shots of Mai Tai before the food even arrived. I thought that Mai Tai was a fruity Caribbean rum cocktail; however, it also happens to be a near-neat alcohol spirit that the Chinese love. It comes in white and red bottles, which I now know to steer well clear of and have never touched a drop of since. I don't remember much about the meal that followed, but I do recall being in the Stage Door pub opposite Victoria station, chatting to Paul Shane and Su Pollard from the TV program *Hi-de-Hi!* They were performing at the Victoria Palace Theatre next door, and I am not quite sure how we got talking to them or what we talked about. Anyway, the next thing I remember after that encounter was walking along a path by a castle wall, briefcase in hand, having just gotten off a train I had obviously caught at Victoria Station. I meant to get off at Beckenham Junction, where I was living in a flat at the time, but I definitely wasn't there. Having been born and brought up in London, I thought I knew the city pretty well, but looking around, I certainly didn't recognize where that place was.

The streets were pretty quiet, and I came down off the path to try to get some orientation and waited by the road until a taxi came past. I flagged the cab down, and before I got in, I said to the driver, "Where are we, mate? I don't think I know this part of London." He replied, "We're not in London, feller. I'm afraid we're in Canterbury!" I'd obviously been out for the count, missed my station, and then overshot it by sixty miles. So, at half an hour after midnight, I didn't have any alternative but to jump in the taxi and head back to Beckenham. The ride was £120, so it worked out to be a very expensive night, and I had a hard start the following day because I had to drive north back to Chester to pack up my Vicars Cross house. I didn't get much sympathy from my colleagues at Esso, who thereafter referred to my error as "The Canterbury Tales!" I had luckily managed to sell the house quickly for a £20,000 profit after just over two years of ownership, so I was pretty pleased. So it was down and onto the London property ladder for me. I found a nice place at 26 Edna Road in Raynes Park—an older end-of-terrace house with a small garden at the back, but it still cost £100,000. Welcome to the London property market!

Another thing that happened before Nick left the group for his new role as a retail sales manager was that he got a lunchtime call from his girlfriend, who worked as a journalist for *New Musical Express* (now known as NME). She had managed to get some last-minute extra tickets for an event to mark the launch of Eurythmics's new video album and wondered if Nick and a couple of his mates were interested in going. Well, that was an easy answer for me and another member of the team, Pete, so off we headed at six o'clock in the evening to a large house somewhere just north of Oxford Street, not really knowing what to expect. When we arrived at the house, there were paparazzi at the entrance and a lot of security, so it looked as if it was going to be quite an event. No one was taking our photos, though, as we walked in. We looked a little out of place in our work suits, but we didn't care, as once we were inside, there was quite a party going on. Bob Geldof was serving behind a small bar, members of Bananarama were chatting in another corner, and I bumped into Sade as I popped in to see the room where Annie Lennox and Dave

Stewart were due to give a mini gig a bit later. We had a great time, and no one could quite believe whom we'd seen when we recounted the story many times over the next few days.

This phase of my time at Esso wasn't all leaving parties and nights out, although the Tiger Club bar in the basement of the Victoria Street office was always tempting for a quick beer after work. One of the projects I was busy on involved helping to choose new suppliers and locations from which to distribute the large and varied amounts of automotive and industrial lubricants that the company sold. I was also learning about the different penetration (PEN) grades of bitumen used for tarmacking. The PEN designation of 30 or 50 was given depending on how thick and heavy the bitumen was and how easily penetrable it was by the standard measuring device. Alongside this, I had also been given the job of pulling together all the planning and budget numbers for the following year across the whole of the business and inputting them into a complex global mainframe system used by all Exxon subsidiaries.

I was definitely learning some valuable skills about how a big company works to add to the sales experience I had gotten in Ron's team, but I was also starting to see some of what I thought were the negatives of the slow-moving bureaucracy and controls that were in place. For example, if I thought I had a good proposal for one of my divisions, it was dead in the water if my immediate boss didn't see the merit. Even if he did think the idea was good, the process to get overall sign-off and agreement for it would then take so long and involve so many changes that by the time it eventually got to go live, the opportunity would be missed or so changed and watered down that it would no longer be good enough. One of the first lessons I talk about is starting before you're ready, which is a very difficult thing to do in a large corporation, with all the inherent controls it has.

This frustration was definitely the start of me beginning to think about my longer-term career and whether a really big corporate entity such as Esso was going to fit well with the work characteristics I was starting to develop.

Another unexpected change was also about to happen in my life as I set off in February 1989 on a two-week skiing trip to Andorra with six male friends and one female. I am not sure how James's girlfriend, Claire, managed to sneak on the boys' trip, but she did fit in pretty well, although we gave James a lot of stick about it. My skiing was not of a great standard, having only been on a couple of trips before. One of these was a school trip to Livigno in Italy when I was thirteen, and the other was a boys' trip to this same resort in Soldeu, Andorra, the previous year. I think we chose Soldeu because not only was it the cheapest place for hotels and ski hire, but it also had the added advantage that all the alcohol was duty-free.

Day one always involved everyone having to ski down a course in front of the instructors before being separated into groups of eight people of supposedly equal standard. I was always more speed than skill and ended up in a better group than I really deserved, much to the annoyance of some of the other people. However, not all the members of my new group liked to see me suffer at the back, and after the first day on the slopes, I started to get to know one in particular—Gill. We spent several hours each day skiing and chatting together, with her giving me extra skiing tips to try to help me keep up. In the evenings, we went our own ways, as we were living in different bits of the resort and had very different itineraries. Our nights usually involved tequila slammers in the room, where we would sit in a circle and continuously pass a bottle around the group until it was finished, before then heading out for food and finishing up with a few beers at the numerous resort bars.

By the end of the week, Gill and I had become good friends, and we exchanged telephone numbers as she was heading home the following day after a seven-day trip. I had another week to go but promised to call the following Saturday night as soon as I was back in Raynes Park.

On the Wednesday evening of that next week, on our way back from dinner, I had what was to be the worst accident of my life. I have only other people's recollections to give me a rough idea of what happened that night because no one was actually with me at the time. I am sure the beers and tequila we had been drinking didn't help, but it was relatively early in the evening, and by all accounts, I hadn't been too drunk when I left to walk home. I was missing from the group for over forty-five minutes before one of the guys eventually found me at the bottom of a forty-foot lift shaft in a half-built apartment block located somewhere between our hotel and the restaurant where we had been eating.

The first thing I remember was waking up at an Andorran hospital with one of my best mates, Duncan, who had come down with me in the ambulance. There was a second patient in the room, whom I later decided was an English expat involved in some form of smuggling operation because of the continuous stream of dodgy-looking men who visited, asking for instructions about shipments over the mountain pass!

I had broken my right wrist, which was already set in plaster, and torn ligaments in my left ankle. I also had a nasty knee injury. The side of my face had been badly scraped, and my left eye was completely bloodshot, so I wasn't a pretty sight. The next day, the surgeon came in to see me and said I needed an operation to repair the ligament damage and that they would do the operation on Friday. That was a pretty terrifying experience, as I remember not getting the general anesthetic until I was actually on the operating table with all the staff gowned up around me. The following Thursday, I left Andorra with my right arm and left leg in full plaster and a huge scab across my face where the scrape was beginning to heal. An ambulance to and from the airport at both ends was arranged by the insurance company, which had also insisted on a checkup at Kingston Hospital before I was finally allowed home. I made it back to Edna Road just before midnight and decided to give Gill a call, even though it was nearly a week after I'd promised to, and that was the start of our relationship.

Having already been away from the office for three weeks, I was keen to get back to work as fast as possible, and one team member who lived nearby kindly agreed to drive me to and from Victoria until I was fit again. It was soon after I got back from skiing that another piece of the jigsaw puzzle of why I wanted to eventually leave the large corporate environment fell into place. Having been away for those three weeks, I realized that nothing had changed in my area and that, actually, I was not really very important to the running of the business. I also suspected that in my current role, if I went in every day and did nothing but pretend to play on spreadsheets, my boss wouldn't pick up on it, and time would just pass by. (That wasn't what I was doing, by the way!)

I'm not sure of the exact date the final piece of my thinking happened, but it was probably around June of 1989. We were at a reunion of all the graduates from our milk round intake, and I remember there being some discussion among us about our salaries and salary groupings. I wasn't unhappy with where I was, but I was definitely surprised to find out that, in our group of nearly thirty people, we were all being paid within a couple of hundred pounds of each other. Some of the group were extremely good performers who should have been progressing faster, in my view, and then at the other end of the scale, there were quite a few who should have been exited. This lack of individual differentiation, as well as what I considered to be poor performance management, was not a good way to manage talent within a business. There'll be a lesson on this later.

Overall, I thought I had a lot more I could give to the company than the environment I was working in would give me. This was a real shame because I had really enjoyed the prior four years, especially the two in my sales job, and I had also made some great friends among my colleagues. Shortly after that get-together, I knew it was time to start thinking seriously about what I should do instead. I also thought that if I didn't have a go at something different now, when I had no family or other commitments, then it would only be a harder decision later. My current boss began talking to me about my next rotation, and I knew I needed to act soon, as I didn't feel it would be right to accept a move when I knew that before long, I would be leaving, especially when the company had been so good to me.

Given that I had always had thoughts about going to live overseas at some point in my life, I started looking at international jobs in the weekend newspapers. *The Sunday Times* and *The Telegraph* were always full of opportunities, although I didn't really consider myself experienced enough for most of them. I also started to think about maybe doing an MBA, as I had very little financial knowledge and could see that it definitely gave people a boost in the job market. MBA studies would also give me more time and perspective to think about what I should do with my own career. I had also kept in regular touch with John Atkinson since I moved south and began to think more seriously about the new bunkering company we had often talked about. I started to put a little more meat on the bones of the concept to see if it was now a realistic possibility.

With these three different career routes in mind, I set about applying for jobs, looking for where I could potentially study a relevant business course, and finally started to put down on paper a proper spreadsheet business plan for what I had provisionally called "Network Fuels."

I didn't know at this point which route I preferred, but I would have to decide soon, as I got my first job interview after the summer in early September with a company in Norway called Protan that harvested seaweed for industrial uses. I also caught a flight to Paris to visit EAP International University who had a really interesting International MBA course. Finally on the third route I met up with John at Cannizzaro House on Wimbledon Common to talk through my more detailed ideas for Network Fuels. I remember the hotel well, as it was the first place I had been where they offered you a glass of sherry at reception as you checked in. Funnily enough, I have been back to the hotel a couple of times recently when having lunch on a corporate invitation to the tennis at Wimbledon.

These were nice reminders of my meeting with John, when it had all started.

I had obviously kept Mum and Dad updated on what I was doing, and I think Dad thought I was crazy to give up a good job at Esso, where he had spent and enjoyed his entire career. Like a lot of people from his era, he talked about how good the job security is in a big company and what a generous pension they give you. However, in some ways, this security and comfort blanket was what I was trying to get away from. Another interpretation I once heard from a Belgian friend who used to work for Total Oil was that it was like working in a *cage d'or* (golden cage) because of all the positives that you had alongside the restrictions and limitations. *Fur-lined rut* is probably an easier idiom to understand!

Two things then happened quite quickly: I got a rejection from Protan in Norway and an acceptance for the two-year course I had applied to at EAP. I had been very impressed after my trip to Paris, so I really thought that I was down to two potential options—the MBA course or Network Fuels with John. In the end, I found a way of not having to choose between these final two. I contacted EAP and asked if I could defer my place by a year, thus giving me a chance to have a go at the diesel business before probably starting the MBA the following year. So, in November 1989, I went in to see my boss to hand in my resignation, and thus began a countdown to Christmas and the start of a completely new challenge.

This is where the format of the book changes a little and where the educational element or lessons I talked about begin. As I start to chart the history of the business, I have preluded each chapter with one of my lessons and tried to link the lesson with that part of the story to try to bring it to life by giving some practical examples.

As I said earlier, I don't expect you to necessarily agree with all of them, but these are the lessons that have been important to me and contributed enormously to the success Radius has achieved over the last thirty-five years.

THE RADIUS STORY

LESSON 1

CARE FOR EVERY POUND AS IF IT'S YOUR OWN.

I did nearly call this lesson "treat every pound of the company's money as if it's your own" and then realized one night that some people might take that message literally, so I decided to reword the title to "care for."

I can give so many examples across all the areas of Radius where employees have spent too much on consultants, contractors, third-party graphic design work, expensive hotel rooms, tanker-loads of diesel, office furniture, mobile phone handsets, pay rises for their team, and the list goes on. Let me also not forget the fact that most IT managers I've met seem to think that if overheads can be capitalized, then these costs are almost as good as free money!

Controlling expenditure was easy enough when I just had a small team and oversight over absolutely everything we were doing. However, now that we have nearly three thousand employees in twenty countries across five continents, with a turnover nudging towards £5 billion, it is simply impossible for me to manage our costs in the same way. I am therefore now reliant on a lot of my senior and junior team to keep this ethos in place. The bigger the company grows with its increasing layers of management, the less people seem to think about whose money they are actually spending and more that maybe it does really grow on trees! When I do find a person who follows the principle of caring for every pound they are spending, they also tend to have other good traits, and it's these people whom I and the company want to nurture and help develop. In our current management long-term incentive plan (LTIP), which I will talk about in more detail later, this trait is one of the key criteria for how we judge which employees should get an LTIP and also how much it should be.

I am sure a significant part of the reason behind my thinking the way I do, beyond the fact that I think my parents gave me a good early grounding in money as a child, is down to the way that the business was originally financed. The only external shareholder money that has ever been put into the business was the initial £58,000 (that's about £150,000 in today's money) from my two partners, John Atkinson and John Dunning. This happened at the end of 1989 when UK Fuels (the original company that eventually became Radius) was officially formed. I'm not saying that £150,000 isn't a lot of money, but compared to most of the start-ups you see now, it is a very modest amount.

I didn't even own any of the equity myself at that point in time, as I didn't have money to contribute, having just lost it all in the recent property crash. It would be another year, and only after we had properly started trading, before I would actually become a share-holder. Despite this, as well as the fact that neither of the two Johns was actually going to work in the business, I believed that I was on my own and that it was all down to me to make this new venture work.

Just for clarification before I go on, some of the articles you might have read online about Inflexion investing £150 million back in 2018 actually relate to it buying shares from exiting partners rather than putting money into the business, so no more money ever went into Radius after the original capital. Not only did we have just £58,000, but we also had no overdraft facility—just a current account with Midland Bank. This meant that we had to rely on our initial pot of equity cash to pay salaries, rent an office, buy stationery, purchase diesel, and get everything else we needed for the business until we either ran out of money or started making a profit. Although this very tight budget obviously meant that we could only grow slowly, it taught me the strict financial discipline that has been critical for our long-term success.

Over the last decade, I have met many young people in the early stages of their own start-ups, and all they talk about is seed capital, their next funding round, Series B raise, etc., as being more important than what they are actually doing in their business. I find it sad, and it doesn't usually end well. In most cases, these people leave a trail of destruction behind them in the shape of huge debts and generally let down a combination of investors, employees, and banks. This sort of person will never be able to understand the very important principle of caring for every pound of the company's money as if it were their own; rather, they have the alternative view of "every good entrepreneur has a few failures" as their excuse! These people defi-nitely fit into the category of treating the company's money as their own, which I joked about at the start. After what I hope should seem a fairly obvious first lesson (remember, not many of your employees will actually show this trait), let's get on to what was a really exciting part of the journey: the very start.

MY FIRST EIGHT WEEKS

After a week's holiday with Gill and some of the Bromley Boys at Aviemore in the Highlands of Scotland, where we celebrated the last few days of 1989, including a great New Year's Eve party, I headed down to Cheshire in my red Peugeot 205 to try to figure out the first things I needed to do to turn Network Fuels (now UK Fuels) from the very basic plan I'd written on ten sheets of A4 paper to a real working business with a network of truck stops and transport companies using its new bunkering service. Only during the formation process, a couple of months earlier, had we seen that the name UK Fuels Limited was still available at Companies House, so we had made a quick decision to choose this instead of my original plan name of Network Fuels, as we thought it would make us sound bigger and more established!

I had already put my house in London up for sale, but, unluckily for me, this was right at the start of a very serious property crash. It did not look as if I was going to be able to sell it quickly, so I needed a temporary solution. John, who was still living in Pulford just south of Chester, kindly offered for me to stay at his old house on Croxteth Park in Liverpool, so that's where I headed after I got back from my holiday in Scotland.

My first official day at work was Monday, 8th January 1990. I count this as the first day of the business, even though the company had actually been registered towards the end of the previous year.

The first thing I had to do was find an office. As I was going to be doing a lot of driving while I was out looking for customers across the whole of the UK, I had already decided that I wanted to be based near the M6, so I started looking in Cheshire around Junctions 17, 18, and 19. Another factor in this decision was that a former Esso colleague of mine, Joe Harker (who had recently retired at age fifty-eight), was interested in helping on the project. Joe worked in the same region as me when I started as a sales rep four years earlier, but he was in the lubricants division and lived in a small village called Biddulph. He also knew John because he had been supplying lubricants to the M6 group when I had been selling John diesel, so we were quite a good match.

Luckily for us, Joe knew of a small single-room office on his high street (with no windows!) that we could rent at very short notice and on a monthly basis. Given that we needed to get an address and base as fast as possible, we signed up and moved in the following week. Meanwhile, I continued searching for something closer to the motorway, with a bit more space than the very dark, ten-foot-by-ten-foot room we were squashed into.

Something else that was fortunate about teaming up with Joe was that, alongside his lifelong passion for golf, he had also developed a keen interest in computing in his later years. This would become very useful, as he effectively took on the role of looking after IT and finance while I set about trying to build a truck stop network before the important task of trying to find some customers.

The heart of our original site network was made up of the M6 group truck stops at Flamstead (M6-J9), Saredon (M6-J12), Crooklands (M6-J36), Tebay (M6-J36), Carlisle (M6-J44), and Sinderby

(A1-near Scotch Corner). If you look at these on a map, what you will see is that they are fairly central to the country and much stronger in the west than in the east.

Before I go on, I thought I would let you know that I did consider putting some pictures and photographs into this book, for example, of the original site network, but I decided to keep it to words only. However, I have pulled together some of these and put them on my website in the "About Radius" section, if you are interested in having a look!

The next few weeks were spent trying to fill in the gaps to build a geographic coverage that would allow a truck with an eighty-gallon (350 liters) tank to pretty much get anywhere in the country and back to one of our sites without the need to fuel elsewhere. Given that most trucks could do at least four to five miles to the gallon, I thought that about another ten strategically located sites would suffice for our starter network.

Alongside setting up the office in week one, I had also been to the local Peugeot garage in Chester and swapped my red 205 for a dark-blue diesel 405, a car which I was going to be spending a lot of time in. So, as Joe set about building a database to handle the fuel card transactions and finding a simple business accounting package as well as, obviously, a bank to manage all our customer receipts and payments, I set off to Scotland to start filling in the gaps in the site network.

As there are basically two main trucking routes above the central belt of Scotland that head further north, I needed a site up towards Aberdeen on the east coast and one that could service customers using the A9 up the center of the Highlands towards Inverness. To complement these two sites further south, I also wanted one at the top of the M74 near Glasgow and something equivalent on the A1 south of Edinburgh.

After several trips in my first few weeks, I found site number one at Brechin, number two at Aberuthven near Perth, number three at Motherwell just south of Glasgow, and number four at Belford near the border at Berwick-upon-Tweed.

These trips all tended to involve staying at Trust House Forte (THF) Travel Lodges and eating two Little Chef meals a day. My go-to combination was invariably an Early Starter at about nine in the morning after three hours of driving, followed by a Chicken Platter for lunch after my meetings. I got to know where nearly every strategically located Little Chef in the country was, as well as many of the Travel Lodges—a special trick of the trade that could be used to take advantage of the fact that they were all part of the THF group. More on that later!

Sites in the east and south of England followed, where I added Immingham, Colsterworth, and North Petherton to complete our fourteen-site starter network, which I was confident would suffice for nearly every trucker in the country. I still had a lot to learn! The site network, however, was just one critical thing that had to be done before we would be able to get up and running.

We also needed fuel cards, a method for recording the transactions at the truck stops, a database and reporting package, a business brand, and all the associated printed materials. This was the age of letterheads, compliment slips, branded envelopes, and business cards, when your local printer was a vital partner. We found our local printer, a nice guy named Ian Douglas at Creative Copy and Colour, and together, we set about designing all the things we needed to get going. For the fuel cards, we needed a specialist supplier and approached a company called Plastic Card Company (PCC), which was making cards for all of our main competitors.

After four weeks in the Biddulph office, it was already starting to feel like we were working inside a large cupboard. Luckily, a more spacious option closer to the motorway became available. So in early February, we had our first move and headed to Arclid, where we rented a larger open-plan area inside an old chapel, only one mile from the M6. This made life much easier for me, given all the miles I was doing then, as it was closer to where I was living in Liverpool. It also had the unforeseen advantage of us being able to pretend the office owner's secretary, Elaine, worked for us when suppliers and potential customers wanted to visit.

The concept of a database and reports was completely alien to me, but Joe was already making good progress on an initial system. He had chosen a package called SMART, which was a combi system that included a database, word processor, and spreadsheets. The key fields we would need in the database were customer name, customer number, and card number to set the account up, and then site name, site number, transaction date, registration number, fuel volume, lubricant volume, and gas oil volume to record the transactions at the truck stops. Our competitors were already well underway transitioning from manual zip-zap–style NCR to magnetic stripe cards and automated transactions, and there was no way we were going to be able to master this technology in just the few weeks before launch, so we opted for a manual-only system. We got our printer to create a nice green NCR bunkering sheet that could record fifteen transactions at a time. Alongside these, we printed some reply-paid envelopes to enable the sites to send the sheets back to us easily once they had been completed. We did, however, play a bit of a sneaky trick by using cards with a blank magnetic stripe on the back, so as far as the customers were concerned, we were using the new technology and were just as good as our competitors.

With this preparation underway, all we really needed to get going was a customer. Given that our bunkering business model didn't involve actually selling diesel and competing with the oil companies but was about providing a network for them to use this fuel, I decided it was OK to talk to Alan at Sherwood's Transport. He was one of the many friends I had made while out on the road selling tanker-loads of diesel. Sherwood's Transport was an existing Keyfuels customer, but given our competitive handling charge of 1 ppl and the friendship I had developed over the two years I had sold bulk diesel to Alan, he agreed to give me and UK Fuels a chance with a few cards. I didn't actually tell him that he was our first customer, so we chose customer number 1120 for the first batch of cards that we ordered from PCC.

After sending the cards out to Alan and asking him to put an initial thirty thousand liters of stock into one of the sites on our network, we were ready to go. All we had to do was wait for one of their drivers to turn up at one of our sites with a card, and we would be away and running.

LESSON 2
START BEFORE YOU'RE READY.

The concept of starting before you're ready is one of the biggest contributors to the difference in success between a fast-moving entrepreneurial business and an aging large corporation.

Older companies become obsessed with research, planning, modeling, and process design as they try to develop what they think is the perfect product for a new market or geography. I think of this as "chasing nirvana" and believe it wastes enormous amounts of money and time and that a more learning-on-the-job approach is actually a cleverer mentality for launching something new. Another drawback is that after the large time investment and expenditure, it is very difficult for employees to go back to senior management after only a few weeks or months to say they got it wrong and now need to make expensive changes and scrap loads of things they developed. This results in either their project limping on unsuccessfully or coming to a complete stop.

It is very difficult to understand all the dynamics and factors involved in launching a new venture when you are about to set out, and it's very likely that you will have to alter nearly every element of your plan once it is up and running. This might mean changing your design, the market sector you have tried to attack, the best supplier, your pricing strategy, marketing message, or one of many other elements.

As we have launched new divisions and entered into new geographical markets, we have moved to a more trial-and-error approach, in which we know from the start that many things probably won't work perfectly. This means we are also ready to change things quickly and keep modifying our ideas, which gives us the best overall chance of success. Hence, getting your project going faster and starting to engage with customers as soon as you can, even if you feel you are not quite ready, should be prioritized over too much preparation. Obviously, you need to make sure you have the business basics in place and the ability to invoice your products and collect money from your customers, but most sales and marketing elements should be left flexible and not overworked so that you can shape them once you start to understand the market.

Many graduates leaving business school tend to be in this overplanning mode. (I call them "the spreadsheet kids"!) I see it as my job to add a bit more trial and error to their way of thinking so that I can help them become more entrepreneurial and faster at delivering new products and services for Radius.

This was a concept I had to learn very quickly right from the start, as we were very low on capital and absolutely desperate to start earning income quickly. Over the years, as we have expanded into new areas and geographies, it has become an embedded part of my thinking as a critical way to run all our projects and one I want many of my team members to understand and adopt.

THE FIRST TRANSACTION

After double-checking that Alan at Sherwood's Transport had given out some of our cards to his drivers, I rang the two or three sites that he had said they were going to use on a daily basis, desperate to find out if we had our first transaction. On 1st March 1990, just eight weeks after that first day in Biddulph, the phone rang in our office, and it was the manager at site number twelve in Birmingham. A Sherwood's Transport driver was there but had forgotten his card and was asking if it was OK to give him some fuel and write it on the sheet manually. Not quite the smooth start we had hoped for, but we were underway with our first diesel drawing of two hundred liters. I still have the framed original bunkering sheet with this transaction in our boardroom today, as it was a moment I will never forget and I'm proud to say that Sherwood's Transport is still a customer today.

Now that we had cards in issue, we needed to create a stop list for when either customers lost their cards or we wanted to stop one from using any more fuel for credit reasons. This would add another important manual routine to our daily workload, as the list would need to be mailed out to all the sites every time there was a card added or removed.

We also needed to start getting more customers quickly, and I soon settled into using a combination of the Yellow Pages and spotting to gather a list of potential targets to approach. *Spotting*, in its simplest terms, is sitting somewhere by the side of a road and writing down the names and telephone numbers from the sides of trucks and vans that pass. This can be more targeted if you choose to sit very close to one of your competitor's truck stops in the busy early mornings and late afternoons, gathering the details of every truck fueling up. You don't ring many customers from a spotting campaign who say they don't need fuel out on the road!

So, over the next few weeks, I started to get into a routine of spending a few days in the office calling potential new customers to arrange appointments and the next few days traveling around the country to try to sign them up. I was also trying to increase the number of sites on our network, as I soon started to realize that the original fourteen wouldn't be enough. Scotland was a regular destination on these early trips because I specifically targeted a lot of meat and fish transport companies based in Aberdeen that brought goods to London. They always needed to refuel around the Lake District on both their way south and the return journey north. I still remember the names from those early days, many of whom are around today: Thomas Gibb, Deep Freeze Supplies, ARR Craib, The Shore Porters Society, and many more. The Little Chefs I had visited in the first month now became regular weekly stopping points where I started to recognize some of the staff as I tucked into my Early Starters and Chicken Platters.

Back at the office, we were again feeling cramped, so I began looking for a better long-term home for the business, so we wouldn't have to keep changing the contact information on our stationery.

A couple of miles north of where we were based, something had become available in the small village of Holmes Chapel (now famous as Harry Styles's hometown!). It was effectively a flat above some shops in a small L-shaped shopping precinct. With three rooms plus a small kitchen and bathroom, we would have enough space to expand our team to six or seven people. So in May, after just four months of operations, we moved for the second time to 23a London Road, helped by John's partner Pat, who brought over her daughter's horse box, which we used to move the desks we had recently bought. We were above a hairdressing salon and a selection of other shops, including a small café, newsagent, florist, fish and chip shop, post office, and off-licence. It is this location that I always refer to as our first office, even though, technically, it was our third!

May was also the month when we took on employee number one, Elaine. She had been the helpful secretary from our previous office, and she now took over the task of entering all fuel transactions and speaking to customers to ask them to put more diesel into the network. Fridays were always especially busy days, as we had to print all the weekly reports with our Epson dot matrix printers, separate the NCR copies, put them in envelopes, and drop them at the post office below. This was normally followed by a trip to the off-licence to buy three cold cans of beer for us to celebrate the week's progress and relax. One final thing I used to do most Fridays before heading home was to rake around in the skip that the florist below used for throwing away their out-of-date flowers and make up the nicest mixed bunch I could find to take home for Gill. I think I did eventually tell her where they came from because the flowers stopped a few years later, after we had moved our office again, which definitely made her suspicious!

Although John wasn't in the office at all, I used to keep him updated daily on what I was up to and any progress we were making. This used to happen mainly in the evenings after work, when we would normally meet at one of John's favorite Chinese restaurants. In the early days our most frequently visited ones were The Fortune Palace in Holmes Chapel, The New Village in Tarvin, The Jade Buddha in

Sandiway, the Chinese Delight in Frodsham, and The Summer Palace in Chester, and some weeks we even managed to visit one or another of these on five consecutive nights. John always ordered BBQ ribs to start and sea bass in ginger and spring onion as a main, and then we added whatever else we decided we wanted on that particular night. Funnily enough, these two dishes are still regulars for me today, and Chinese is still my favorite food, followed closely by Indian. Over the next few years, we often joked about writing a food guide about the best Chinese restaurants in Cheshire, as we reckoned we had visited nearly all of them.

So this is probably a good time to tell you a little more about John, besides his love of Chinese food. He was born right next to Crooklands Garage on 22nd July 1933, which is easy for me to remember because he regularly used 22733 as his security code on his home alarm and other devices. Crooklands is a small village in South Lakeland, handily placed alongside the A6. The garage was already a well-known stopping point for Scottish transport companies, and it had four separate lanes for trucks to refuel behind the main petrol station.

After school, John didn't go into the family garage business but instead did an engineering apprenticeship and started his working life at Marconi. It was only when the Penrith to Lancaster section of the M6 motorway was completed in 1970 that the idea of a career change was sparked. Luckily for John and his brother Toby, a new motorway junction (J36) was constructed within a mile of their garage, making their site an even better-located refueling point for any vehicles traveling across the border, especially because there were not yet any motorway services planned on this new section of the M6. Further north, about twenty miles from Crooklands, a local farmer, John Dunning, was also the beneficiary of a new junction being built on land he owned. Soon after Junction 38 at Tebay was built, John decided to build a petrol station and truck refueling point within a few hundred meters of the motorway to take advantage of the new stream of passing traffic. So the new M6 motorway, designed to link two countries together, was very fortuitous for both the Atkinsons and John Dunning, and it wasn't long before they started talking about potentially working together.

John Dunning didn't have any experience in the truck fueling business but had a really well-located site with loads of room for parking, and the Atkinsons already had a good Scottish customer base and knowledge of the market, so they had the makings of a good partnership. John decided to leave Marconi and throw himself full-time into the diesel business. Like I did nearly twenty years later, he began regular trips to Aberdeen to sign up transport companies to their newly formed company, M6 Diesel Services, that initially just had the two sites at Junctions 36 and 38. Over the years that followed, M6 Diesel expanded its network of sites by buying three more on the M6 at Carlisle, Flamstead, and Birmingham and also leasing one on the A1 at Sinderby. This network of sites became the core of the UK Fuels network that I described earlier.

LESSON 3

SELL WHAT YOU'VE GOT.

There are really two distinct sides to the "sell what you've got" issue, with the first one probably being the most obvious. When my sales leadership in a division tells me, "We need to have a CAN linked product in our telematics offering to reach the HGV sector," or "We've got to have driver ID to reach the Fleet market," or "We don't have a good enough price from a certain mobile supplier," or "Our EV charger doesn't have dynamic load balancing," or "We don't have an insurance offer for single courier" ... or, or, or. Every week, I hear from one of our managers about why we haven't got the product they need to sell to a certain type of customer, which is their excuse for why they are struggling to meet their targets.

My answer to this first issue is that managers need to concentrate on segments and parts of the market where we are strong and our products sit best, and then they also need to not believe every-thing they hear from their sales guys as to why we can't sell to a certain customer. Nearly all customers only ever use a fraction of the functionality you offer in any product, and this is especially true in the telematics sector. When you set analysis software, such as Fullstory, on top of one of our platforms, what you find is that a very large percentage of the customer page views are in the live map feature, with a massive drop off as you move to trip history, driver performance, and geofencing features, after which more complex use is almost nonexistent.

This was also a lesson I had to believe in right from the beginning of my journey as I started out selling a UK diesel site network that only had fourteen locations, which seems ridiculous now. Back then, I was happy to explain to customers that they did not need any more sites than that, given that their trucks had tanks with at least eighty-gallon capacity and a range of many hundreds of miles.

The other and less obvious side to the lesson of selling what you've got is that the owner or CEO of a company often obsesses over making their product better and better, with more functionality and complexity, and is always using that as an excuse to put off the launch as they chase the nirvana of a perfect solution. This imbalance, which I also talked about in the starting-before-you're-ready lesson, is normally found in more technically minded people who fail to understand that getting the sales and marketing right is as important as the product and that they need to go hand in hand.

I have encountered this many times in the telematics business. Numerous companies focus a disproportionate amount of energy and resources on product development and very little on sales. This usually ends with a business that either fails or crawls along at a slow pace. So the moral of this story is "Get selling and no excuses, please!"

STARTING TO GROW THE BUSINESS

Not long after we got going, I realized that balancing the diesel stock in the network was going to be a difficult process. Customers would deliver a load of fuel into a single site, such as Birmingham, and then their drivers would draw down on this stock from any one of our fourteen locations. Predicting where they were going to use the fuel was impossible, so every day I had to look at what had been used the previous day and then try to organize deliveries to replenish all the stock. This process became continually more difficult as we started to add new sites to the network at the rate of a couple a month, making the original fourteen-site proposition seem well in the rearview mirror. Looking back, I can't believe how we managed to attract customers with our tiny network. This is a perfect example of having the attitude of selling what you've got and believing in the products you already have, even if you are constantly trying to improve them.

Sometimes, it was not possible to get a customer to put fuel in at a particular time and location, and the only way to keep certain sites stocked was for us to buy a small tanker of fuel. Not only did this obviously start to eat into our very small cash reserve, but we also then needed some customers to actually buy fuel from us rather than just bunker fuel that they had bought from elsewhere. These are called credit customers rather than bunkering customers, and we had to invoice them for the diesel as well as the handling charge, which meant the much larger credit risk of 25 ppl instead of just 1 ppl. So then, I had to chase customer payments at the end of the month and wear the credit controller's hat—yet another new role I had to learn quickly.

We also had our first tangle with a competitor, Port Container Services (PCS), which had started a similar business about two years earlier. PCS was a subsidiary of Russell Davies Group, a large container transport company that had decided to set up a fuel card business to sit alongside its transport, storage, and tire divisions. I went to see one of its big customers, Dual Carriage, based along the dock road in Liverpool, and managed to persuade it to move completely across to our network, which didn't go down very well with PCS's managing director (MD), Roy Sciortino. Roy became a fierce competitor over the next few years as we both tried to build our businesses to challenge Keyfuels, which was at least five times bigger in volume than the two of us put together. Because Dual Carriage's business was truly national, this first big customer meant that our volumes began to increase across the whole network, which gave us a little momentum when trying to negotiate new site acceptance deals.

Meanwhile, I had finally sold my London house in Raynes Park, wiping out all the £20,000 equity I had previously built up in Chester. I bought a small, detached house for £78,500 with a 100 percent mortgage at 2 The Pryors in a little village called Tarvin to the east of Chester. This meant that as I began the business in 1990, I was starting on this new venture with not a penny to my name. Gill and I moved in during the summer, which was good timing, as she was starting work as a physical education and dance teacher at a school on the Wirral in September. Tarvin was not only handy for the office at Holmes Chapel but also close to where John lived in Pulford, making it even easier for us to meet up for our regular Chinese meals, especially with one of our favorites, The New Village, right on my doorstep! Just after Gill started work, we got married in North Berwick on 13th October before heading off on honeymoon to Hawaii—the first proper break since I started work. It was somewhere I had always wanted to visit, having grown up watching the original series *Hawaii Five-O*.

As 1990 drew to a close, we had our first company Christmas party at our local Chinese restaurant (no surprise there), followed by a few beers at the Red Lion pub. Gill and I had invited an old friend from Esso, Ron Clark, and his wife over to join us, so there were eight of us in all, including Joe with his wife Eleanor and Elaine with her partner Sam.

The other thing I had to start thinking about then was whether I was going to take my deferred place at EAP in Paris in September. Given that the business was already showing a very slight profit and that the original concept was definitely working, I decided it wasn't the time to leave; I wanted to keep going. I called the EAP representative to let them know, and they kindly said it was OK for me to defer for another year. John also sat down with me one evening and agreed to give me a 20 percent share in UK Fuels at no cost to me for all the efforts I had put in to date. This was another part of the puzzle that made me believe I was making the right decision. The shares were nonvoting, which was fine with me, but it was a proud moment to think I was now a part owner and maybe even starting to become an entrepreneur. John's generosity and care for his key people were a real influence on me, and I'm sure they have rubbed off on me, as this is something I am always thinking about with my team. I'll talk a bit more about rewards in a later lesson.

Back in the business, all the new volume growth was beginning to put pressure on making sure we got the transactions back from the sites as fast as we could. We also needed to get these transactions into the database quickly; otherwise, all our stock reports would be out of date, and we would be out of sync with the sites. Our first solution was to start using fax machines so that the sites could send us the green bunker sheets as soon as they were completed. We also decided to employ a full-time person to enter the transactions, as it was becoming too much for Joe, Elaine, and me to do with all the other things going on. Hence, our second employee, Karen Shone, joined in January 1991, just after our first-year anniversary. She always reminds me that she failed her interview test, which involved adding up volumes from one of our green stock sheets with a calculator, and I always reply that we were extremely desperate at the time! She stayed for thirty-three years, eventually becoming operations director in our telematics division and one of our best-ever people. She definitely had more than a sprinkling of the qualities I am trying to describe in this book.

This manual solution was not going to be a long-term fix, so it was time to start thinking about how to put real data onto the magnetic stripes on the cards and do fully automated transactions. There were two types of technologies being used by truck stops to accept the cards, for which we needed to build a solution: indoor and outdoor terminals.

I started by looking at the indoor terminals made by Fortronic. These terminals were nearing the end of their product life, and the manufacturer had stopped making new ones a year or two earlier; however, there was still a good market in refurbished devices. The important bits of information that these terminals needed to read from the card were the primary account number, which contains the International Organization for Standardization (ISO) number, account number, card number, expiry date, and product codes. The ISO is a six-digit number used to identify who has issued the card and is also used by all banks for their credit and debit cards. In the first few weeks of the business, we had quickly applied for and had managed to get registered with the number 707865. This had given us 9,999 customer numbers and 99,999 card numbers, which would last us quite a long time.

The other thing I needed to do was meet with Compower, a polling bureau that would dial in to each terminal and collect all the transactions from the sites overnight and package them into a single data file for us to collect the following morning. We also needed to create an electronic copy of our stop list so that this file could be downloaded to all the terminals when they were being polled during the night, which would allow us to control cards being used on the network and avoid having to send out so many manual lists. So, within a couple of months, we bought our first batch of refurbished machines configured with our 707865 ISO number and ordered some dedicated telephone lines at the truck stops to connect them to. We then reordered a new batch of cards with something real encoded on the magnetic stripe for all our existing customers, so we were ready to go. This felt a little like when we had our very first manual transaction at Birmingham, so it was a momentous day when we finally got our first file from Compower. We imported it into our database, thus taking an exciting step into the automated world and towards the start of a huge technological revolution that was coming over the horizon.

In addition to the indoor terminals, there was a completely new concept of outdoor payment terminals that some truck stops were beginning to trial. These terminals were connected directly to high-speed pumps that drivers could use without having to go inside to the operator behind the counter. There were two main manufacturers at the time: Petrovend and Triscan. This type of machine also allowed local fuel distributors to turn their depots into small fuel stations without the need for staff. These could run on a 24/7 basis and became a nice new form of income for them, alongside their traditional home heating, commercial, and agricultural delivery businesses.

In many ways, the technology worked in a similar way to Fortronic, with a new stop list downloaded once a night when the daily transaction files were polled. However, this also presented a new problem to overcome—the need for PINs. Petrovend had designed a complex offline PIN system that effectively used an algorithm to generate PINs from the card data. This meant that as each card was inserted in the terminal, the terminal read all the details from the magnetic stripe and then knew what PIN to expect.

I approached Petrovend and asked its staff to provide me with a copy of this security program, and they replied saying that it was extremely complex and could only be calculated using an IBM AS/400–scale computer and that the only solution was for us to start buying all our cards from them. The pricing being suggested was nearly ten times what we were currently paying to PCC, which would not allow us to be competitive, especially since we were not even charging customers for the cards, as we had included them as an incentive in our launch offer. I kept pressing the company to release the program to me under an NDA and eventually Petrovend agreed, even though I could see that they thought there was no chance I would be able to interpret it. The evening I received it, I stayed late in the office and set to work on our Amstrad PC to try to build a spreadsheet macro in Lotus 123 to do the calculations that apparently needed AS/400 processing power. I obviously can't disclose any details, but I was presented with some maths complexity I had never seen before, even at A level, and it definitely stretched my Lotus skills to the limit. By eleven at night, I finally entered a card number at the top in the input section of my macro, and at the bottom of my Amstrad computer screen, a four-digit number appeared that matched the PIN issued by Petrovend. I was already looking forward to the phone conversation I would be having with Pete, the MD at Petrovend, to let him know that I had cracked the mega-complex code on a little PC in just a few hours!

So, the following day, I came to work and set about getting our first outdoor terminal site up and running with a small fuel distributor. This heralded the start of a new phase of expanding our network, as new sites could be set up quickly with very little manual effort or cost. The big added benefit of this mechanism was that all transactions were automated, so they didn't add to the growing number of green sheets coming in by post or fax every day. One clever trick I came up with to get over the issue of our fax line being constantly engaged when the truck stops tried to send in the sheets was to use rolling telephone numbers. This meant having three extra telephone lines that rolled between themselves at the exchange, so we could effectively receive four different faxes at the same time using a single fax number. We were really impressed with ourselves for getting this simple bit of technology up and running and never failed to show visitors our rank of machines all working at the same time!

As I started to visit the fuel distributors to see if I could do a deal to get acceptance for our cards at their depots, I found that most of them were also selling diesel on the Keyfuels system. They were effectively acting as large customers who put a stock of fuel into the network, often at their own site, and then sell this diesel to their customers on a weekly basis as the cards were used across the whole of the network. Keyfuels used the word *dealer* to describe them, and these dealers were really beginning to drive additional growth alongside their direct customer offering. As I talked to these dealers about card acceptance, I also started to ask if they were interested in using our network, too, as an alternative to Keyfuels. I obviously offered them our very competitive handling charge of 1 ppl (plus free cards), but I also thought I needed something else to try to differentiate us. What I came up with was a chance for them to put their own branding on everything their customers saw, including the fuel cards, the site directories, and their weekly and monthly reports. As this was something Keyfuels wasn't doing, our bespoke offering proved really popular and started to build us a reputation among the fuel distributors. They all talked among themselves, so I started to get calls out of the blue to visit Texaco and Total distributors across the UK. It wasn't long before we were building quite a reasonable dealer network of our own. Back at the office, this added complexity meant that we had to have many different card types and site directory covers, which created mountains of boxes every time we did a reissue. This was happening every three months, given how many sites we were now adding on a regular basis.

This meant our weekly printing process was starting to take much longer, as our volumes and transaction numbers were growing alongside a rapidly expanding range of different branding. The report printing on a Friday afternoon now involved several OKI dot matrix printers all hammering away, and then we had to separate all the triplicate NCR sheets and put them in envelopes for each individual customer. The extra time this took meant that our ritual Friday afternoon beer began to get later and later in the day! We had to endure this ever longer and noisier part of the process for a few more years before the arrival of the new ultraquiet, superfast laser printers came to our rescue. It would then be a few more years still before the transformational change of being able to email reports and invoices to our customers would eliminate this problem altogether.

Something else that happened early in 1991 that proved to be a pivotal step for the business was my first trip to Ireland. One of our larger customers, John Miller Transport (JMT), whose owner was actually a personal friend of mine, rang me and asked whether there was any chance we could open a site near Larne Harbour. Larne is a small town located near a port in Northern Ireland, up on the northeast tip. It is the closest point to Scotland and the port of Stranraer. JMT had a contract to move computers from Mullingar in the south, up across the border, then over the Irish Sea into Scotland and down into England. Back in 1991, diesel was cheaper in the UK, so my friend wanted his trucks to refuel in Larne before they headed south again to pick up another load. The price differential would not always work in the same direction; a little later in the book, I'll get into how important cross-border pricing would become to the future growth of the business. I decided to arrange a visit and booked my flight to Belfast with British Airways for £275, which was pretty expensive back then. This was well before Ryanair got going and before the other low-cost carriers that followed it would change the cost and accessibility of air travel.

I made two appointments for my trip: one with another branded Texaco distributor, Nicholl Oils, based in Greysteel near Derry, and a second with a transport company called Pandoro located down at the harborfront in Larne. After landing at Belfast International Airport, I got my first sight of all the security checkpoints that were in place back then, which definitely gave a different feel to those early visits as I traveled across the country. At Nicholl Oils, I met Gary, the eldest son in a family business. Little did I know at the time that this would be the start of a very important relationship. Although Gary didn't have a site or depot that could suit the needs of JMT, he was interested in having his own branded Nicholl Oils fuel card that could run on our network and was also happy for us to add his depots and retail locations to our growing list of UK Fuels sites. My second appointment proved more fruitful for JMT, as the manager of Pandoro in Larne agreed to accept our card and become a location on our network. So we were up and running with a site in Ireland, even if the transactions were on a manual-only basis.

Back home, I also started to get a few requests from customers who wanted to fuel their trucks on the Continent. The major transport routes to France, Germany, and Italy all tended to run through the southern ports of Dover and Ramsgate, and it would be a couple of years before the Channel Tunnel would eventually open and offer a new way for freight to cross to the Continent. As diesel was generally significantly cheaper on the Continent than in the UK, especially in Belgium, Luxembourg, France, and Spain, customers wanted locations to fuel either at the ports where they landed or close to the main highways on their ongoing routes. This meant that Calais in France and Zeebrugge and Veurne in Belgium were top locations when the trucks just got off the ferry, and Luxembourg and the Mont Blanc Tunnel were really good spots once they were into their journey. If they happened to be heading even farther south to Spain or Portugal to pick up loads of fruit and vegetables to bring back north, then La Jonquera and Irun, both located just south of the French border at either end of the Pyrenees, were ideal places to fill up. Given that the trucks crossing Europe used very large quantities of fuel and had enormous belly tanks that could take more than one thousand liters per fill, this was a potentially really interesting new market for us.

There were already several fuel card companies that specialized in this pan-European fueling: DKV, UTA, and ROUTEX, all of which had vast networks in nearly every country across both Western and Eastern Europe. There were also fully automated operators, such as IDS and AS 24, that ran smaller chains. These two smaller ones had 24/7 operations at every single site on their networks, where they were using outdoor card terminals similar to those that were starting to appear in the UK. They were generally much more competitive on price, which definitely fit in well with our sales and marketing approach. Given that its model was probably more akin to our own, I decided to approach AS 24 as a first step to see if it was interested in some form of partnership. The company was based in Nantes on the Atlantic coast of France and had been founded just a few years earlier in 1988, but it was already growing quickly.

I flew down to AS 24's head office the following week, and after a few further meetings, we agreed that we could become a commission agent to sell AS 24 products to our UK customer base. Given that our network already had several fully automated sites with Petrovend equipment, I also asked if AS 24 would be interested in becoming a customer of ours, too, for when its European truckers from across continental Europe were visiting the UK. We signed this deal and then began getting their card ISO numbers and protocol set up with Petrovend. This was the start of my learning more about the European fuel market and all the different country nuances. This would prove useful knowledge when we later decided to take our first step onto the Continent.

LESSON 4

COMPARTMENTALIZE.

I was going to call this lesson "Lots of pots" but decided it needed a more professional title, so I chose "Compartmentalize." When you Google the definition, it talks about "fear of leaks," and in many ways, this is exactly what I am trying to explain, but not quite in the way Google intended!

I started to learn this lesson as a result of our new joint venture (JV) model (which you will hear about in the next chapter), which meant that instead of building an ever-larger central sales office, we continually spawned more and more smaller regional locations, all run by individual leaders.

What I realized from having a model like this was that it was easier to see things that were going well and to identify parts of our sales operations that were underperforming. This meant it was a faster exercise to fix these issues, which then led to much better overall growth performance. It also had the added advantage that if I found a particularly good person in Ipswich, Glasgow, or Cheltenham who wasn't able to move near Crewe, I could just build up an operation around them.

When you look at the actual economics of a sales operation, the additional cost of having multiple offices rather than one central one is relatively small compared to the advantages of performance from our multiple-pot theory. It also allows us to fish in lots of different employment pools, which is also very important when you have a rel-atively high turnover of mostly young staff. This theory has the further advantage of making lots of different individuals clearly responsible for a specific subset of customers and profitability and spreads people management pressure across many shoulders instead of one.

As I am writing this section today, which is actually one of the final lessons I've written despite it being near the start of the book, I am at an off-site session in the Lake District doing exactly what I am talking about here. Our telematics customer base in the UK is now over forty thousand, with more than two hundred thousand revenue-generat-ing units (RGUs) fitted to a variety of vehicles and other assets. Given that we have built most of this base up organically via telesales from our main Crewe office, it has started to become a very large beast to manage. We are now churning customers too fast, our customer service and account management are under immense strain, and we are struggling to really identify exactly how to improve things despite making lots of changes.

We are therefore using the methodology described in this lesson by splitting this cohort into Enterprise and Fleet and then sub-splitting each of these two new groups into five smaller lots each, thus creating ten pots instead of one. Enterprise will have a mainly geographical structure, with North, Central, South, Government, and Ireland, while Fleet will have a more vertical one, with Transport,

Construction, Couriers, etc. Each of the ten new blocks of customers will have roughly twenty thousand RGUs and an individual director or manager responsible for maintaining and growing their own base. I am sure this new lots-of-pots structure for the business will help us grow faster, as it has been proven many times over the years, so we should hopefully stop the leaks.

A NEW JV MODEL
FOR GROWTH

As the network continued to grow and we became more established in the market, I had my first approach from an individual looking to start their own fuel card business. Colin Sykes was working in Scotland as a sales manager for one of the bulk fuel distributors I described earlier, and he had decided that there was an opportunity to start a fuel card–specific reseller company of his own. He had also come up with the catchy name, Thistle Fuels. So, after a quick chat over the phone, I set off up the M6 to meet Colin at a town called Biggar in Scotland to talk through his idea to use our network as a platform to create a new type of dealer. His plan seemed pretty good, especially given that he had great sales experience in the transport sector and also had loads of local contacts across the whole of the Central Belt of Scotland.

The biggest problem I could see was that he was going to need a lot of credit to finance all the diesel purchases he was going to need, which would not only stretch the financial resources of UK Fuels given we would be supplying him, but would create a second problem by giving us a very concentrated individual credit risk with this new start-up company. I talked through the issue with John over one of our regular Chinese meals, and over the next week or so we came up with a creative idea to try to solve this problem. Instead of being just a supplier we would propose for us to become a partner in his business and inject some capital to help finance the diesel purchases. Secondly, we would suggest that UK Fuels provide all the customer vetting and credit management services centrally to ensure that Thistle Fuels would manage its credit policy in accordance with our very strict rules and not put us at any increased risk.

John and I arranged to meet Colin for dinner the following week to talk through our idea of a 60/20/20 percent partnership, which would free him up to concentrate all his efforts on sales, as he wouldn't have to worry about buying diesel or managing credit. Although this structure would give him a larger part of the long-term financial benefits, we would split the voting share on a 50/25/25 percent basis, thus allowing us to have equal control because we would always need to agree on major decisions. We chose to meet the following week at Penrith, just south of the Scottish border and about halfway between where Colin lived in Berwick-upon-Tweed and where we were based down in Chester. This dinner would be the start of many return visits to Junction 40 of the M6 over the next few years.

After taking a few days to think about our proposal, Colin called to say yes, so it was all systems go for Thistle Fuels. We decided it was best to keep our direct investment in this new dealer quiet so as not to potentially upset our other dealers. I used a friend of mine in Edinburgh as a nominee to hold the shares on John's and my behalf. Over the next few weeks, we designed a new logo for the cards and site directories, formed a new company, and found a small office in Berwick-upon-Tweed. Colin then resigned from his job, and he was asked to leave immediately, so we were all ready for our new JV. Colin then set about racing around Scotland and the Scottish Borders in his white Peugeot 309, visiting as many transport companies as he could in the weeks that followed. This meant that the volumes began to build almost immediately. Within a few months, it was obvious that Thistle Fuels was going to be a success and that we had added another string to the UK Fuels bow to accelerate our growth.

Before I go on, I think it is important to cover some key principles that were established as part of the formation of this new JV. The costs within Thistle Fuels were kept very low with Colin accepting a salary significantly below his market rate as well as having a much cheaper secondhand diesel car. The reason for this was that he was getting a 60 percent shareholding, and the success of the company was therefore paramount for all of us to get a return. The faster the company achieved profitability, the faster we could have a dividend and get some reward for all our hard work. This extra money would then allow Colin to catch up and significantly overtake his previous remuneration, as well as build some capital value in the new business. This concept of caring for the company and then the company caring for those who have looked after it is central to my entire way of thinking about culture, and I talk about this more later. We also set off without a shareholder agreement, which meant that we were all needed for approval on all key decisions, with none of us being forced to do something we didn't want to do.

It wasn't long before another very similar set of circumstances occurred with an employee at one of our main diesel suppliers, Phillips Petroleum. Ian Watson, who managed a team of bulk fuel sales reps across Scotland, had also become interested in potentially leaving and doing something along the same lines as Colin. We soon began talking seriously with him about a second JV, and we came up with the novel three-word name Fuel Control Services (FCS). These three-word names would become very common over the next few years as we started to accelerate this new JV model and actively look for potential new partners.

A further difference in the structure of FCS was that I decided to give Steve Gent, my sales director, and Mike Goldstein, my IT director, a 5 percent share each as a new type of incentive. This meant that the shareholding in FCS was 50 percent Ian, 20 percent John, 20 percent me, 5 percent Steve, and 5 percent Mike. This was the start of the LTIP for my senior team, which would prove critical for driving growth over the next decade and beyond. It was also a growth scheme that we would mirror even after we brought all the businesses together nearly twenty years later, and it's still operating today. The key principle of this scheme is that the shares are not worth anything on the day they are given and will only become worth something after a lot of time and hard work. These two new JVs were also the early proving point to me of the compartmentalization theory, as we now had three separate offices all driving their own growth plans in different geographies, with various customer types and sales and marketing approaches, all contributing to the increase in our bunker network volumes.

I can't remember the exact date we broke through the million-liter-per-month mark, but I remember it being a very momentous date for UK Fuels. And surprise, surprise, we decided to celebrate it at The Fortune Palace, our local Chinese restaurant! There must have only been about twelve of us at the time, but it was a loud and noisy party, after which we didn't show our faces back there for quite a few weeks! Over the years, we haven't spent much time celebrating our successes, despite the conclusion you might come to after reading this book. However, I think this was an early example of when we do have a party, we want everyone to enjoy it and forget about work. It was probably around this point that I also had to make a final decision about whether I would take up my place at business school in Paris. Given the momentum we were now building, I knew that continuing with the UK Fuels project was the right thing to do, so declining my spot was an easy choice in the end. John was also kind enough to give me a further 10 percent share in UK Fuels, so I was now a 30 percent shareholder and felt like a proper equal partner.

Another thing that was starting to become obvious was that Joe and I were not going to be able to do all the jobs within the business ourselves if we wanted to scale, so we needed to get some more specialists to join the team. Tim Robins was the first of these. He was a trained accountant working for Baker Tilly who joined and took over all the finance jobs Joe had been doing. I'd known Tim from Lancaster University, where he had been studying with my best man, Justin.

Mike was next to join as the IT director. Given that the only way we knew how to increase computing power was by simply adding an additional un-networked PC, we obviously needed help! The daily operational tasks as well as the end-of-day backups now involved using a ridiculous number of floppy disks, and we were getting close to breaking point on data management.

The third key person we took on about this time was Steve, who joined as sales director and had lots of industry experience that he had picked up during his time at Triscan. This was the other main manufacturer of outdoor terminals, alongside Petrovend. I had also gotten to know Steve quite well over the previous couple of years and thought he would fit in well with our culture.

My new, bigger team was in place by the end of 1994, which suddenly gave us significantly more resources and capability and therefore the ability to project ourselves in a stronger way with the major oil companies. Although we didn't know it at the time, these relationships were going to be another key building block in the development of UK Fuels.

The Christmas parties were also becoming bigger and more raucous, and after the first one at the Chinese restaurant in Tarvin, we moved to Warmingham Grange, where they did much larger organized events that enabled us to book our own tables for twenty people or more among a larger overall group of a few hundred. Everyone looked forward to these gatherings, and they always created a few stories that would be talked about back at the office for months and sometimes years to come. As we didn't spend too much time celebrating our successes during the year, it was a good time for everyone to let their hair down a little and come back in the New Year ready for the fresh challenges that lay ahead.

Before the next chapter, I thought I would tell you one of my favorite stories about the early days and one that relates in particular to my regular Sunday trips north to meet up with both Colin and Ian from the two new JVs. It always makes me smile when I think back about it.

One thing probably not many of you will know is that when THF, one of the world's largest hotel groups at the time, was at its peak in the early 1990s, it had a little-known special deal: If you went to check in at one of its hotels and it was fully booked for that night, you could get a referral to its next closest property at the same price even if it was a far more expensive hotel. Because Thistle Fuels and FCS were based in Scotland, the town of Penrith in Cumbria was the perfect halfway point for meeting up. I would regularly drive up on a Sunday to meet with one of them for an early dinner and catch up before staying over for the night and then finishing off our meeting the following morning.

Right next to the junction, there was a Little Chef restaurant with a Travel Lodge behind it, which provided a perfect meeting spot for these regular get-togethers. A lot of other businesspeople obviously also had the same idea, and this Travel Lodge was reputedly the busiest one in the whole of the UK at the time and one you absolutely had to book in advance. Well, that was if you didn't know about the special deal, combined with the local knowledge that just a few minutes' drive away was the Leeming House hotel—a beautiful country house perched on the banks of Ullswater and also part of the THF group.

So imagine the scenario as Ian and I arrived at the reception to check in on a Sunday evening and we opened with the usual question of "Have you got a couple of rooms for this evening, please?" Only to get what became the regular response of "I'm really sorry, sir, but we are fully booked tonight, as this is one of the busiest Travel Lodges in the UK. You really need to book in advance, especially on a Sunday evening, if you want to guarantee a room."

Then came what would become our standard reply, "Do you know of any other hotels in the area that might have a couple of rooms available?" followed by, "We do have a sister hotel down the road called Leeming House that's only a few miles away, and I can refer you both there if you think that would work for you. If they do have rooms available, they would be at the same price as you would have paid here, but I'm afraid that wouldn't include breakfast."

We were obviously very happy with that arrangement, as we preferred coming to the Little Chef for our regular Early Starter breakfast anyway.

A phone call would then ensue, which always resulted in rooms being available, as the weekend tourist–oriented Leeming House was always deserted on Sunday nights.

Then, on to the part of the tale that Ian and I will never forget and still makes us laugh today. The next question from the receptionist was normally, "Could you give me your last names, please, to confirm the booking so that Leeming House can be ready for you?"

I replied, "Holmes and Watson," to which the receptionist responded, "Really?" with a smile on her face, not believing us!

Until that day, neither Ian nor I had ever put the Sherlock Holmes link of our two surnames together. When Ian eventually retired many years later, he kindly bought me an original first-edition copy of *The Hound of the Baskervilles* in memory of that famous day as well as the great partnership we went on to build.

Although there were several different receptionists at the Travel Lodge over the next couple of years, we got to know them all well, and soon, we didn't even have to pretend what we were up to. If, on a rare occurrence, there was a trainee or new employee who wasn't aware of the special deal, we soon put them right!

A final corollary to this story was that I had lunch recently at Brown's Hotel in London, which is part of the relaunched upmarket Forte Hotel chain, and Sir Rocco Forte approached the person I was dining with, who was an old friend from the business world. After they had finished chatting, I introduced myself and gave a brief recount of this story, which definitely made him smile too!

LESSON 5

DO MORE OF WHAT'S GOING WELL AND STOP WHEN IT ISN'T.

This seems a fairly obvious lesson, but I don't often see that many people in our company move quickly enough to reduce resources in one of their weaker areas of the business and then ask to reallocate this overhead to one that is going well.

Over the years, not everything I have tried has worked out, so it is important to become good at recognizing poor performance as early as possible so you can make the often-difficult decision to stop quickly. This normally includes having to let several, or sometimes many, of your employees go on very short notice, which is probably why many managers often ignore this problem and leave it to linger rather than tackle it immediately.

When I read about entrepreneurs in the papers or see them on television extolling the virtues of going bust and what an excellent learning experience for the future it is, I cringe. Generally, these so-called entrepreneurs have been blowing investors' money on completely uncontrolled, wasteful projects and definitely not caring for every pound of the company's money as if it were their own. They tend to leave a trail of destruction behind them, including shareholders and banks that end up losing many millions of pounds, and blame everyone but themselves for the company's poor predicament. I have never wanted to owe anyone a pound, either personally or in business.

So, whether it's adding people to a sales team that is performing well, starting more JVs (as per our model), or pulling out of a country, sector, or relationship that isn't working, I have always tried to work according to this principle. I want my team to be able to recognize these instances in the business and make recommendations and implement them rather than just sit there waiting for me or someone from above to make the tough decisions for them. This is a philosophy that I think about every day as I try to plot the best course for the future of Radius.

On the positive side, for the last twenty-five years, I have told my teams that there is absolutely no limit to how many salespeople they can take on (even if it is well above budget) as long as they all individually meet their monthly sales targets. What you tend to find is that if they build their teams too large, the average performance starts to drop below an acceptable level, and the system becomes a self-leveling one that maximizes the managers' individual capabilities as well our ability to recruit enough local talent.

This derestricted way of working negatively impacts short-term profitability, as it increases overheads, but it has the advantage of giving us better long-term growth. It is also one of the advantages of being a private business, as it is not something that is easily replicated when you have the quarterly reporting constraint, such as in a publicly quoted company (PLC).

Even within private businesses, not that many owners adopt this long-term growth philosophy. Those who don't are generally adhering to the rule that dividends are more important than investment and growth, meaning they are running their companies more as lifestyle businesses. Radius has never fallen into this category.

BORDER BUSINESS AND THE BIRTH OF DCI

Over in Ireland, our relationship with Nicholl Oils was going well, and we had established a good network of more than fifteen sites in the north, with lots of volume starting to build on the personalized branded card we had created for them. On top of this progress, however, something far more significant was happening at the border that would have a greater positive impact on our business and the development of our operations across the whole of Ireland.

For the last ten years, there had been a specific, busy business that had been going on at the fuel stations just on the north side of the border because of a price differential. The cheaper prices in the north that had driven all this volume were now being neutralized, and the pendulum was beginning to swing the other way because of the UK government repeatedly increasing excise fuel duties on diesel and petrol in every annual budget. The effect of this on Nicholl Oils was that a significant number of its commercial customers were now asking if it was possible for them to have a fuel card that would work on the south side of the border so that they could take advantage of the new cheaper fuel conditions there.

Gary and I had been talking over the idea of a new JV similar to those I had started with Colin and Ian in Scotland, and we decided that the time was now right, so early in 1995, Diesel Card Ireland

(DCI) was born. We agreed on a 50/50 split between Gary and me on the company ownership. John was supportive of this new venture without being a shareholder. Then, both Gary and I set about doing deals with site owners located at all the major border-crossing points, from the one at Dundalk in the east to the one at Bridgend in the far northwest, and nearly every road in between! Where there wasn't an existing site, we looked to rent a small parcel of land and put down a self-contained bunded unit as an alternative. These units were effectively a fifty-thousand-liter diesel tank with two high-speed pumps and an automated card reader at one end. All you needed on-site was power, a telephone line, and a graveled area, and you could be up and running very quickly with a site that could work 24/7. These soon became commonplace for us right across the border, with tanks delivered to Dundalk, Lifford, Tyholland, Emyvale, Ballyconnell, Swanlinbar, Bridgend, Muff, and many more. Some of these places are literally only a few meters south of the official border line.

DCI began to grow really quickly, driven by an ever-increasing price differential that was heading for more than 20 ppl as the UK government continued to pile on the excise duty. We continued to add more locations, some of which were much farther south, and I was soon into a routine of flying to either Dublin or Belfast two or three times a month. Our network soon included sites in Dublin Docklands, Naas, Cork, Limerick, Portlaoise, Galway, Sligo, Mullingar, Rosslare, and many points in between. We also started to promote a branded card offer to local fuel distributors and soon built up strong relationships with Emo Oil, Tougher Oil, and some of the local Texaco fuel distributors. Back at the office, we agreed to set up a separate finance function for DCI so that the costs were clearly segregated from UK Fuels, and we appointed a second finance director, Malcolm Joyce, to work entirely on this project. I'd gotten to know Malcolm at my local gym in Chester, so he was yet another new senior employee I'd managed to find without having to pay a huge fee to external recruiters!

I remember there being lots of comments by competitors at the time that I was wasting my time in Ireland. These were generally centered around why I was bothering, as it was such a small country, and it would have been far more fruitful to launch into Continental Europe. How wrong they were, as our business there has kept growing for the last thirty years. Ireland is still our number two country today, well ahead of Germany, France, Italy, and even the US. From the very early days of DCI, when we were rapidly expanding our border network to many of our more recent endeavors in Ireland, this has been an excellent case study of doing more of what's going well. However, you will have to wait a little longer in this book for some examples of stopping when it isn't!

Back at our office in Holmes Chapel, we had expanded twice during these first few years, initially by taking the adjacent flat on our left-hand side, number 25a, and then by taking number 21a on the other side. This meant we had to go outside to the back balcony and knock on the front door of one of the other flats if we wanted to move between our three offices—definitely not an ideal setup. Staff numbers were going up, and by late 1993, we were heading towards twenty people, including the first members of my new senior team. Things were definitely starting to feel cramped. We had also begun to talk more closely with some of the major oil companies about partnership deals, and our current office setup of three separate flats did not present the right image of a professional, tech-based management company.

So it was back to looking around for a new office again, and probably having to move out of the village we were in, to somewhere a bit bigger with more choices of commercial property. After hunting for a few weeks, I found something that was more than double the size of where we were, in the center of a small town a little further south, next to Junction 17 of the M6. It was an old co-op building where the first and second floors were available to rent. The space sat above one of the new everything-low-price shops, and the on-street entrance was located beside Woolworths. So within a couple of months, we moved a few miles down the road to 12 High Street, Sandbach, using a removal van this time instead of Pat's horse box! We had loads more space there and could start to lay out our growing number of departments in a more organized way. One of the first things we did after moving was get some nice, embossed signs made with Cards Department, Finance, Operations, etc., printed on them for each of the room doors. This definitely made us feel more structured and professional, especially when we were showing visitors round.

The only problem with leaving Holmes Chapel was that I had signed a twenty-five-year lease for the original unit at 23a. I decided to use this as our off-site storage for the growing number of copy reports that were building up. We had rented the other two units on three-year leases, and they didn't have long left to run. I promised myself that I wouldn't make this same mistake again, as it was proving impossible to sublet them. From then on, we would only sign up for maximum five-year rental periods, and in nearly all cases, we would have a three-year break clause.

The other thing that was becoming urgent was that we needed to start making some serious changes to our IT systems, which were beginning to creak under the pressure. We now had more than thirty PCs, none of which were networked together, and we were not going to be able to last much longer on our floppy disk method of transferring files. In addition, our "smart" database was starting to run very slowly as well as fail regularly, given the amount of transaction data we were now processing.

Mike set about solving these two problems, and within twelve months, he had networked the new office and moved all transactions onto an Oracle database. Looking back, we were actually fortunate to have delayed this development step, as it allowed us to effectively stay on PC hardware versus having to change our setup completely to an AS/400 platform similar to the ones both our main competitors were using. This meant we could ride the exponential wave of PC processor speed improvements and keep our IT costs relatively low, even as the business started to accelerate faster. Once the new database was up and running, Mike and his new IT team (of one person) started to write some of our processes in Oracle Forms to ease the strain on all the manual work that had been steadily building up. These new programs would go on to last us for more than twenty-five years until Oracle finally decided to sunset them just a few years ago.

The internet, which I knew very little about in its early form, was starting to become more important too. Every company now needed a nice website if it was going to look professional, even if there wasn't really any functionality. So we registered UKFuels.co.uk and DCIcard.ie and got going with our first versions. Mike and his tiny team didn't have any experience in this new software language, so like a lot of companies at the time, we fully outsourced the development and hosting of the sites to one of the new micro businesses that had popped up. The biggest impact for us was that we got email addresses, which enabled us to communicate with our customers much more efficiently, as well as sign new ones up in days rather than weeks. It would be quite a few years before we would eventually take on our first marketing person and begin to understand some of the other advantages the internet could bring us in this new digital world.

On the personal front, things were also about to change in a big way soon, as Gill was pregnant. The house in Tarvin was definitely going to be a tight squeeze with a baby, so we started to look around the area for something a little bigger. We settled on the village of Tarporley, just a few miles down the road. By the spring of 1993, we had moved to 10 Springhill just before the birth of our first daughter, Lauren Rosie, on 13th July. Our new home was in a nice estate of twelve houses and had a small garden at the front and back, and it was just a few minutes' walk to the village center, where there was a good selection of shops and pubs.

DON'T SPEND TOO MUCH TIME AND EFFORT HUNTING WHALES.

This particular way of thinking is one I acquired very early in the life of Radius and one that has stuck with me over time, despite the fact that I have actually managed to land a few whales along the way!

It's very easy, when you just start off and are desperate to grow, to get starry-eyed at a particularly large opportunity that suddenly presents itself. The first and most obvious thing to be wary of when this happens is that there will probably be several other companies quoting for this contract, making your odds of success naturally lower than with your classic customer engagement. The second obvious fact is that it will more than likely be at a very competitive price, hence a lower-than-normal margin for you.

If you take both these facts as acceptable risk (given the size of the prize), you then need to realize that these types of customers tend to have several key components about them in common that start to lead to a gradual increase in the risk, without you noticing it is happening.

To start with, they tend to have more complex product and solution requirements, meaning that your core offering will need significant changes and enhancements. This can be costly as well as consume more of your IT development capacity and senior management effort. This inevitably leads to a much longer lead time before you can actually start trading with this customer, giving a further negative effect on your base case economics. If you are selling a physical product as part of your overall service, there can also be hidden cash flow effects that start to emerge because either you have to hold higher inventory or the customer wants longer payment terms.

If you do finally make it through all these issues and land your whale on board, the next thing you start to learn is that they need much more servicing than you had imagined. To keep them happy, you now have to continually change and personalize your product as you receive a never-ending flow of new requirements, sucking ever more resources from your core development activity. To top it all, if trading does actually build up significantly, you now realize that you have created a new large risk for yourself, as you are now over-reliant on them because of the percentage of your business they now make up, which means if you lose them, they leave a very big hole.

Over the last thirty-five years, I have stuck to concentrating our efforts on catching tuna, haddock, and plaice and left most of the whales I've spotted to someone else!

THE OIL COMPANIES

As our bunker volumes continued to grow and the amount of diesel we were needing to buy for our direct credit customers increased, the relationships with our fuel suppliers were becoming ever more important. The biggest of these were the ones that many of you will recognize from the retail petrol stations you drive past every day—Esso, Shell, BP, Texaco, Total, Gulf, JET, etc. There are also ones that operate in the commercial markets only, such as Mabanaft, Harvest Energy, Prax, Greenergy, and, in the old days, Phillips Petroleum (now P66).

The fact that we were working with many of their branded distributors helped get us closer to them, so when Gulf Oil decided to go out to market for a supplier to run a new fuel card, we decided to put our hat in the ring even though it felt against my philosophy of not spending too much time and effort hunting whales! Gulf Oil, based down in Cheltenham, was trying to build a national network of unmanned diesel sites—many of them located alongside its existing fuel distributors. It had branded this new format of sites as "G Stops," which always caused a few smiles! The company was looking for a partner to provide all the backend processing and card-issuing capabilities as well as a strategic motorway and trunk road network to fill in the gaps where it didn't have its new G Stops. Keyfuels and PCS were also bidding, but I think the combination of our superlow 1-ppl handling charge and the personalization package we had developed won us the day. I remember going up to the Lake District for a professional photo shoot at a truck stop as part of the launch, as Gulf Oil had high expectations for how its new concept was going to drive additional business for it.

A similar opportunity to this came up with Total Oil, in which we had also already been working with many of their branded distributors, including Chandlers Oil & Gas, E. Cunnah & Son Limited, Southern Counties, Total Heat, ABA Fuels, Ford Fuels, RPD, and Prince Petroleum. Total Oil wanted its own bunker card that it could market to its direct commercial clients, and this soon began to add a few customers and continued to help grow our volumes. The company was also becoming one of the biggest bulk diesel suppliers in our network, which meant we were soon added to the favored list of invitees for its annual rugby Five Nations (now Six Nations) trip to Paris. These weekends had always been by coach from London, and drinking started early on a Friday morning alongside a bacon sandwich at a bar near Victoria station. This was followed by a long drive to Paris, including a ferry across the channel. On my second trip, transport changed to Eurostar and the Channel Tunnel, with beer and sandwiches moving to The Fire Station pub in one of the arches underneath Waterloo Station. Our host from Total Oil, Tim Shepherd, our main sales contact, always led the post-match singing in a cordoned-off area in a small bar in Paris near Parc des Princes, whether we had won or lost.

The trip I actually remember most was one year when I decided to make it even easier for myself and fly from Manchester, when I ended up traveling with the Hodge brothers, who ran the Preston-based distributor, Ribble Fuel Oils. After dropping our bags at the hotel, we headed straight for lunch at the Eiffel Tower in the first-floor restaurant. We had some very nice red wine with the meal, and the manager ended up giving us a lock-in all afternoon. We eventually had to leave after the evening dinner guests started to arrive! I do remember the evening afterwards, when we were meant to be meeting up with all the other guests and our hosts from Total Oil, who had arrived that afternoon by train, being a bit of a write-off!

These two new cards from Gulf Oil and Total Oil had their own ISO numbers, which added a new complexity to our systems, as up to now, the only difference between the branded distributor cards had been the artwork designs on the front. Each new ISO needed to be set up at all the electronic terminals across the networks and involved both new transaction file formats as well as separate stop lists.

Ultimately, neither of these deals would prove to be the block-busters we had hoped for, despite all the effort we had put in (lesson 6 learned!). It would not be until our third oil company deal that we would finally land one that would actually give us a return on all the time and money we had invested in the bidding and delivery phases. Gary Nicholl's father, Hugh, also played a key role in helping us win this deal because of his influence in the Texaco branded distributor world. At many of the quarterly council meetings, he had recommended us to several other companies within its UK membership, including Watson Petroleum, Peak Oil, and Askham Oil Supplies Limited, which had all proved successful. So when Texaco started to think about launching its own card into the commercial market, Hugh was very much our inside man, using his influence to promote UK Fuels, the smaller newcomer, rather than Keyfuels or PCS, both of which had much bigger networks and longer track records. Texaco appointed a manager on its side, David Gower, to run the project, and over the next few months and many meetings, we began to shape a new concept with the code name *fastfuel*. Once this had been finalized, we had to put together a detailed proposal of how we would handle all the transaction flows and the financial reimbursement of Texaco's network of company-owned and dealer sites. This was the first time since the start that we had entered a complex tender process and had to put together a really professional presentation and contract document.

After not much short of a year of meetings and negotiations, we finally found out we had been successful and were awarded the contract in September 1995. I think Keyfuels felt it was the firm favorite to win, so this was probably the first time it began to see us as strong competitors, even though, after we had been awarded the contract, it thought the project would fail given our lack of scale and resources. So we set about doing the biggest bit of IT development we had commissioned to date, which involved lots of new file formats and data interchanges, as well as an enormous addition to the number of sites. This was because Texaco was including its entire network of nearly six hundred sites—a number that completely dwarfed our current network of a little over one hundred locations.

We also needed a completely new brand for fastfuel, and Texaco engaged a third-party agency to develop some concepts, as it wanted to make a big splash with the launch. It did feel a bit like déjà vu with another big oil company, but I had my fingers crossed that it would be third-time lucky. This new card also needed yet another new ISO number, which then had to be set up at all the Texaco sites, so there was plenty to do. Within three to four months, we were ready for launch and issued a few cards to some of our direct customers to get the ball rolling and create a few live transactions on the system.

The final thing needed as part of our contractual commitment was to create our first real web-based portal to allow customers to log in and download their transactions online. We thought this was cutting-edge technology even though it was already commonplace in the market, so again we had to use external software developers to help us build it. We called the new system Webfuels, and although it wasn't the nicest-looking system, it worked and would end up having to last us for over a decade before we would replace it. The sales and marketing plan was always that the Texaco team and some of their branded distributors would sell the card, with our role being a pure processor and administrator of the service. Within six months, volumes were well below the original plan, and it was looking a little as if Keyfuels might have been right about the project failing. From our perspective, all the systems were working really well, and the customer proposition in terms of the size of the network, pricing, and quality of locations was strong, so we didn't see any product reason why it shouldn't be a success.

Specifically, there were also a lot of urban locations on the Texaco network alongside its trunk road and motorway sites, which meant fastfuel allowed access to a much wider range of SMEs, such as builders and plumbers, who tended to refuel more locally.

To try to accelerate things, we decided to offer this product to all our existing resellers to complement the branded versions of the UK Fuels network that we were already supplying them. Within a few months, this began to change the growth trajectory, and volumes began to accelerate.

However, it would be another change that was going to really get fastfuel going and one that would go on to be the most important single factor as to how the business would develop for the next thirty years. You'll have to wait for the next chapter to find out what this change was!

These three new relationships were important in shaping our market thinking that the oil companies were going to be more partners in our business model rather than competitors. This was a very different philosophy from the other players in the fuel card world, which were much more focused on promoting their own brands as the only strategic pathway to growth.

Hugh Nicholl started kindly inviting me to the Federation of Petroleum Suppliers (FPS) annual conferences. They were always a good opportunity to talk to lots of our existing distributor customers as well as make a few new contacts. As there was always a strong contingent from our competitors, too, these were always lively events, with each of us trying to get one over on the other. They were always in April, and for twenty years, I only ever missed one in 2008 because of a back operation in which I had the bottom few vertebrae of my spine fused. I'm afraid to say that this annual industry get-together eventually fizzled out, probably because of the rapid consolidation that started to happen in both the bulk fuels business and the fuel card sector.

LESSON 7

MAKE LOTS OF SMALL IMPROVEMENTS.

At the opening of our new telematics office in Crewe in early 2024, I was reminded when doing some research on our guest of honor, Martin Johnson (England's Rugby World Cup–winning captain), that then-coach Sir Clive Woodward had a very similar approach to what this lesson talks about, but it had a much fancier name—the kaizen concept. Clive had introduced lots of new innovations, including a lighter streamlined kit, fresh kits for players at halftime, new nutritionists for individual team members, different exercise regimes, and so forth. This methodology was also something that Dave Brailsford used in the Olympic cycling world but under the slightly different name of aggregation of marginal gains. Well, you now know who was really the first to have this idea over ten years earlier? Bill Holmes at UK Fuels! Well, only joking, as I know I am not the only businessperson ever to have thought this way.

People in Radius are surprised at all the meetings I attend and the specific details I get involved with, as I am still trying to make lots of small improvements every day that collectively add up over time to make a significant difference to our progress. Those senior managers who see me diving into their areas and making these changes as a problem rather than thanking me for my help are soon in my group of "Are they going to make it or not?"

If I list out the number of small things I classify under this category, I think that three a day is probably my average at the moment—and more like seven a day on my recent three-day trip to a location where performance has definitely dipped in the last six months! Today, quite a few of these changes involve moving and developing people and changing their reporting lines, whereas in the early days, it tended to be designing a new logo, altering product pricing, adjusting sales targets, or changing the invoice frequency on a particular product.

Imagine if every employee worked in this kaizen way (we have almost three thousand people now). You can understand how these small changes can soon add up to an enormous amount of improvement every week (three times three thousand times five)! This culture is something you have to foster and work on constantly, as even if just your directors and managers worked like this, your business would soon be on an unbelievable business improvement curve!

TELESALES, THE BEATING HEART OF THE BUSINESS

Up to that point, the actual selling of diesel on a credit basis was something we had needed to do only because it had allowed us to balance the stocks in our bunker network and keep all of the truck stops fueled. Our sales team consisted of me and two or three new starters looking through the Yellow Pages and calling all the companies in the road transport and haulage sections, supplemented with some regular spotting campaigns. When we came upon smaller customers that were not interested in bunkering, we offered them the chance to have a credit account and work on a pay-as-you-go (PAYGO) basis. As I alluded to earlier, this gave us a much bigger margin of between 2 and 2.50 ppl but also came with the added credit problems of both collecting the money fast enough at month's end and actually getting paid at all, as the transport sector was notorious for insolvencies and liquidations. Even very small transport companies with just two or three trucks could easily use £500 of diesel per day and therefore build up a significant credit exposure very quickly.

After we introduced fastfuel to our resellers, we thought we might as well use it as a secondary product for our own team to offer, as well as the UK Fuels card. We soon found that this gave us a much higher rate of success per call, as there was a greater chance that there was a local site for the customer, and everyone we spoke to had heard of the Texaco brand, which made it easier to at least get past the gatekeeper and speak to the boss. There was also another significant difference between the products, which was that they gave us the ability to appeal to a much wider customer type and not just transport companies. These new customers covered almost every sector of the SME marketplace, from plumbers and builders to shopfitters and couriers. Although the companies didn't use as much fuel on a per-vehicle or per-customer basis, we could make a higher unit margin of 3 to 4 ppl, and they were generally more creditworthy and easier to sign up on direct debit.

We soon expanded our team and started to think about PAYGO as a business in itself and not just a way of helping us balance the bunker network. It wasn't long before UK Fuels was not just the processor of the fastfuel card but had become its biggest reseller as well. When you combined this new growth with what we were already getting from the other partners we had signed up, fastfuel was starting to be a real success for both Texaco and ourselves. Over the next couple of years, the telesales team got steadily bigger, and we started using the old offices in Holmes Chapel as a separate, dedicated sales office instead of just file storage, which made me feel a little better about the twenty-five-year lease that still had nearly twenty more years to run!

By 1997, everything in the business was starting to run faster, with Ireland and DCI growing well and the UK having found this new growth area with fastfuel. However, we were about to get some worrying news. We came in one morning to see a fax that Hugh Nicholl had sent. It was a press release from Chevron (Texaco's parent company in the US) to say that they had signed a memorandum of understanding to merge with Shell. The fact that we had no relationship with Shell in the UK, combined with the knowledge that it already had its own existing card-processing platform, made us immediately concerned about the future of fastfuel and whether it would just be closed down and absorbed into this much larger system after the merger had been completed. Given that fastfuel was now more than 50 percent of our income in the UK, it represented a really big risk for us and a good example of why it isn't a good strategy to build your business with just a few big customers or whales.

I immediately decided to approach Shell to try to start a relationship and see if it was interested in UK Fuels becoming a card reseller for it. It already had a couple of existing ones that were selling exclusively Shell cards, so initially, I think it saw us more as a competitor than a potential new partner. However, after several meetings in which I showed them our steadily expanding telesales operations in Holmes Chapel, I eventually persuaded them to give us a chance. If Texaco was considered a B brand at the time in terms of network size and strength, Shell was definitely in the A category, with a full national network alongside those of BP and Esso. This new deal was going to give our team an even better set of products to sell with service stations in nearly every town in the country and an even stronger brand to help us open conversations with potential new buyers. We expanded the sales team further and took on another small office round the corner in Welles Street, Sandbach, to give us more room as the team continued to grow.

The UK business was starting to pivot at this point, and rather than concentrating our main effort on building the UK Fuels bunker network, our number one priority was now trying to grow our PAYGO volumes with Shell and Texaco. Funnily enough, about this time, we also heard that the Shell-Chevron merger was off, so fastfuel was no longer under threat, and what had been an enormous risk now turned into a bigger opportunity.

This early success with fastfuel also resulted in Texaco asking me to its head office in Canary Wharf to see if we were interested in running its account card. This was a long-standing product that Texaco had been selling for many years and was effectively used as an account card for each of its service stations to give to local businesses. The card was based on pump price only, and customers could apply for one by picking up and filling in a paper leaflet available on the counter and returning it in a reply-paid envelope. This card had been outsourced by Texaco to a company called PHH (better known for its Allstar brand), and as it was coming to the end of its current contract, Texaco offered us the chance to tender to see if we could put in a more compelling proposal. We quickly put together an offer and, within a few months, signed a deal and started working on a plan to migrate thousands of Texaco's existing customers onto our platform. The big advantage of this deal was that there was already a large number of both customers and volume running on the card, so we would be getting significant income from day one.

As our telesales team numbers began to grow, we started to realize that we needed to constantly work at improving the efficiency of the team if we were going to optimize the growth we were getting on a per-person basis. First, we noticed that we shouldn't be targeting geographies as wide as an individual county when calling a potential new customer. Just because Texaco had twenty sites in Lancashire didn't necessarily mean it had one in Blackpool, and a plumber in Blackpool was never going to drive to Preston just to fill up their van and save a few pence per liter. Second, we realized there were certain dead call times during the week, and it was more useful to get our team to do mailshots during these hours rather than customer calls, especially late on a Friday afternoon. We also started to use the phone system software for call monitoring to make sure that all the team members spent a minimum number of minutes on the phone each day. Once this was introduced, the stats soon showed that the salespeople who worked hardest in terms of actual talk time ended up being the most successful at growing their volumes.

The lesson of making lots of small improvements is alive and well today across all our divisions as we try to optimize the use of what is our biggest investment in terms of capital: our global sales teams. I believe these teams and our overall go-to-market capability in the SME sector really differentiate us from our competition. The next lesson, which goes hand in hand with this one, talks about probably the single most critical component to making these teams successful: relentless performance management.

This was also the first time we found that salespeople get up to all sorts of tricks to try to beat the system and do less work. We found that one of our guys, who had very good call times but a low number of new applications, had been boosting his daily minutes by calling the Speaking Clock! For those youngsters among you, that was a service first introduced in France in 1933 that enabled people to call a number and listen to a recorded voice telling them the exact time. Our sneaky salespeople liked calling it, as it would never hang up, no matter what you said to it! There would be many more instances of this sort of behavior over the years, and our managers had to get cleverer at working out the ever more sophisticated techniques that the salespeople were using to cheat the system.

One way we ultimately kept issues like this in check was that we always operated a very performance-based pay system, even for senior management. We had a relatively low basic salary with various commission elements added, linked to the number of new customers, total volume drawn, and amount of gross profit earned. This meant that the top performers had a very good overall package, and the poor performers were soon highlighted and subsequently weeded out quite quickly. This way of thinking about remuneration has been a very important factor in the success of the company over the years and is one of the significant things that tends to differentiate entrepreneurial businesses from large corporates. Big companies tend to pay in a much flatter, less differentiated structure, which has the result of incentivizing poor performers to stay and good people to leave, and it definitely isn't good for a company with big ambitions.

Now that we were onboarding lots of new customers every day, the credit department also became its own definitive group with its own nice sign on the door, even though its office was just a small box room with a skylight in the ceiling. We also set up online links with Dun & Bradstreet and several other service providers, so we could now check new customers and their directors faster, which allowed us to speed up the time it took from initial receipt of the application form through to decision-making and card issuing. We took on a new credit manager, Steve, and eventually a credit director, Angela, as the live customer numbers really started to increase. We also began using credit insurance, which specifically allowed us to take on larger transport customers, as a single customer bankruptcy could result in a bad debt of £100,000 or more, and this was a risk we couldn't afford to take. These steps helped us grow even faster and put a new rigor into how we were checking and then approving or rejecting all the application forms as they came in.

These improvements in both sales and credit vetting were really starting to change the shape of the business as we got closer to the oil companies with our strategy of aiming to operate in the sectors of the market that they either didn't want to participate in or couldn't because of their expensive cost structure.

One final thing happened, probably about a year or so after we got going with Shell. Esso also finally agreed to have a meeting with us about becoming a reseller. It already had seven or eight existing partners selling its card, and over the last couple of years, it kept telling us that it was not going to appoint any more. I think the thing that finally changed Esso's leaders' minds was seeing the success we were beginning to have, growing volumes with some of its main competitors. This latest step increased our network even further and meant that we were able to reach an even greater percentage of the SME market and therefore continue to improve our conversion rates from the growing number of calls our sales team was making. The only major brand we didn't have now was BP, and it would be another couple of years yet before we managed to finally get a deal with it over the line.

Also around this time, I came up with a new idea for the bunker business to offer a unique service that our competitors didn't. This was built around the fact that most of our customers had bulk diesel tanks at their home depots and were also using our fuel cards when they were out traveling on the road. These owners were obviously keen to monitor their trucks closely and make sure that they were using fuel efficiently, as well as trying to prevent fraud. If they didn't watch out, some of their unscrupulous drivers would steal from the tanks to either sell to a third party or use in their own personal vehicles (most truck drivers have diesel cars!). In order to control this, every month, they would have to bring together all the transaction details for every bit of diesel used by each individual truck and combine this with the start and finish odometer readings from the cab, and then calculate the exact miles per gallon (mpg) on a vehicle-by-vehicle basis. If they came upon a truck that had an mpg of 4.7 when the fleet average was 6.8, they knew they had a problem! This process of control was fraught with difficulties, as most of these customers just had a manual plastic key control system at their home depot, which depended on the driver filling in little paper slips correctly every time they filled up.

We came up with the idea of installing a commercial card reader at their home depot that we would poll every night, which therefore meant that every transaction for each vehicle could be collected on an automated system, with the odometer readings collected at every point throughout the month. This system still relied on drivers to enter information correctly but was a vast improvement over what most of these owners were doing at the time. We called our new offering fuel management services (FMS), and we put together a comprehensive report at the end of every month to save customers the hours of manual effort the reports had previously taken. This new service started to give us an edge and allowed us to sign up some much bigger customers, including the famed Eddie Stobart.

As our volumes increased and the size of our stockholding at each individual truck stop went up, there was another risk we had started to take, one that had not even crossed our minds. It was only when one truck stop went bust and we lost the seven thousand liters of stock we had been holding there that we understood this new potential risk. From that point on, we had to start credit vetting every new location as well as all the new customers and begin looking for warning signs of problems before they actually happened. The biggest of these was when the site owner started asking us for more stock than we actually needed. Typically, we would hold one week's stock as the maximum, so asking for significantly more than this was a bit of a giveaway that they were actually using our diesel stock to finance their own business. If they were doing that with us, they were also probably doing it with

Keyfuels and PCS, which could mean that they were effectively selling many tens of thousands of pounds of our fuel to help with their cash flow issues. Given how little money we had in our own business, we could not afford to lose a big chunk of stock, so this was an issue we would have to pay significantly more attention to now.

This problem happened a few more times over the next year, and each time the problem arose, we took faster and tougher action, which meant that we minimized our losses, usually at the expense of one or both of our archrivals. Probably the most memorable instance that will give you a feel for how seriously we took the job of protecting the business back then was when we noticed that our site at Forfar in Scotland started asking for deliveries of fuel when, according to our records, we already had plenty of stock there. What then suddenly put us on a red-alert status was that some of our customers called to say they had been turned away from the station and not given any diesel. When I called, the site owner told me it was only a temporary hiccup and that a couple of loads of fuel had just arrived from our competitors and they were up and running again. I didn't get a warm feeling from the conversation, and given the experience I had built up over the last couple of years, I thought the problem was much more serious and probably terminal, and we needed to do something about it fast. One thing we had never done in this situation was actually going to retrieve our stock of diesel from a site using a tanker with a hose and pump. Given that it would take several weeks for our customers to naturally draw down the thirty-five thousand liters we had there in individual transactions, I decided to take some faster and more direct action. The only company I knew of that could potentially help me—because it had a fuel depot and therefore tankers in the area—was Brogan Fuels. If you remember from the first few weeks when I was looking for sites in Scotland, Brogan's had provided us with a filling point in Glasgow that became the third location on our original network of fourteen. Alan Tait, one of the owners, had become a good friend over the last few years, so I picked up the phone to ask him a big favor.

Alan said that he could organize two of his tankers from the Brechin depot to come down to the site at about six in the afternoon after they finished their normal shifts. He also asked if we could get someone from our team on-site at the same time, in case there were any questions when their tankers turned up. Mark Tabb, who was our first on-road sales guy, was definitely the man for this situation. His do-anything, go-anywhere, go-anytime attitude was perfect for this set of circumstances and definitely counts towards why he is still working for us today. I gave Mark a call and said he needed to leave straight away to get to Forfar and that I would think of a plan for what he would actually need to do while he was en route.

This was a very unusual set of circumstances, given the fact that I don't think any bunkering company had tried to do something like this before. Contractually, we owned the stock until it was given to our customers. However, even though we had the right to pick up unused stock, it had never been tried before. But given that the owner had actually been selling our stock and was therefore in a negative position himself, we felt we were perfectly entitled to collect it, especially as the site had broken our contract and stopped dispensing diesel to our own card customers. After the conversation I had with the owner earlier that day, I decided that ringing him in advance and asking him if it was OK for us to come and pick up our stock was not going to get a positive response, so instead, I let the next few hours tick by as Mark drove north.

I decided that I would ring the owner and engage him in a long conversation about future business, etc., so that he would be on the phone with me while we were picking up the fuel. Mark would turn up at the site and go into the shop, so he would be there to tell the on-site manager what we were doing after Brogan Fuels' two tankers arrived and started pumping the diesel back out of the forecourt tanks. Hopefully, the on-site manager would understand the situation and respect our contractual right to pick up the fuel. It was a well-executed operation, as Mark first introduced himself and told the manager that he was from UK Fuels and that he had come to pick up the Fortronic card reader. Having started the conversation, it soon came out that she was an unhappy employee and knew that the site was about to close and that she was about to lose her job. Mark then told her that we were there to pick up the stock that we owned, as well as the card reader, and that we were terminating our dealings with the site. Once we had all our diesel pumped out, the two tankers left the site to head north back to their depot. I finished my conversation with the owner, and Mark bid farewell to the young woman, leaving her to deliver the bad news to her boss as he headed off straightaway down the A90. Mark decided that instead of staying up locally as originally planned, he would get a bit further south and over the border before getting his head down for the night! I then rang Alan at Brogan's to thank him and his guys and promised to treat him to a few beers and a curry next time I was up near Glasgow. Thirty years on, and Alan and I still meet up for the occasional beer and curry (normally at my expense!) and always recount this story from the old days.

The Sandbach office was already beginning to feel a little cramped, and I had already had to move out of my nice attic room to give it up for our growing accounts team. We had only been there for four years, so as I started my search again in 1998, I decided that we needed to get something significantly bigger and with a more open plan to allow us plenty of room to expand and get more organized. It soon became obvious that there was not going to be anything of the necessary size locally, so I began looking at options near the next motorway junction south on the M6, in a town called Crewe.

I had only visited Crewe before when I had passed through several times on the train heading north on holiday to the Lake District as a child. It is most famous for being a historic railway town at the center of the English rail network, but it has found fame more recently as the home of Rolls-Royce and Bentley. Rolls-Royce eventually moved to a new factory in the south, leaving Bentley as the largest local business, with a new fuel card company about to arrive and eventually claim second position!

We were also in the same situation at home, in which we needed something bigger, but I wanted to stay in the village, if at all possible, as we had made quite a few good friends. After looking at a few places, we found a nice new estate at the top of the village and moved for the second time to number 12 Heatherways.

LESSON 8

RELENTLESS PERFORMANCE MANAGEMENT.

One area of the business in which it is easiest to monitor the differences between people's individual performance is sales. Whether it's how many new customers they have signed up, how much volume they've pumped, how many trackers or mobile phones they have sold, how much new gross profit they have earned the company, how much gross written insurance premium they have signed up, or any number of metrics like this, at the end of the month, you can make an unequivocal ranking list of your salespeople.

As our salespeople are onboarded, they are given very clear and relatively low monthly targets. The onboarding includes a ramping-up period as they build their pipeline and go through training. Over a period of four to five months, the targets build up to a level that will give us our planned return on investment over the longer term. For example, in the fuel division, it might take a new salesperson twelve to eighteen months to get to the company's monthly breakeven and twenty to twenty-eight months to get to a cumulative breakeven position before we have to start making a profit. This means we have to monitor new salespeople's weekly performance extremely closely, and if they're falling significantly off their flight path and we can see that they aren't going to make it, we have to make the decision to let them go very quickly, or our whole delivery plan economics fail.

Telesales is a tough job and one that I did for the first few years after I started. It does not suit everyone, so you have to be prepared for relatively high rates of people churn. For instance, if we are starting a sales office in a new town or country and want to get to a team of ten, we are probably thinking we will need to go through thirty to forty people before we will form a team with an average performance that is at the right level. One more thing that soon stands out from the numbers is that top performers are not just 10, 20, or 30 percent better than average; they are 100, 200, or even 300 percent better. Poor performers tend not to be just below average as well but are more likely to be 60, 70, or 80 percent below average!

Most of our best sales managers started on the front line, and they are also rewarded on a volume/margin basis, so they learn to be able to make the tough decisions to get their teams working. However, in the central functions, such as finance, credit, IT, marketing, and people, the senior teams have not been brought up in this same disciplined way, which means they all tend to be much softer when it comes to managing people. Just as in sales, good people in these central divisions are much better than average and bad ones a lot worse, although it is much harder to have an accurate stick to measure them against. Personal judgment is much more important here, and you want your team to be able to identify the very good ones and bad ones quickly so they can start making the tough decisions in a similar way to the sales teams themselves.

One final thing to note that definitely gets missed sometimes is that when you have a poor employee that you have let stay longer than you should have (before you eventually bite the bullet and exit them), the other members in their team are not actually thinking you are the axe man and being too hard but more often than not are thinking, Why has it taken management so long to come to that course of action?

The main lesson here is to make decisions and changes quickly, even if it feels tough, as the longer you leave them, the harder it gets.

RIDING THE CELTIC TIGER

While the UK business was starting to grow faster in volume and revenue, so was Ireland, which was definitely helped by the fact that the Irish economy was doing really well and there was a lot of growth, especially in the SME sector, where we were strong. I'm not sure exactly which year it happened, but in 1996 or 1997, our Irish business overtook the UK division in monthly gross profit, and it would be many more years before the UK would finally get its nose in front again. The reason for this was that we had gotten ourselves into a strong and unique position at the border locations, where we now had the largest and most automated fueling network. Our main local competitors were mostly smaller operators that had sites at only one or two crossing points and that couldn't provide a complete service.

In addition to this network advantage, because customers were saving themselves up to twenty pence on every liter of fuel they bought, the price competition was not as aggressive as usual, so our margins were a bit larger than we normally expected. With this level of border pricing differential, every trucker and commercial vehicle operator in the north would send their vehicles to fill up at night once they had finished their day shift, so the pumps would literally be busy nearly twenty-four hours a day. We used to joke that even Grandad would come down in his fifteen-year-old Mondeo on a Sunday afternoon to fill up his car to last him for the week ahead.

We had started this business doing all our sales calls from the Nicholl Oils office at Greysteel near Derry, but given the fact that we now had customers right across Ireland, we were going to need an office in the south. We also needed someone to head up our operations there, and the only existing contact that came to mind was David Gower, who had run the fastfuel project for Texaco. Although he wasn't Irish, he was married to a woman from Tuam, just north of Galway, and had always spoken about going to live in Ireland at some point if he got the opportunity. With that in mind, the next time I was in London having a review with him about the progress of fastfuel, I brought up the subject to see if he was still interested in a move and potentially coming to work for DCI. He jumped at the chance, and within a few months, we were looking for our first international office in the fabulous city of Galway. We were soon up and running and looking for employees to start trying to mirror the telesales team that was now working well back in Sandbach. My trips became more frequent, and at one point, I was traveling to Galway, Dublin, or some other part of Ireland almost every week.

I got to know the Galway pubs pretty well, too, and we soon got into a regular routine of having our first Guinness at The Quays, then walking up to The Kings Head before finishing up at The Skeff Bar on Eyre Square. These pubs were quite different from those back home, as most of them looked quite normal on the outside but opened up inside into huge, cavernous spaces, all with live music every night. Galway has obviously expanded and developed a lot since we set up there in the late 1990s, with lots more supercool drinking venues, but the good news is that our old favorites are still there, and the city has an even more friendly and vibrant atmosphere than ever. I am often asked which is my favorite office and where would I like to go and base myself. Well, Galway is definitely up there, and the only thing that could potentially go against it as being my first choice is the weather! Dublin had a great selection of bars as well. Gary and I used to regularly stay at Temple Bar Hotel and start our evenings at Buskers Bar downstairs before moving on to The Porterhouse or Zanzibar, followed by Café en Seine, and finally ending up at The River Club if we fancied a late one. I'm sad to say a couple of these have gone now, although Café on Seine is still around and remains a fixture on the much less frequent times I stop over in Dublin today. Lee and I also now enjoy a beer at Bruxelles pub on Harry Street where it's always good to see the statue of Phil Lynott from Thin Lizzy just outside reminding me of the great concert I went to back in Leeds in 1985.

Over the next year, volumes continued to grow, and I started to work hard on increasing the number of sites on the network. It was nice not to have Keyfuels and PCS bothering us and was a very different experience from growing the UK network. Ireland's biggest oil company at the time was Statoil, which had bought its network from BP several years earlier and was top of my target list with which to agree on an acceptance deal. I had tried many times over the last couple of years, and it was only after a few senior management changes on Statoil's side that I began to have more serious conversations. It wasn't long before we got a trial going with a few of its most strategic truck stops, and after this proved successful, we started to roll out further across more of its company-owned and dealer sites. At one of my Dublin meetings, Liam, our main supply contact, asked me if we were interested in running Statoil's retail account card in a similar way we were doing for Texaco. The company was also unhappy with its current supplier, and having heard about our success in the UK that had resulted in enhanced volume growth, it was interested in whether we could do that for Statoil too. Statoil had a much larger and more complex set of customers, with a lot of bespoke requirements, so we set about getting a plan together to put our best foot forward in the tender process. Within about six months, we convinced Liam we could do the job and put a very competitive price proposal forward, so it was full steam ahead again on yet another significant oil company deal.

We also got approached by one of our customers and suppliers, Emo Oil, about whether we were interested in buying into a small fuel distributor site it had in Dundalk and developing it into a twenty-four-hour truck stop. Owning physical sites was definitely not part of the original plan, but at this very strategic location, it would give us some real security of supply over the long term and help keep our other suppliers at the key border crossings competitive. So for thirty-five thousand punts, we bought a 50 percent stake in an acre site just off Coes Road on the outskirts of Dundalk town. Within a few weeks, we had installed a new MCS card reader and started to pump some volume through our first company-owned site.

Back at home, my search for a new office in Crewe ended with an option to take the sixth floor of Rail House, a large, old concrete sky-scraper (fifteen floors!) situated right next to the main railway station. It was in a dreadful state, but I thought that with a new carpet, a lick of paint, and new power and computer cabling, it could look pretty good. Having made the mistake of taking a long lease in Holmes Chapel and now having a little understanding of how landlords try to rip you off for dilapidations at the end of a lease, I decided to take my own home video camera into the office. I did a full recording to show just what state it was in as we were taking it over, in case of future problems with the landlord insisting on us returning it to the condition that we took it over in. I used one of the huge, old cameras with cassette tapes, and the recordings got put up in my loft at home alongside my many home videos of the children.

The outdoor terminal market for unmanned sites had two players, Petrovend and Triscan, both of whom could accept our full range of card ISO numbers as well as all our competitors' cards. This wasn't an ideal situation for us, as Petrovend, which was by far the strongest in the UK in the new truck stop sector, was very close to Keyfuels and was always trying to charge us more for switching our transactions or setting up new card formats on the network. We also didn't like the fact that Petrovend knew all of our volumes at all the locations where it had terminals, which gave it a deep insight into how our business was developing. We weren't that surprised when one day, we received a communication to say that Petrovend had sold out to Keyfuels, which made us even more concerned about the information it had and the fact that it was a key supplier.

Triscan, on the other hand, wasn't particularly aligned with any of the bunkering companies and was a bigger market player, especially in the commercial sector, in which it installed units at truckers' home depots. We had started to build quite a strong relationship with Triscan as part of our new FMS and were also starting to use it in the Irish truck stop market, where we were now buying from its local distributor. It wasn't a perfect relationship, however, as it was charging huge sums for call-outs and repairs at these sites, which we believed should have been included in the manufacturer's original warranty when we bought them. So when a completely new supplier, Team Overgaard from Denmark, came into both the UK and Irish markets, it seemed like a good opportunity to try to get close to it to see if it had a good alternative product. Bjarne, the Danish owner, was over nearly every other week, and we started to install the company's modern-looking terminals at some of our border sites as well as recommend him to many of the other truck stop owners whom we knew. Instead of having to go through a third party to pick up our transactions and download a new stop list every night, we now had the protocol to do the polling ourselves, which gave us much more control over our data as well as privacy from our competitors about our volumes.

This new relationship continued to develop, and I started to make regular trips to Naestved in Denmark, where I was able to start influencing some of the hardware and software development myself. Naestved is a small town about an hour or so south of Copenhagen and one of the quietest places I've ever visited. There is very little nightlife, so it is completely at the other end of the spectrum to Galway and Dublin, and after eight in the evening, the streets were always completely deserted, even at the weekends! During my regular stays at Hotel Kirstine, the only place we found that was half reasonable for dinner was the Raadhuskroen pub. It actually did a pretty decent schnitzel, which has always been one of my favorites, as Mum used to cook it regularly when I was growing up.

The only major oil company we didn't have a reseller deal with was BP, which probably had the best network in the UK at the time, especially on the motorways and trunk roads. It also only had a very small number of partners, with one of them being Fuel Card Services from Leeds—probably the biggest fuel card reseller in the country at that point—and it had obviously benefited from the fact that the BP proposition was so strong. It had grown under the radar over a number of years and, in some ways, was the pioneer to have the branded reseller model as the core part of its business. If it was number one at the moment, we were now definitely hot on its heels, and instead of just being aligned to one main supplier, we saw the advantages of having several. We had tried to talk to BP several times about a deal during the last few years without success, but with the advent of DCI and our growing relationship with Nicholl Oils, we now had a different route to explore. As part of our DCI development in Ireland, we had also needed a UK trading business to manage the small number of transactions our customers had on the more expensive UK side of the border, and we had called this company Direct Fuels.

Gary now approached BP, with whom he had a strong bulk supply relationship, to see if it was possible for this new UK subsidiary of DCI to sell BP cards as long as it didn't sell other brands. Within a few months, this got agreed on, so then, across all our businesses, we were the only company to have a full range of oil company reseller products. This was the stimulus to start increasing our number of salespeople even faster and go about catching up and then getting past FCS as fast as we could.

On the IT front, we also introduced another bit of clever technology to help improve and centralize some of our manual processes. My concept was to have websites with a process name rather than a normal name that all our staff and customers everywhere could use to complete certain tasks or actions. The fact that all the dot-com addresses were available made me think that I was probably the first person in the world to come up with this idea as a use case for a website! We just created simple web page forms for entering the data and then set the link to terminate to a comma-separated values database in which the relevant person or team could manage every single transaction from one place. Our new websites included copyinvoice.com, enteratransaction.com, bankacheque.com, customercreditnote.com, changeofcustomerdetails.com, archivefiling.com, transactionquery.com, orderadirectory.com, and a few more besides. This technical solution made a huge difference to our operations by speeding things up and vastly improving our overall customer experience as well as being an extremely low-cost solution!

LESSON 9

DO THINGS IN THE RIGHT ORDER.

When you arrive home in the evening and have planned to watch a movie that night, it's important to try to get whatever other activities you need to get done out of the way in the fastest possible time.

Doesn't it bug you when your partner says that they have got an important bit of work they need to complete on their laptop and will order the Chinese takeaway as soon as they've finished their PowerPoint presentation (which they expect will take them about thirty minutes)? Given that the Chinese takeaway always takes at least forty-five minutes to arrive, wouldn't it have been more sensible for them to stop work on their presentation, order the takeaway, and then complete their work in perfect time to pour a glass of wine or beer before the food arrives? You've just saved yourself an extra thirty minutes of time to watch your movie and therefore won't have to go to bed before the end!

This may sound very obvious, but these situations occur every day in the office, and not that many people seem to be capable of constantly reassessing the tasks at hand to make sure they are spending their time wisely so that they can get projects done in the shortest possible time frame.

For example, if you are launching a new product and you need to train the sales staff (two weeks), design and create some new content for your website (four weeks), do some software development on Salesforce (five weeks), and review your terms and conditions with legal (two days), what do you do first? Get on with the Salesforce work—it's not rocket science!

Although not directly relevant to this particular issue, and because it was a particularly short lesson (and hopefully easy to follow), another important element of managing your tasks well was simply explained by a good businessman I met many years ago, who has gone on to be extremely successful.

He used to say, "Don't make a decision today that can wait until tomorrow," which is definitely different from Benjamin Franklin's famous quote, "Don't put off till tomorrow what you can do today."

Both these phrases have relevance to this lesson, as many times over the years, I have felt overwhelmed with the number of different things that I am trying to do at any one time. It can creep up on you without you really knowing it, and what generally happens is that you end up doing little bits on all of the topics but not actually completing any of them. The famous "spinning too many plates at once" scenario, in which, sooner or later, a few of them start to fall and crash on the floor, is very true.

Whenever I reach this point, I have learned to take a step back and really look at the tasks, both in order of their importance and whether the work or decisions actually need to be done or made immediately. The first phrase is very relevant here, as putting off tasks that don't need a decision today actually allows more time for their consideration and for potentially more facts to be available before you make the decision. This isn't just a lazy way of working! Reducing your list into bite-size chunks and finishing each one until completion before picking up the next one then becomes a clearer way of making progress. Now you can go home each evening with a sense of achievement, and the things you have agreed on can start to get implemented and begin positively contributing to the development of the business.

I try not to ever lose sight of this when I'm feeling underwater. Go back to the basics that your mum used to teach you, of finishing something off before starting something new!

FIRST STEPS ONTO THE CONTINENT

Sometime in 1999, after we had been operating for nearly a decade, we moved into Rail House in Crewe (conveniently located next to the famous railway station!). I definitely thought we were a proper business now, as I had my own parking space outside in the car park and the building had a lift and a security guard who welcomed me every morning. After the higgledy-piggledy offices in both Holmes Chapel and Sandbach, we now had two huge open-plan floors, and we could begin to lay all the departments out exactly as we wanted them. We had an air-conditioned server room, albeit with the exhaust pipes from the portable unit sticking out through a hole cut in the glass window. We even had a separate small canteen room, where people could eat their sandwiches at lunchtime. The salmon-pink carpet tiles I had chosen, however, proved less successful and were very susceptible to big brown marks from spilled coffee. This would be the last time I would pick anything different from the patterned black that has become our mainstay across the globe today. The overall move went pretty smoothly, but one thing did come to light as we emptied the Sandbach office that answered a couple of questions we had been trying to solve over the last few years. Why did we get such a large batch of post with our green bunkering sheets on the first day that the employee normally responsible for entering them was on holiday?

Second, why, near the end of the month, when we called the sites to chase up their sheets, did they often say to us that they had already sent them several days or weeks earlier?

Well, as we lifted the filing cabinets up to move them from Sandbach to Crewe, we found hundreds of green bunkering sheets under each one—the hiding place the employee had found to help him reduce his workload. When he was due to be off on holiday the next day, he'd put the latest ones due to be entered inside new reply-paid envelopes and repost them in the Sandbach High Street post box just near our front entrance. The sheets would then turn up the next day in a huge bag for our temporary cover staff to enter, while our employee had his feet up on a beach somewhere, sipping a beer. Needless to say, he didn't last long after we found out.

Not long after we had moved into our nice new office, we had another bit of good news in terms of an exciting opportunity. Conoco, a large American oil company that owned the JET retail brand, approached us about tendering for its account card business. It had also heard about our positive deal with Texaco and was interested in a new company pitching new ideas to try to stimulate some new growth. I remember Steve and I taking our huge forty-two-inch plasma TV screen (extremely heavy back then!) down from the boardroom and putting it in the back of my car to give our presentation down at Conoco's Warwick head office. We must have looked like delivery drivers as we carried it across the car park, sweating heavily after we arrived on what I remember was a very hot day. Six months later, we were live with yet another card and brand, which now meant there were even fewer places across the UK where we didn't have some form of card offering that we could give to potential new customers.

The AS 24 deal we had signed a few years ago had proved quite fruitful, and we now had a good number of customers fueling on the

Continent, giving us a reasonable amount of commission. The other extra perk of this relationship was that, not long after we had begun, AS 24 started to have an annual rewards trip for its top-performing sales staff. Even though UK Fuels was not strictly part of the group but rather an agent, AS 24 kindly included us in these competitions. Over the next few years, I had some great trips to lots of places with a French influence, including Guadeloupe, the Dominican Republic, Djerba, and Crete. These trips were always really well organized and involved some interesting experiences, such as a catamaran cruise to Marie-Galante, a 4×4 drive into the Sahara Desert, including a night in a Bedouin tent, and even a tour round a local Rum factory, which I remember being particularly good. They were educational for me as well, as I started to learn more about the European fuel card market and how it operated. French was the official trip language, which always tended to mean that the non-French people created a separate splinter group in which English was more commonly used. I always seemed to end up mixing with these guys who usually included the Germans, Belgians, Dutch, and Portuguese. Not only did my French improve every year, but I also made some good friends from across the Continent, who would prove very useful for the next part of our journey. These overseas incentives also provided me with a good blueprint for fastfuel, in which we were soon to start doing some reward trips of our own.

One of the contacts I made on my visit to Guadaloupe, Koen Sturtewagen, became a particularly close friend. So once I decided that Belgium would potentially be the best place to start for our next country after Ireland, I thought I would meet up with him to talk through my ideas. There was obviously the immediate advantage of Belgium being very close geographically; however, what I thought would be the biggest benefit was the fact that it was also a low-diesel-tax country and so would have good international diesel volumes as well as local ones. I did ask Koen if he was interested in potentially leaving AS 24 to help start this venture, but I think at that point in time, he was too comfortable where he was at Total Oil. Instead, he introduced me to a very old industry friend of his, Marc de Vos, whom he thought would potentially make a good partner. Marc had a traditional bulk fuel distributorship at Eke-Nazareth, quite close to Ghent, so it was back on the plane again to go and see if I could persuade him that there was an opportunity for a new fuel card company. He was immediately positive, and Diesel Card Belgium was born just a few months later, which soon got shortened to DCB. I gave Steve the role of driving the project from a sales and marketing perspective, with Mike helping with all the new IT requirements that would be needed. I also gave each of them a 5 percent share in the new company as an extra part of their long-term incentive.

The things we needed to do with the longest lead times were to set the new company up and get our VAT registration organized, as well as a bank account and direct debit facility, so we set about these immediately. Second, the IT work for collecting all the new transactions and then creating multi-language invoices needed to be started so that we would be ready for launch. Third, all the sales and marketing materials, including the new orange DCB cards, needed to be designed and printed before the final phase of recruiting the new sales team could be started. As we were using Marc's existing network of seven automated depot locations as our launch network, this was one problem we didn't have to worry about initially. Making early decisions about relative time frames for each of these tasks allowed us to launch in just three months, so it was a big advantage to do things in the right order.

Soon, Steve and I were going over every couple of weeks to build out the site network to improve our coverage as well as set up a new telesales team in Eke to start looking for our first customers. We had regular lunches at Mac Pudding, a funny Scottish-themed restaurant along the canal from the fuel depot at Eke, followed by a few cheeky *pintjes* at a nice little bar next to De Pinte station. This became a favorite watering hole and was run by a friendly Moroccan guy whom Marc knew well. It was a great spot before we jumped on the fast train back to the airport. When we stayed several days, we always went into Ghent, where we inevitably ended up in the rib shack by the canal, and if we went into Brussels for a meeting, we normally popped into the famous Delirium Café. This particular place happens to hold the Guinness World Record for the most beers sold from around the globe and is just off the main square.

The new network we were building was predominantly commercial fueling locations, and it was going to take quite a lot of time to get good coverage, so lots of visits followed over the next year. Our UK success as an oil company reseller meant that we also started to explore similar opportunities in Belgium, but it is fair to say that new entrants were not normally welcomed with open arms by the locals, so this would take time too.

Around this time, we also had our first foray outside the fuel card business into the world of tires. It seemed quite an obvious product for us to cross-sell, given that all our customers had vehicles of various types, but we would soon learn that this was not as simple as we first thought. For a start, there was an enormous myriad of brands, sizes, and models, with a pricing structure that was much more opaque than the world of fuel. These prices would also change regularly and without any notice, so it was very difficult to provide quotes for customers and have any confidence that we were competitive on price. We set up a small team to work specifically on this new product and called as many of our customers to talk to them about their requirements. I can't remember exactly how long we continued to sell tires before we decided to stop, but I do know what happened that was the final straw that broke the camel's back. One morning, we were speaking to a very small local customer in Crewe who had a few vans, and our salesperson was trying to sell the virtues of our group buying power and the price benefit that this enabled us to give them. When she eventually told us that she had rung her local store (from the national company we had a deal with) and been quoted a price for a single front tire at £20 less than we could even buy one, we realized that this was not going to be a very easy model to scale. This was a very good example of doing more of what's going well and stopping when it isn't.

Now that we had a bigger business with so many strands, I had to start to put in place a more formal budgeting and targeting plan each year. I decided that it would be a good idea to get out of the office to do this so that we could properly get away from all the day-to-day activities. We held the first of these sessions up at The Pheasant Inn in Burwardsley, not far from Crewe, and the following year, we went a bit further afield up to Underscar Manor, a beautiful country house on the shoulders of Skiddaw mountain in the Lake District. Every single product line would have last-twelve-months' and forward-twelve-months' volume graphs, which initially meant a lot of separate acetate sheets on the overhead projector! Thankfully, at some point, when we had settled on the Glenridding Hotel as a regular venue, these graphs finally went digital, although it was always a slog going through two hundred different slides in the sales and marketing session. I remember at one of these meetings when we decided to substitute the current year's finance plan with the one from the previous year to see how long it would take our financial director, Tim, to notice as he went through his presentation. Well, I think he got about halfway through before realizing what we had done, which left us all rolling around laughing for the rest of the afternoon.

LESSON 10

TELL YOUR BOSS.

With UK fuels over ten years old now and not only growing in terms of total head count but also becoming spread across quite a number of locations, including our new offices in both Ireland and Belgium, the task of keeping control of everything that was going on day-to-day was becoming much harder. These next two lessons are about the good and prompt communication you need in your management structure to enable you to continue to scale without losing the immediacy of action you get when you are in start-up mode.

Definitely every week, and occasionally it feels like every day, I find out about an issue or problem that I should have been told about days, weeks, or sometimes even months earlier. Invariably, there are issues that, if I had known about them when they first happened, I would have taken them more seriously than other people did, responded faster, and often taken a different course of action. This time delay normally results in the problem having both grown significantly and an associated customer becoming more unhappy, which then usually leads to a much higher cost to resolve than if we had acted earlier.

One of the mantras I repeatedly tell my senior team members is that they need to tell me about every problem that is going on in their area, no matter how small they think it is, and this is why I never say to them, "Why have you bothered me with that?" If they don't live and breathe their own job this way, then they also don't encourage their direct reports to work in this manner, too, and this poor communication culture tends to cascade right through their divisional structure. As I keep reminding them, once they have told me about it, then it is my problem and one that we need to agree on a solution to together, but if they fail to tell me, then on their head be it. Hence, when I have someone on my team who never comes and talks to me about problems, I am not thinking that I have a division running really well. On the contrary, I am thinking that I have a sick structure in which I need to make some urgent changes. I regularly dig down into these divisions to see what is really going on under the surface, under the "don't believe anyone; test everything" lesson that I will talk to you about a little later in the book.

The issues and problems I am talking about might be that we overpaid a supplier, we debited a customer's invoice twice, we failed to turn up to install a customer's vehicle tracking boxes at the correct time, we couldn't get our hosted telephony platform to work through a customer's firewall, we promised a customer a new van when we didn't actually have one in stock, a customer suddenly went over their credit limit and our employee didn't pick it up on our monitoring report, we had an IT problem when running our weekly invoices, or any one of a thousand other things.

People who don't follow this way of working tend to fall into one of three categories. Probably the most common of these is the manager who thinks that because they don't hear about problems in their area, there aren't actually any going on. These people have often just worked in large corporations or professional organizations and have not had the experience of working in multiple departments or at the coalface of a smaller private business. If they had had this experience, then they would have gotten to know that new problems do occur frequently and that you always need to keep improving processes and strengthening your team as you are trying to grow a business.

The second category is the employee who finds out about a problem but then thinks that they are protecting their boss and doing a good job by not bothering them with it. In this case, I always remind them that if they had a small business of their own with ten employees and their employee had not told them about a £50,000 problem, what would their reaction have been?

The final type of person I come across is one who thinks they are so senior that they don't need to tell their boss about the problem, as that would be a sign to their team that they didn't have a high level of authority.

Whichever one of these three categories the person falls into, the really important thing that they all fail to understand is that talking through and solving problems with your manager is a very important part of their learning. There is also a high likelihood that their manager will have some previous experience that will give them a better chance of finding the best and fastest solution.

Unfortunately, there is a long list of my historic managers and directors who have had to learn the hard way about telling their boss, as however many times I told them what to do, it still didn't sink in. Lacking this mentality is one of the main reasons I have had to then exit many of these senior Radius people over the years.

Maybe they should have read a few books by Dorothy L. Sayers, who even back in the early 1900s came up with the famous quote, "A trouble shared is a trouble halved," in her series of detective novels.

RAPID EXPANSION OF OUR JV MODEL

Thistle Fuels up in Berwick-upon-Tweed continued to do really well and established itself as our biggest reseller with hundreds of predominantly Scottish transport companies. Its size attracted the attention of Roy at PCS, who started making a few acquisitions following the takeover of the Russell Davies Group by Securicor. Unbeknownst to Roy, when he approached Colin to see if he was interested in selling Thistle Fuels, the first thing Colin did was to call John and me, whose shareholding, if you remember, had been hidden because of the nominee share structure we had put in place. Even though we weren't particularly interested in selling, we agreed among ourselves to let discussions continue and see what sort of offer Securicor might come up with. I think because Roy knew it was our biggest customer, he was keener than ever to do a deal, and within a month or so, he came back with an offer of £1.5 million, which seemed an incredible amount of money for a fuel card business at the time.

The legals progressed, and Roy got all the approvals he needed from Securicor, so the last thing that needed to happen was Colin's disclosure letter. These letters are the last chance for a seller to tell a buyer any important information that they think they should know, that hasn't yet been given, and that is a normal requirement in every M&A transaction. On one evening, just a few days before we were expecting to exchange contracts, Colin dropped the bombshell on Roy that John and I were actually partners in Thistle Fuels and the real owners behind the nominees, so far from being upset by the deal, we were going to benefit massively from it. I think because the deal process had gone so far already, Roy didn't want to pull out, so the following week, in June 1997, the contract was signed, and a few weeks later, £300,000, amounting to my 20 percent share, dropped into my bank account. This was an eye-opening moment for me as to how valuable a card reseller business could be, and although it gave UK Fuels a short-term dip in volume, it spurred us on to expand our JV model further. One of the other downsides of selling was that John and I had gotten used to regular Sunday nights at the fabulous Tillmouth Park Country House hotel just on the outskirts of Berwick-upon-Tweed. It had a lovely old castle feel, and John and I would always have a game of snooker in the evening after dinner, and I would enjoy the excellent local kippers for breakfast, another of my childhood favorites.

I already had a good idea about what I wanted to spend the money on, as I had always liked the thought of having a cottage in the Lakes because I had had so much fun at the one my parents had owned in Glenridding. Also, because Mum and Dad had retired in the area, it made perfect sense so that they could see more of their two granddaughters, Lauren and Becky, as they grew up. Mum was soon scouring *The Westmorland Gazette* newspaper for me on a weekly basis to look for anything suitable, very much like her mother had done for them all those years ago. Pretty much the first thing she came across was the front wing of a five-hundred-year-old Grade II–listed, converted farmhouse set up in the hills just a few miles from Windermere. The drive was a kilometer long, and the house was set up on a hillside six hundred feet above sea level and off-grid completely in terms of gas, water, and sewerage. Driving up towards it, Gill and I knew before we even arrived that it was somewhere quite special. It had fifteen acres of land, a separate garage, and stables, and you could literally walk out the front door straight on to a myriad of local tracks well away from the hustle and bustle of visiting tourists. We didn't spend much time looking at anything else and put in an offer of £245,000, which was almost exactly what was left from my share sale after I paid capital gains tax. The offer was accepted within the next week or so, and it was all systems go.

Pretty much as soon as we took ownership and after furnishing it with some nice old chunky pine items we found at a shop in Chester, we started a ritual of going up every other weekend, which gave our two girls their first proper taste of the great outdoors. Within the first year of ownership, I also completed a walk that I still think of as the hardest ever physical activity I have undertaken—the Lake District's big four. This is the summiting of all four of the Lakes' three-thousand-foot mountains—Scafell, Scafell Pike, Helvellyn, and Skiddaw—including walking in between and starting and finishing in Keswick in under twenty-four hours. My brother and I, along with a good friend, completed the forty-five miles and over ten thousand feet of ascent in twenty hours and five minutes, which we thought was a pretty good effort. We were completely wrecked at the end and pretty much dead on our feet, but I still look back on it as a great achievement, as parts of the route are not that easy to follow, especially as you have to do one of the big ascents at night.

The experience with Thistle Fuels gave me renewed vigor to repeat the model of doing more of what's going well even more, and over the next few years, we started a new UK JV nearly every six months, all with a similar 50/50 structure in which I gave several lots of 5 percent to members of my management team. There were Forecourt

Fuels in Brighton, Fuelling Services in Worcester, Fuel Cards Direct in Burnley, and Dieselcard in Liverpool. We varied the model slightly when we bought into a couple of existing businesses, such as Fuel Card Solutions in Birmingham and Roadstar in Cheltenham. All the new partners came from the industry, and the shareholding model with its associated low salaries meant that everyone was super incentivized to grow quickly so that we could start paying a dividend sooner rather than later.

One of the most important of these new partnerships came from a very surprising angle. Roy, my long-term rival at PCS (now called Fuelserv), who also became a friend, confided in me that he was thinking of leaving the group. Securicor had sold the transport division, including the fuel business, to DHL, which had then subsequently been sold to Deutsche Post, and Roy had begun to get fed up with the constant change in ownership and the restrictions on his ability to make entrepreneurial decisions. I had often joked with him about starting a business together, so when we next met up, we started to have more serious discussions about that. Keyfuels had also approached him about a potential role, so it was going to be interesting to see which direction he would jump. Well, within a few months, the decision was made: Roy left Fuelserv, and Infuel was born in an attic room at his house in Ipswich. It wasn't long before he began renting a small office, and he was soon underway growing his reseller business in a faster and more professional way than most of the other JV partners we had. If I describe myself as a volume guy, Roy was definitely a margin man, so we actually made quite a good pairing when it came to bouncing ideas off each other.

Not long after Roy joined, Fuelserv changed hands again and was bought by Retail Decisions (ReD), as Deutsche Post decided that fuel cards were noncore, so I think Roy was pleased that he had moved.

Our JV element of the business was growing rapidly now, and we had so many different companies to administer that we now took on a third financial director, Peter Coxhead, to look after all the partners and manage all the separate invoicing, direct debiting, payments, and monthly accounts.

In Ireland, we also started a new JV, Direct Fuels, in Greystones, just south of Dublin. Our partner here had been working for one of our customers and had looked after their fuel card operations there, so they were able to get up and running quickly. We also bought a minority stake in Fuelwise, an established reseller up in Coleraine, so it was definitely all guns blazing on our new partnership model.

At Rail House, we took on extra wings on both the eighth and first floors to cope with our expansion. We moved all the hard-copy customer application forms downstairs, as they were starting to become quite a handful in terms of both numbers and variety of brands, as well as putting the post room closer to the front door! We had already changed enveloping and franking machines several times, and we now had pretty serious and very expensive equipment to manage all the hard-copy invoices we were producing. The suppliers of these machines were notorious for very long-term, one-sided contracts that you could never get out of, but the good news was that things were about to change.

First, laser printing arrived on the scene, and it allowed us to retire the noisy OKI dot matrix printers we had used for more than ten years. We were not going to be able to cope with all the printing and posting much longer without a major rethink, especially as most of our PAYGO invoices were weekly. Mike and the team started to look at whether we could convert the invoices into digital documents instead of printing them so that we could potentially email them directly to customers as a way to solve both of these problems at once. The customer service and sales teams started to gather email addresses, and within a few months, we were starting to eat into the enormous manual process as we converted customers from paper to digital. This felt like a huge breakthrough and a perfect use for the internet, which was something we were beginning to understand and starting to embrace a little more.

We also started our own fastfuel incentive trips and made the first one to Moscow, which proved quite an experience. Drinking two bottles of vodka between the fifteen of us before the food was even served definitely had the effect of getting the night going with a bang. We headed to New York the next year, followed by Kraków, Reykjavik, and then Dubrovnik, and we always tried to mix a little culture with fun, which was how the AS 24 trips had worked.

As the growth continued, we needed more office space, so when a modern unit became available just round the corner on Macon Way, we decided to take the plunge. Within a year, the unit next door came up for sale, and we took that one, too, followed two years later by a whole block of five on the adjacent wing. This new block was the perfect size to move the DCI back office into and to properly separate this business physically away from the UK operations and give it room to breathe and expand.

LESSON 11

ASK YOUR BOSS.

As discussed in the last lesson, having a very close overall relationship with your supervisor is critical, but instead of it being about telling them your problems, this lesson is about asking for their advice.

The most common problem that occurs with this issue is that people from larger, non-entrepreneurial organizations get into the mentality that if a particular decision is within their authority level (is within their remit), then they don't need to speak to their boss about it. Many of them also see it a little as a power thing and get hung up on the level of expenditure that they are allowed to authorize, whether it's £25,000, £100,000, or £500,000. The situations I'm referring to could be about setting credit limits, purchasing telematics boxes, hiring staff, choosing a hotel for an off-site meeting, onboarding a new installation partner, buying a telecoms customer out of their existing contract, buying new vans for stock, signing a new fuel supply contact, choosing shower fittings for a new office, or any one of similar small decisions that go on in the business every single day.

What you need to understand is that your boss might have some other knowledge to add to the decision-making process and that, far from bothering them, you are taking advantage of tapping into their experience. It's very easy to do and takes no time to either speak to them face-to-face if they are close by or simply copy them into an email.

This is about using common sense and raising up decisions through the layers quickly to get second and third opinions. Even in a big company with thousands of employees, you will be surprised by just how many of these smaller decisions a single senior person can touch on and have input on if they wish. This is all about learning and passing on experiences as well as instilling good communication as a central company philosophy. When one of my guys comes to me for advice, I see it as a real sign of maturity and someone who is keen to keep learning by understanding what I would do in their set of circumstances. These are exactly the sort of people the company needs.

One final thing to try to help you remember lesson 11 is that we have also used the phrase "as much use as a chocolate teapot" for many different things over the years, and a manager who doesn't understand the importance of asking your boss definitely falls into this category!

OSS1 AND THE CHIP CARD BATTLE

My trips to Team Overgaard in Denmark continued despite the sleepy nature of Naestved, and my knowledge of the technology was improving with every visit. I did actually take Gill and the girls over for a weekend to do a little exploring and managed to find a bit of fun at the BonBon-Land amusement park as well as at a nice summer house near Karrebaeksminde. We also visited a beach where there used to be an annual competition for who could sit longest on a flagpole set into the sea, which seemed a very strange tradition (only in Denmark!). The Team Overgaard finances weren't in great shape, however, and the business was living very much hand to mouth and really needed an injection of some cash. It was becoming quite an important supplier now, and no one we wanted to see fail, so in tandem with another one of its major Swedish customers, we decided to help out. Between us, we took a 50 percent stake in return for putting £250,000 into the company. This had an added benefit of giving us more control over both the development projects and the day-to-day activities. One thing I started to get Team Overgaard to work on was a replacement for the indoor Fortronic terminals, which were becoming increasingly difficult to both source and support. We also renamed the company Modular Card Systems to fit in more with the products it was selling, which soon got shortened to MCS to make it easier.

This new acquisition was about to prove more critical than we could have imagined, as before long we found out that Keyfuels was planning a major technology shift with a plan to replace all their magnetic stripe cards with new ones containing a "chip." They had also given their new technology a name, "Oasis."

This would make the cards more akin to what you would see issued by banks and potentially provide a big technological step forward. The marketing pitch was that the chip cards were going to be much more secure than the traditional cards. First, the chip was going to allow Keyfuels to introduce PIN security on indoor card readers, which had never been possible, and second, the new fuel cards would be virtually impossible to clone. Card cloning had raised its head in recent years, in which a fraudster would somehow get a customer's card details from either a collusive driver or other employee and then copy them using a fairly simple encoding machine onto a new blank card. The card would then be used at one of the many indoor sites that didn't require a PIN to be entered for authorization. One of the weaknesses of the fuel card market was that the authorization of the card was still offline and still relied on new stop lists being down-loaded every night. The terminals were now running out of memory to manage the huge lists of cancelled cards, and there was always a twenty-four-hour period between each poll that the criminals could exploit if they knew what they were doing. Keyfuels's plan was to introduce this new technology that could either force us to completely move our cards onto its platform at a very high cost or, if we didn't agree, put both ourselves and ReD (formerly Fuelserv) at a significant long-term strategic disadvantage. There were quite a few meetings between the three bunkering operators down at the Keyfuels office to try to agree on a compromise to make an open system that we could all use and share the development costs of Keyfuels's Oasis platform, but to no avail.

This potential threat had the effect of getting us closer to our archenemy, ReD, and we started to open discussions between ourselves about finding an alternative solution. We also brought in the two outdoor equipment suppliers that had also been excluded from the Oasis project, so both Triscan and MCS were now part of a new team of four to look at how we could create our own chip card platform quickly. Each member of this new group hosted a two-day meeting over the course of a few months, always with a fun night out as part of the agenda (only after we had finished all the extremely technical discussions!). The first of these was in Ipswich near the ReD office, and we ended up at one of the ReD staff members' favorite party venues, where there was a drag party night that they all later claimed to know nothing about. The rest of the group never let them forget, and when it was the turn of Triscan, which were based in Blackburn, we booked Funny Girls in Blackpool as a surprise for our southern guests.

Over this period, the team at MCS came up with a new protocol as well as a supplier who could provide the chip cards. Triscan and MCS then started the development work to implement this solution on their outdoor terminals. The new indoor terminal project I had kicked off at MCS six months earlier also now needed some modification to add a chip reader alongside the one for magnetic stripe cards. We also thought that the platform needed a name so that it would look professional when we started talking to the truck stops and other sites about updating their equipment. We eventually settled on Open Smart Standard 1 (OSS1), much to the annoyance of Keyfuels, so now it was a VHS-Betamax–type battle similar to the one that took place in the 1980s in the videotape world, only this time it was Oasis versus OSS1. Each of us tried to get the upper hand with the site owners as we started issuing cards on our new platforms. The owners weren't particularly happy, as it meant having three different card terminals on their countertops—one for bank cards, one for Keyfuels, and one for UK Fuels and ReD. This battle went on intensely for the next couple of years, with none of us getting to a winning position until another technology twist really sounded the death knell for both new platforms that had consumed so much time and effort. The sites were starting to get rid of all of their standalone card readers in favor of fully integrated systems that managed the whole of their shop products as well as fuel. The suppliers of these new systems had built them ready to accept the full range of fuel cards and would allow all users, including the banks, to utilize online authorization (OLA) technology. It was this shift to OLA that made nearly all the advantages of the chip card platforms redundant. This was a game changer, and over the next year or so, the battle died down and finally stopped, after which we all returned to issuing magnetic stripe cards only and controlling our security through OLA.

One of Keyfuels's newer recruits, Tom Pickles, had quite impressed me during our interactions over chip cards, even though we hadn't managed to actually do a deal. With the UK and Irish businesses both growing quickly and our fledgling European move in Belgium underway, we were definitely ready to strengthen the team further. I invited Tom up to show him round Rail House and have lunch with Steve and Mike, and within a few weeks, after a bit of extra persuasion, he agreed to jump ship and join us. This was much to Keyfuels's surprise, as they always liked to portray us as a tiny operation that worked out of a small portacabin by Crewe station. With Tom on board, I gave him the sales leadership of the UK and Ireland to look after as well as MCS so that Steve and I could concentrate more of our time across the channel on developing in Europe. Shortly after

Tom joined, we took on Tim "Sheppy" Shepherd, another of my UK contacts. He had been the organizer of the famous Paris rugby trips. Tim came in to be sales director at Fuel Control Services, now our largest and fastest-growing JV—a mantle it had taken on after the sale of Thistle Fuels.

Over in Ireland, a further opportunity to invest in a border site had popped up, as the owner of our best location just north of Monaghan had decided to retire and was putting his site on the market. This was one of the few places that was literally a stone's throw from the official border and a site where we were already pumping over thirty-five thousand liters a day through two of the bunded tank units I talked about earlier. This wasn't going to be like Dundalk, as there were lots of bidders for this exciting opportunity, so we decided to team up with Statoil, which was also keen to get a foothold there. After much negotiation, we paid the enormous sum of 1.5 million punts, 750,000 punts each, for us to secure a very grotty but extremely well-located truck stop at Emyvale, just over the border from Aughnacloy.

Back in the UK, we also had a second attempt at launching a new product to cross-sell to our customers, and this time, we decided to have a go at the van and car leasing business. As before, we set up a new small, dedicated team led by a friend of mine who had joined from the industry, and a little bit like before, we started fax-shotting and mail-shotting thousands of our existing customers. For the second time, we found ourselves in a very competitive industry in which it was really difficult to understand what a good supply price was, and once again, our customer success rate ended up being very poor. In a similar way to tires, after about a year of trying, we eventually gave up on leasing and took the doing more of what's going well and stopping when it isn't approach. It would be many more years before we took the plunge and tried our hand at another product.

However, the good news for us, which we didn't know at the time, was that it would be third-time lucky!

LESSON 12

DON'T BELIEVE ANYONE; TEST EVERYTHING.

Having talked about the need for fast and effective communication in the last two lessons, those lead nicely to this next one. In this one, I am saying don't necessarily believe what your direct reports are telling you, and also, if they are not saying anything to you at all, that is probably not a good sign that everything is going well. In either scenario, you need to check up on them continuously.

I regularly pick up my phone in a meeting and actually call one of our telesales people, or a software developer, or a finance team member, or even a supplier to ask them whether what I am being told is actually correct or true. My normal finding when I do this is that I am either being given a rose-tinted view of the world or that the person doesn't actually know what is going on, as they haven't tested what their team members are actually saying to them.

Another way to think about this, if you have watched the original *Jurassic Park* movie, is the chaos theory that the mathematician Ian

Malcolm warns about. He predicts that although the scientists think they have covered every angle for a long-term stable environment for the dinosaurs (which were meant to be all female), the island will actually instead quickly proceed to behave in an unpredictable fashion, and that it is an accident waiting to happen. Needless to say, the dinosaurs do start breeding, and the T. rex and velociraptors escape after the fences fail, leading to a vast amount of chaos and havoc!

In the world of work, this means that any processes you have put in place at a point in time as you are growing your business will inevitably either deteriorate or not be able to cope with the growth as you go forward. They therefore need to be changed regularly to avoid a *Jurassic Park* situation. In practice, this does not happen unless you have the right mindset and adopt an approach along the lines of the title of this section.

Let me give you a few examples. If you write a nice sales letter template for all your new prospects and tell your team that it shouldn't be changed within six months, it will soon look like something you can't even recognize, with appalling grammar and spelling. If you agree to a relatively simple software enhancement to the front end of your platform and don't stay close to the project, you will end up with loads of new suggested functionality and a project that takes five times as long as the one that was originally planned. Your marketing team will produce your new Salesforce screens with information asked in the order that they think is best as tech people rather than what is easiest for the salesperson to use as they are talking to customers. They will also probably add twice as many fields as you actually need. Credit will change the vetting criteria and reject customers you should be accepting, and/or they will also not be chasing unpaid invoices as fast as you used to. Sales will be spending too much time calling customers that are either too small or in a customer category in which you have lower conversion rates, etc., etc.

Managers who aren't happy when you display this constant checking characteristic will almost certainly not be doing testing themselves in the same way, and you will be almost certain to find problems in their areas. Good managers won't mind, as they will be doing the same with their team and will see your actions as ones that are helping them to improve systems and processes in their group rather than a lack of trust in them individually.

Remember also that the spreadsheet kids I referred to earlier often believe that the computer can never be wrong and just present you with data and reports without doing some manual sense checks or applying a bit of common sense. I am always finding cases of supposedly senior or intelligent people (normally from finance) presenting volumes and margins on numerous graphs that simply can't be right and expecting me to make very important decisions on the back of them. They normally come up with the excuse that one of the cells in their table has been copied incorrectly!

A NEW EUROPEAN DIESEL CARD

Our new business in Belgium was now live, and it felt a little bit like déjà vu with our initial network of twelve sites trying to find customers using the Golden Pages as our lead source. Steve set up our telesales team in an upstairs corner of Marc's office by his fuel depot, and I was out on the road with Marc, meeting some of his many contacts and trying to add sites to the network. It was very slow going for quite a long time, as one thing we hadn't counted on was how few transport companies were actually based in Belgium, as well as the SME market being right at the micro end of the scale. The customers we were getting were much smaller in size than usual, with lots of cars on their fleets, which meant volumes crept forward very slowly. The Belgian highways were, however, full of trucks from other countries, with a fair complement of these coming from the UK. This made me think that we should start offering our fledgling Belgium network to our UK customers in addition to AS 24 cards, as we now had a very competitive local supply price that was several cents per liter better than our current one.

It didn't take long to decide that we needed a new company for this venture with a European brand. This would allow us to design our own billing system and pricing mechanisms tailored specifically for cross-border customers. The tax and VAT regulations were very different on the Continent, and the invoices all needed to show both the customer's language as well as the local country's language where the fuel was drawn. True to form, yet another three-word company was born, European Diesel Card, one that we knew would quickly be rounded down to EDC. Our initial network was Belgium-only, and Marc and I managed to do a deal with Romac Fuels, a company that owned one of the busiest international fuel stations in Europe, located alongside the main highway just on the Belgium side of the border with France. This was the main route for transport companies operating between the UK and Northern Europe, where the trucks would come off the ferry nearly empty of fuel and then fill up their huge belly tanks with a thousand liters or more. One single fill like this was the equivalent of the amount of diesel that four DCB customers would use in a month. This was a little bit like the Irish border business because the customers were saving so much money that we could have a bigger margin than normal, so this was the best of both worlds.

I now set about visiting the other big fueling locations across Europe, whose locations I had a pretty good idea about from the volumes we were doing at them on the AS 24 card. As I visited the various countries, I always tried to meet up with one of my friends from the incentive trips so that I could get a bit of local knowledge that would help with the negotiations. Before long, we had a core network of sites where we had agreed on very competitive acceptance deals at most of the big-volume locations used by British and Irish trucks. This was important, as it was our existing customers we were going to target first when we began our initial EDC sales campaign. In Spain, we had Irun and La Jonquera; in Luxembourg, Capellan; and in the Netherlands, we had managed to do a deal at Meer to add to the sites we were already operating in the DCB network in Belgium. At Calais, a notoriously dangerous area at night for the drivers because of all the migrants who congregated there and who wanted to sneak into their trailers, we potentially had a different solution. Colin Sykes from Thistle Fuels, who, following the sale of the business to Securicor, had decided to start again on his own, actually owned a small site here. It was really just a patch of rough land in the dunes with a tank, some pumps, and a card reader. Because of his noncompete in the UK after the sale, he also had the idea a couple of years earlier to try to create his own European fuel card network and also offer European VAT reclamation services, which was another thing all the international truckers needed. His volumes were very small, though, and he was struggling to make the site viable, so we agreed to buy it for £100,000 and give him a very competitive access deal so that his own customers could continue using it. This was now the third site on our company-owned network, alongside Dundalk and Emyvale in Ireland. Not that long after we had done the deal with Colin for the Calais site, I also asked if he was interested in selling the whole of his European card business, given that he was starting to realize that on his own, he probably was going to struggle to get it to long-term viability. He agreed, and within a couple of months, the deal was completed, and this gave EDC more momentum in terms of volume but also added quite a few more sites to the network that made our overall offering more appealing to new customers.

Infuel in Ipswich was starting to grow quickly and had already moved to a larger office. Roy was also helping with the sales effort on the new EDC card as well as bringing his skills and experience to bear in the UK to our diesel purchasing, in which we were now forward buying blocks of fuel and selling them in advance. These futures deals were only possible because we had a huge stock of customer fuel in the network that we could physically sell today and then take delivery of at a later point in time. This helped us to balance our stocks as well as allow us to take advantage of the ups and downs in the European

Platts product market, which created excellent positive cash flow. The swings could also be up to several pence per liter at a time, so it was a great extra income source as well.

I'm not quite sure exactly where the idea for our next project came from, but in early 2003, Roy and I started talking about developing a new concept to try to accelerate our UK volumes even faster. The premise was to launch a card with which every single customer was on the same very competitive weekly price, regardless of size, and this price was to be listed on the front page of a website on a daily basis, which no one had ever done. Additionally, it was to be a low-cost operation in which customers could only sign up online, and they had to receive their invoice electronically, which was still quite a new concept. Up till then, pricing had always been done individually for customers and communicated by phone or email so that competitors didn't know at what level you were selling. We were now saying that every customer was equal and that they no longer needed to ring different card suppliers each week to barter them down to the lowest level.

The next thing we needed was a name and a design to create a completely new-looking card. After a brainstorming session one day over a few beers, as I remember, we settled on Smartdiesel, which we thought was very appropriate given the new concept with an all-black card design. We began preparations and set the launch date for the 1st of July that year, with an ambition to get to a million liters per month within six months. We decided to do an advertising campaign in the trade press, which we had never done before, and to rent one of the best unofficial motorway hoarding signs to advertise this weekly price. The site we chose was near Stoke, between Junctions 15 and 16 on the M6, seen by thousands of truckers a day, and which was certain to annoy Keyfuels and Fuelserv! The location was very close to quite a tight bend in the road, which meant it was in the perfect eyeline for drivers heading north. We asked our printers to create a giant-sized weatherproof price sign that we could change every Sunday night. To give an extra edge to the launch, we also decided to use some of Roy's futures bulk purchase gains to make our price even more competitive in the market for the first six months. So when launch day came, everyone was super excited to see how this completely new idea would be received by the market. Well, a trickle of applications started to come through, which soon became a torrent, and the phones started to buzz in the office, with everyone asking what was going on and how it was possible to offer every customer the same price at such a low level. We weren't even pumping a liter yet, and our competitors were already under pressure with their customers saying they needed to match Smartdiesel, which was at 79.90 ppl! Well, we got to our million liters per month within just a couple of months, and by the end of the year, we made it to a million liters a week, massively ahead of our original target. At the next FPS conference in Harrogate, we took our biggest contingent of staff ever and combined it with a celebration of our Smartdiesel success.

LESSON 13

YOU CAN HAVE VOLUME AND MARGIN.

Having talked about the importance of communication in the last three lessons, this one is back to more of a basic business mentality that I needed to learn relatively early in my journey. Managing the careful balance between volume and margin is critical if you are going to grow a large, successful business that is sustainable over the long term. I have had many people work for me over the years who have had the you-can't-have-both mentality when it comes to this question, and Tim "Sheppy" Shepherd was a prime example! If you can't break away from this methodology, it ultimately leads you to have either a small profitable company that never grows or a larger business that doesn't make much money.

I definitely started my working life as a volume guy, in which out on the road at Esso, I would try to sell as many tanker-loads of diesel and other fuels as possible. With my bigger customers, if the pricing wasn't within my authority, I would always be asking my boss for his support to get me a higher rebate from the planning team in the head office so I could get a particular deal over the line. In my defense, we were never given details of the entire economics, and I didn't have a profit target, so I never actually knew whether the diesel I was selling was at a positive or negative margin anyway!

Over many years and with the experience of lots of different situations, I have learned that in most of our markets and divisions, you can have both if you have the right quality of data and account management combined with a determined mindset. There have been some exceptions to this mantra, when it literally wasn't possible because of the specific sector we were trading in or particular competitive tensions, and here, I normally decided that this was probably a vertical that we shouldn't be developing.

Another thing to always keep in mind is that when a member of your team tells you that competitors are pricing at a certain level, don't necessarily believe them, as they probably haven't dug into all the details that surround this particular comparison. These competitors might have higher up-front charges, some form of ongoing account management fees, or many other means of making money away from the headline product price. On most occasions, everything is not always as it appears from just the raw price that a salesperson has been given by their customer!

So, how do we go about improving our volume/margin balance? The first thing you need to do is make sure the quality of your data is in good shape. Then, segment your customers into several groups according to their size and pricing. Next, systematically test these groups using small cohorts of customers, with a mindset that you are going to change margins to the level you need but do not want to lose a single customer. Your account management teams need to be on alert to escalate all the negative customer interactions in real time, so you can then make quick decisions to either reduce prices again to save a specific customer or sometimes make the tough decisions to shed some clients that will never be profitable.

A good example of this was our business in Italy, where not long after we had taken over the customer portfolio, we found that the bad debt was significantly worse than we had planned. Our margins there were very thin already, and there was no way to negotiate a lower price from our supplier as a solution to our problem. I therefore sat down with Sheppy and then subsequently our local leader in Vimercate and told them that we had to make a radical change to our model and introduce a monthly management fee of 1.25 percent. This new fee would have to be charged across the whole customer base if we were to get back to our original business model plan for gross profit. They were both vehemently against this and said we would lose all our customers overnight as soon as we started to implement this change. My response to them was that if this was really the case, then we didn't have a viable long-term business and would have to close down our Italian operations. Anyway, I enforced the change, but as a compromise, I did say to our local manager that if any customer rang in to complain, then he was allowed to waive the new fee. Well, to Sheppy's and the manager's surprise, only two customers out of our total base of over three thousand at the time actually called in to complain, so within weeks, we were back to feeling good again about the future prospects for the Italian operations. Today, Italy is one of our best European businesses, with nearly fifty thousand customers, many of whom are now using our telematics solution in tandem with their fuel cards.

EXPANDING ACROSS EUROPE AND THE SON VIDA SUMMIT

Our operations in Belgium were beginning to gather a bit of momentum now and sat nicely alongside our new European card proposition. While I had been out looking for sites for EDC and meeting up with some of my old contacts from AS 24, another one of them expressed an interest in a potential JV deal. He lived in Breda at the southern border of the Netherlands, which seemed as good a country as any for our next step, given its adjacency with Belgium. Over the next week, we started talking more seriously, and before long, Diesel Card Services was born. Then, in a similar way to Belgium, we started to do a few site deals to create a small network as well as recruit some salespeople to find new customers. As the initial network was predominantly truck stops, the new customers here were mainly transport companies, so it was more like how we had started originally in the UK. As with Belgium, we also explored the possibility of a reseller deal with a major oil company that would allow us to accelerate faster and target the SME market, which was really helping us grow back home.

Portugal followed next with another friend from the AS 24 trips, and he started to look after network development across Iberia. Given that diesel was cheaper here than in both France and Portugal, it made sense to put most of our time and effort into looking for strategic locations in Spain to complement the two sites we already had on the EDC network up near the border with France. This network would be good not only for the new Portuguese customers as they headed north and east across Europe but would also be perfect for the British and Irish ones who were coming down to Iberia in the hundreds to pick up fresh fruit and vegetables to bring back across the Channel. We opened a small office in Caldas da Rainha, about an hour north of Lisbon, and also began exploring if we could do a reseller deal with one of the local oil companies. BP had a good presence here, but just because we had a good relationship in the UK didn't automatically mean that this would extend across other territories, as BP's European management structures across the Continent were completely independent.

In France, we started with the same JV concept, but instead of trying to build a truck stop network, the two new partners concentrated their efforts on doing more of a retail card management deal with one of the French hypermarkets, similar to some of the account card deals we had signed in the UK. We found a small office in Saint-Denis in the suburbs of Paris and, after a few trips over, signed a deal and began selling to small SME customers located close to one of the hypermarket locations.

Spain followed next with an office in Valencia, where we started looking for trucking customers to use the network that we had already established for EDC and the Portuguese business. One thing we soon began to realize was that credit in Europe, and especially in Spain, was much tougher than in the UK. Our bad debt levels as we got going were running at one to two cents per liter, nearly ten times the UK, and put a very big hole in our business model, so growth slowed down here as we tried to figure out what to do. We had to use a different credit insurance policy, which had very high rejection rates and much higher premiums, so this was definitely part of a new learning curve as we realized we couldn't just replicate our UK model overseas.

Given this, when we started to think about Germany, we decided that instead of starting with our own brand of card, which was what we had done nearly everywhere else, we would wait until we could persuade one of the local oil companies to give us a reseller deal. Many meetings in Hamburg later, we finally managed to do a deal with Esso, which was helped by the fact that our UK volumes were really starting to develop locally, and we were now its fastest-growing UK partner. Employing people was also very different in Europe, where there were vast differences between salary costs and workers' rights across the regions. Germany was a perfect storm of being very expensive, having very low unemployment and very strong employee protection. This was going to make the process of recruiting and building a team that much harder, and for a variety of these reasons, we decided to base ourselves in Berlin, which at that point in time was a much cheaper place to run a business. We opened a small office near Schönefeld Airport, found a manager there instead of a JV partner, and got going selling Esso cards.

The rescue of the MCS business in Denmark had thrown us together with another one of its major customers that was Swedish. At our regular quarterly board meetings, we always joked with Sven and Claus over a few beers at the Schnitzelhaus about starting a fuel card business together there. With Germany up and running, we thought now was a good time to give Sven a call and see if he and Claus were really serious about starting a project. The two of them were different partners from the ones we had found elsewhere, as they actually owned a good-sized network of fully automated service stations right across the country already. The geography of Sweden is such that the roads are very quiet and run dead straight for miles and miles through forests and lakes, with the occasional village. Hence, there were lots of very small sites with just a single card reader and two or three pumps that ran twenty-four hours a day, seven days a week. With their network already in place, all we needed was a small office at their existing HQ. This was located in Norrköping, an hour and a half south of Stockholm on one of their fast trains. Credit was not going to be a problem, as it is illegal to write a check in Sweden when you don't have the funds to pay. On the other hand, margins, customer size, and wages were all issues to be faced, and it soon became a very difficult business model to get to try to work. After a couple of years of trying, with some very pleasant trips to Stockholm in the summer, we decided enough was enough. We sold our half of the business to them and decided to concentrate our efforts on more fruitful geographies. (Do more of what's going well and stop when it isn't—lesson 5!)

We also explored an opportunity in Denmark, where we decided to go and see one of the local automated network operators, OK Petroleum. We thought we would pitch our Smartdiesel concept to see if we could do something similar. Bjarne from MCS kindly offered to chauffeur us for the trip and picked us up from Copenhagen Airport before driving us across to Aarhus in Jutland, where OK Petroleum was based. We decided to go the night before so that we would be fresh for the meeting the following morning, and we arrived well in time, at about four in the afternoon. After a quick change, we headed out for a wander about to find somewhere to eat and explore the city. This was somewhere I already knew, as I had really enjoyed my ten-week summer internship working in the laboratory there while I had been at the University of Leeds. Well, not for the first time, we located a rather nice bar, and after a couple of beers, we decided to try some of the local drinks. After a few Nordsø Oil licorice shots, the night went downhill as we tried to drink every spirit along the counter, with a small beer chaser in between each one. The bar was also doing five shots for the price of four, so we each took our turn at a double on every fourth drink. Well, as you can probably guess, the next day didn't go quite as well as planned, especially as Bjarne had lost his car keys the previous night and we were nearly late for our meeting after having to grab a cab. After introductions and a reviving coffee and croissant, I gave the presentation, and afterwards, we left OK Petroleum's offices thinking we had done an excellent job and pulled it out of the bag. However, we never heard back from the company, which wasn't a great surprise in the end, so Denmark never happened. It is definitely an evening that Tom, Malcolm, and I will never forget and resulted in all of us taking a lengthy course of abstinence to recover once we got back. It is also one that is definitely in our memory bank when we get back together every now and then.

The final piece in Europe that happened next was that we got an approach from our Shell UK senior contact to ask whether we were interested in buying a portfolio from them in Italy. This was not a country I had any knowledge of, but I jumped on a plane to Milan to find out more about this opportunity, face-to-face with the local team. We had never had the chance to start with a base of customers that would provide income from day one, so this would allow us to have a slightly bigger office and team from the start if we could get a deal done. I gave Sheppy the project of finding somewhere to base ourselves, and after a few reconnaissance trips across to Italy, he whittled down an initial long list of ten to a final choice of three. After a bit of haggling over price, we signed a contract with Shell and opened on the sixth floor of a nice office block in Vimercate. This town is in the northeast suburbs of Milan, significantly cheaper than locating ourselves near the center of the city.

Needless to say, the credit situation was again much worse than planned, and the business was immediately underwater. We were therefore desperate for an increase in our unit margins. After initially trying to negotiate a lower supply price from our network provider, which was unsuccessful, Sheppy and I flew to Milan to talk to our local manager about the alternate plan I had come up with to turn the business around. As I outlined in the last lesson, and contrary to what they both thought, you can have volume and margin, as the changes we made proved successful, and we got Italy back on track.

With all these new countries, the amount of traveling Steve, Tom, Sheppy, and I were doing was really increasing, and Caffè Nero at Manchester Airport T3 became a regular meeting spot for an early-morning coffee. We all knew each other's orders, and I started to acquire a penchant for a fresh almond croissant! Funnily enough, the café is still there now in the same place opposite the Ryanair check-in desks! Many of the new countries we had added over the last year or so were farther away, so most of the trips were now two nights away instead of the singles we had been doing to Ireland and Belgium.

With all this growth and an increasing number of customers, our Webfuels customer portal was really starting to both look dated and lack functionality versus the ones our competitors were now offering. We therefore decided to set up a separate office on the eighth floor and start a project to create something that was market leading and really different in terms of the user interface. We wanted something that was intuitive and driven by simple icons that would be very easy to use with no training required. After nine months of hard work by the team, Velocity was born and released, which jumped us significantly ahead of the pack, a better position to be in, given that we had been trailing for so long.

As soon as the team finished this project, they started working on another critical bit of work that we also needed to do before our credit team drowned under the weight of the hard-copy application forms. The number of these that we were now receiving a day from across Europe, combined with the fact that many of them could take many days or weeks to check and approve, depending, meant that on any one day, there could be several hundred in credit at the same time. When you combine this with all the documents that then had to be printed off and stapled to each application, this made for a lot of paperwork. This new project was revolutionary and would create a completely electronic application form with which we could gather the customer's bank details over the phone without the need for a signed mandate. This could then be passed immediately to credit, where the necessary checks could be done and appended electronically and then a decision made. It would not only allow us to reduce the time period from receipt to acceptance but also completely eliminate the mountains of hard copies we were now filing downstairs in the racks that were bulging on the first-floor wing. We could also retrieve these in the future without having to send someone down in the lift to hunt around for hours among the myriad of lever arch files. We nicknamed the system Cruise, which, alongside Velocity, definitely moved us many steps forward and gave us a stronger platform for further growth. This was probably the first time that I began to see that IT could be much more than just a means to an end but could be something that gave us a strategic edge. Instead of just managing transactions and creating invoices, this new software was now part of our product and what made us different in the marketplace.

The business was now in its eighteenth year, and our innovative JV model that had really helped to drive growth while keeping central costs at a low level was starting to creak. For several reasons, the model was going to have to change, with the biggest pressure coming from suppliers, for whom we now needed an ever-growing amount of credit because of our insatiable demand for diesel. There was also the fact that several of the partners were starting to think about retirement and beginning to wonder how it might be possible to release some capital from the business. Although, in many ways, we were operating like a group, it was also becoming increasingly difficult to explain our very complex financial structure to the banks, as in most cases, there was no formal link between the businesses apart from me being a common shareholder.

I decided that we should get all the shareholders together to talk through the alternatives for moving forward that could potentially solve some of these issues. Rather than doing this locally in Crewe, I thought it would be nice to go somewhere a little warmer and nicer and set Tom "Big Tom" Pickles and Sheppy (who had slowly acquired the reputation and responsibility of entertainment secretary) to find somewhere suitable. Tom, who had previously worked as a holiday rep in his early years, took the lead, and the two of them came up with several options for hotels, all of which were in and around the city of Palma on the island of Majorca. So a week or so later, we set up an overnight trip to go and look at four hotels and pick a venue for the June trip.

The first one we saw was the Castillo Hotel Son Vida, just off the ring road and nestled in the hills that overlooked the beautiful bay below. As soon as we arrived and walked through the entrance of this old castle, we knew it was the perfect spot and that we were not going to be able to find anything better. We went to the next hotel out of courtesy and then decided to cancel the afternoon and have a few well-earned beers instead. In the evening, we found a fabulous little tapas restaurant called La Bóveda near Plaça de la Llotja, which was an instant hit and I still class as my favorite place to eat today, so you will have to pay a visit. We also had a very large gin and tonic in Bar Abaco, which is just round the corner from the restaurant and a must if you are visiting. We nicknamed it "the fruit bar," as there were hundreds of lemons, oranges, and other fruit strewn all over the old floors inside, which I never quite understood the significance of.

So six weeks or so later, we all headed out to Majorca for the first-ever get-together of all of the JV partners. There were about forty of us, and I had put together a pack of information to highlight the growing credit requirements of the group and the need to have more of our financial strength in one place where it was clearly visible so that the suppliers and banks could start to treat us more like a single business. I went on to talk about some of the other benefits of creating a strong single entity. The fact that we could use this as the vehicle to buy out partners if they decided to sell shares when they retired was definitely an idea they liked. That we all genuinely believed that one big business was actually worth more than the sum of the value of lots of smaller ones also made the idea more compelling. I then outlined a plan in which, rather than one big-bang merger (which I imagined we all thought would be difficult to agree on), we would try to go on a journey in this direction and start to reduce the number of entities on a progressive basis by doing some smaller mergers first. This would then allow us to create a model and work through all the different valuation mechanisms we would need on a more gradual basis, with a couple of partners at a time. Some businesses had bigger trucking customers but lower unit margins. Some had smaller, more local business customers with lower bad debt. In addition, older busi-nesses tended to have a better net-profit-to-volume ratio, as they were now not in their rapid growth phase and had lower overheads, so there were a lot of different factors to consider. Some of the partners were definitely keener and bought into the consolidation concept more than others, so we agreed we would start working with them but keep talking to everyone else as we went along. We set a target date for overall completion of spring 2013, which was six years away. I thought that was achievable and wouldn't put too much pressure on the project.

Now that the work element of the trip was over, it was time to relax, and Sheppy had found the perfect idea that we thought would appeal to everyone. We had booked four motor yachts that we would join at Puerto Portals and then cruise down to Sant Elm for lunch at a nice cliffside restaurant. We had a fabulous lunch of calamari, jamón ibérico, and Padrón peppers. Roger, one of the partners, also asked his father-in-law, who lived in Andratx, to pop down to join us for an hour or so. He had been an F1 driver many years earlier and recounted some great stories about the old days when he had also been a competitive skier in the offseason. The F1 drivers today would definitely not be allowed to do anything as dangerous when they weren't racing. I think the most they are allowed is to play on the Xbox. After a pleasant swim stop in the afternoon, we went back to the hotel for a gala dinner, which, if my recollection is right, not everyone managed to make because of overindulgence in wine earlier in the day! The Son Vida was the perfect venue and made me think that it was time to finally change the location for our annual management off-site meeting. This had moved from Glenridding to Windermere in the last few years, but the warmth and sea of Majorca was no competition. Palma was also very easy for everyone to fly to, given that we now had a much more European spread in our senior team.

LESSON 14

THINK EVERYTHING'S GOING BADLY.

This next lesson is one that I think is very difficult to learn, unless you have worked at a young start-up business where all you are faced with every day is a huge number of things to fix. Many young people who start their working lives at a large, successful corporation never get exposure to this front line of numerous problems and therefore live in a false world where they think that all the systems and processes are working well. Not enough of our management today thinks like this, which is why, in our relatively new graduate program, we give them exposure as early as possible in their careers to the fact that not all our customers are happy and that we need to constantly strive to improve the way we work. Hopefully, this next example will add a little color as to the way we try to get our people to think a bit differently.

Although the location, exact format, and number of people attending have changed a little each year, every June, I try to get away with my senior team for an off-site management meeting. These get-togethers are both to reflect on the previous twelve months' performance and to look forward to where we want to go over the year ahead. I also try to include more relaxed team building to make it a fun few days.

Many of these have been in the Lake District, where we have been to Underscar Manor on the banks of Skiddaw, The Glenridding Hotel nestled along Ullswater, and The Burnside Hotel, located in the busy town of Bowness-on-Windermere. Alongside the normal two days of presentations, in which I always insisted on monthly graphs for every product line (in every country), there were always boozy nights at many of the nice local pubs, which consistently made the start of the second day a bit of a graveyard slot!

In the last fifteen years or so, the venue for these meetings has moved from the relatively local Lake District to the warmer climes of Majorca, where we have usually stayed at the fabulous Castillo Hotel Son Vida. Although the end-of-the-day pub crawls have changed to boat trips along the coast, the endless sets of graphs for all the countries and divisions remain a constant. This means that every year, we have to flick through an ever-growing number of slides even faster, especially as we now have six divisions, whereas we used to only have one. At least now everything is digital, which is very different from the old days when each sheet had to be photo-copied onto an acetate for us to display using an old-style overhead projector, which was always a bit messy.

So what has all this got to do with the very important message of this lesson and a trait that I said is all too rare among my senior managers? Well, it was one of these annual management trips to Majorca that really highlighted the difference I described above about people who haven't experienced a bootstrap culture.

I remember that at the start of the first day of the conference, we were running through the figures for the fuel division, with each of the country leaders talking about their individual volumes and margins. All of them were explaining the problems they were having—weak members of their management teams, difficulties in recruitment, not enough quality digital leads, competitor aggression, etc.—followed by the associated changes they needed to make. This was despite the fact that in most cases, all their countries were either on or ahead of their budget numbers.

Then we came to one of the central services presentations, in which we had a new director who had only been with the group a couple of months. He proceeded to talk about how well everything was going in his department and how good his figures were, with not a single mention of any problems.

Well, at the end of the meeting, two things happened. The first was that he started talking to some of the other senior members of the team, saying he hadn't realized how badly things were going in the business, which I think was probably making him question why he had given up his good corporate job to join us. This was followed by me speaking to him to tell him that I didn't want to have another presentation like the one he had given and that I only wanted him to talk about the negative issues that he was having in his group, how he was planning to fix them, and what help he might therefore need from either me or other members of the team.

This mentality is one that has been with me since the outset of UK Fuels back in 1990, that I think about as I head to work every morning, and that determines what I spend my time on during the day. It is also one that I try to encourage in our new, younger generation of managers just starting out on their journeys.

ARRIVAL OF THE AMERICANS

You probably won't be that surprised to know that the two largest fuel card companies in the world at that point in time (and it's still the case) were from the United States. However, FleetCor (now Corpay) and Wright Express (now WEX) both started life in very different ways. FleetCor had only been founded in 2000 but was already a very big business in 2005, with a market capital of over $2 billion, having grown very quickly and aggressively through M&A. WEX, on the other hand, had been around since 1983 and had grown much more slowly and on a mainly organic basis, although that had started to change in recent years, I think in part because the new kid on the block had already overtaken them.

The first time I heard either of their names was when someone called me in 2006 to tell me that Peter Vallis, the owner of Keyfuels, had just sold to a big American company called FleetCor. Not long after this, I found out that the CEO, Ron Clark, had been across to the UK, making an initial tour of some of the main oil company reseller businesses to meet up with the owners. Within a few months, FleetCor had purchased a couple of the larger ones and put offers on the table for several more. There was a real buzz around the market-place, with everyone a little surprised at how much the company was prepared to pay for what was effectively just a customer base with very little associated infrastructure.

A month or so later, I was honored with a lunch invitation to a nice restaurant in Covent Garden that still sticks quite clearly in my mind. The subject of the meeting was very much about not if I wanted to do a deal but how much money I wanted and how I would like to be paid. The FleetCor representatives gave me a long list of who else they were talking to and effectively said that, at some point, everyone was going to sell to them, and that included me! I had no intention of selling, and we joked about it back at the office. However, over the next year, many of the names they had talked about began to fall like dominoes, and the new beast kept getting bigger. FleetCor's acquisition model was very different from our organic growth one and involved cutting costs and centralizing functions in combination with increasing margins and charges. This modus operandi had some unexpected upsides for us that we hadn't really considered as it began to take control of the new companies it had acquired. First, FleetCor was slowly taking out some of our fiercest rivals, which began to ease the pressure on our weekly pricing calls with customers. Second, its model meant that the company shed quite a bit of volume into the marketplace, which had to go somewhere, and because of the size of our growing telesales team, we were one of the big beneficiaries. Maybe the arrival of the Americans and two big new players was not going to be such a bad thing after all, as it was making lesson 13 easier for us—you can have volume *and* margin!

However, FleetCor's ninth acquisition in 2009 of ReD for £21.5 million suddenly changed the dynamics in the original bunkering business, in which there had only been the three of us. It now controlled well over 80 percent of this particular market, and our friends at ReD from the OSS1 project were now swallowed up into the Keyfuels machine. Dark clouds were brewing, and it wouldn't be that long before our current reasonable working relationship with our much bigger rival would take a serious turn for the worse. One positive thing that came out of the purchase of ReD was that we started talking to Lee Everett, one of the old Fuelserv employees who had been Roy's protégé and who wasn't really enjoying his role there. After a bit of gentle persuasion at Roy's house in Ipswich, followed by a nice dinner at The Last Anchor restaurant in the docks, Lee resigned from FleetCor in January 2010. Just over six months later, after serving out his noncompete, he joined Roy's business, Infuel, in October. Within six months or so, it was obvious that Lee needed to have a bigger role in the group going forward, and he moved north to Cheshire early in 2011 and became the MD of EDC, our rapidly growing European fuel card. Little did I know at the time, but thirteen years later, Lee would eventually take over as CEO of what would become a much larger and different business.

Rail House was now bursting at the seams and also starting to feel not the right sort of office to portray the quality and scale of services we were now able to offer. During my new search for space, I came across an opportunity just across the rail bridge from the station, where a developer had bought a scrappy bit of land that was being used to park buses overnight that backed onto the West Coast Main Line. They were planning to build some industrial units similar to some close by, but it wasn't too late to see if we could get planning changed for something different. We approached the council and managed to get a change of use agreed on, and we began to put plans together for a purpose-built office that could become our new HQ. The design wasn't going to take up the whole plot, so it would leave space for a second building should we ever need one, which, given our current trajectory, would probably not be too long a wait. Our new two-wing building with a central core got passed, and we signed off on a design and build contract with a builder. We set up a camera on-site so that we could monitor progress and ended up with some great time-lapse footage, which we put on our website so all our employees could see the building progress.

After just over a year, everything was complete, and we began the move across from Rail House to our brand-new home. It was also handy, as it was located on the same road as our Macon Court office, where DCI was now based. It had the added benefit of a McDonald's at the end of the street, which went down well with the sales teams as well as most of the senior management! We named the building Eurocard to show off our new European credentials, and before the builders had even signed off on the final handover, we decided we might as well get on with constructing a sister office next door, as we were certain we would need even more room before too long.

As we talked with the old landlord at Rail House about our departure, we got a very unpleasant shock one morning from the managing agent when he presented us with a very large dilapidations bill of £50,000. The landlord insisted that we return the building to the "pristine state" he claimed that it had been in when we took possession nearly ten years earlier. You'll perhaps recall something I did a decade ago as a precaution. Luckily, I remembered, too, that video I'd taken at the time with my old camera, and I went up into the loft at home to root around among my old family videos. After making a copy of the relevant tapes onto a disc, we sent a very tongue-in-cheek reply, saying that we would be happy to return it to the original state, as we had taken over some very run-down accommodation. Needless to say, after the landlord watched the "gruesome" video, the £50,000 problem promptly disappeared!

THE FIRST OF THE FIFTIETHS

Steve "Genty" Gent, one of the first members of my senior team to join the business, was rapidly approaching his fiftieth birthday in the summer of 2009, and I started to think about doing something a bit different to celebrate this occasion. Since the famous Moscow trip, when we tricked Steve in a vodka-drinking game (Mike and I were drinking shots of Evian!), he was definitely already on the lookout for any trickery relating to his birthday, so whatever we were going to do would need some careful planning. After much consideration, I settled on a one-night trip to Palma, Majorca, with about twenty of the team and then put my mind to work on how we would keep it secret and what special surprises I could work into the plan.

The first thing I did was decide on a date, the 19th of June, and having done that, I enrolled one of our Scottish customers, Alistair Brogan, into the ruse to arrange a faux meeting in Crewe on that day to make sure Steve would be about for his surprise. I suggested that Alistair give Steve a call and offer a couple of alternative dates and also say to Steve that it would be good if Bill was about so that he could join the meeting. It was literally only an hour or so after the call that Steve was on the hook, as he came into my office to ask me about the meeting and whether the 19th or 20th of June would work for me.

I replied that I was already committed on the 20th, so the date was set.

Next, I knew we would need to get his partner, Ann, involved if we were going to get hold of his passport without him knowing—an essential part of the plan if we were going to fly to Spain. So I called her up, and we agreed to pretend to Steve that we were going for a night out in Manchester and would swing past his house to allow him to change out of his suit. She said that she also wanted to do a little surprise for him and have a birthday cake and drinks at the house for us when we stopped, so that was added to the itinerary. She agreed to find his passport and said she would slip it to me when we stopped by for champagne and chocolate cake.

So flights were booked for just after lunch on Wednesday, 19th June, and I also sorted a stretch limo pickup from Crewe so we could get the party started early.

I knew Steve was very close to his older brother, Martin, and thought that he would make a great surprise as an extra guest if he was free that day. I gave him a call, and he was really keen to join the team, which then gave me another opportunity to add a further twist to the plan. Martin agreed to play the part of a scruffy hitchhiker holding a scribbled "M6 North" cardboard sign on our planned route as we left Crewe. On the day we agreed on, we would hide his overnight bag along with those of the rest of the team so that Steve would not realize that we were going to the airport until the last minute.

So with everything set, the countdown began, and it didn't take long for the 19th to come around. In the meantime, we also arranged to book a fake dinner with Alistair for the evening of that day, with an overnight stay planned in Manchester to make sure that Steve didn't make any of his own plans that would derail our surprise.

So on the morning of the 19th, Steve was relaxed as usual, and everything appeared normal. We were all in our work suits, and there was no sign of our overnight bags, which were safely tucked away in the cleaning cupboard.

A meeting at the rear of the new sales office was arranged for Steve so we could keep him out of the way when the limo arrived. It was about his favorite subject, fastfuel invoice processing, so he duly obliged and crossed over to the other building with a spring in his step! Once the coast was clear, we quickly retrieved our bags, changed into jeans, and loaded the luggage into the back of the limo before jumping in and closing the door. Steve was then called and asked to come back over to the head office because there was an urgent problem. I think he knew the game was up when he saw the limo, but if there was any doubt when we opened the door and all shouted, "Happy Birthday!" the trap was sprung. We told Steve we were going to swing by his house so that he could change, too, and he literally just jumped straight in and grabbed a glass of fizz.

As we left Crewe on the main road, the driver suddenly braked and pulled over onto the verge, and we all groaned and shouted, "What's going on?" The driver leaned back and said that he had seen a hitchhiker, and as we were going that way, he thought it would be kind to stop (he was also in on the plan). We all groaned again as the hitchhiker approached the limo door, but as soon as it opened and Steve saw his brother Martin smiling under his hoodie, it was his turn to groan! Martin jumped in, and it was another glass of fizz all round as we headed north towards Holmes Chapel to Steve's house. When we got there, we parked at the end of his road, and Steve said he would just take two minutes to change and that Ann would be very surprised to see him, as she was working from home that day. Anyway, as soon as he was out of sight, we all got out and started to follow him down. By the time we got round the corner, he had already been inside and seen the cake and drinks that Anne had prepared and was back at the front door ready to welcome us all in. Ann slipped me his passport, and after half an hour or so and yet another glass of fizz, we headed off with Steve changed and ready for what he thought was a night out in Manchester. As we approached the airport junction of the M56, there was a lot of joking, and when Steve noticed we had turned off, he immediately said, "I can't go anywhere, as I don't have my passport with me."

As we went up the ramp to Terminal 1, I pulled his passport out of my pocket and gave it to him. Steve then spluttered that he didn't have any bag or clothes with him! We all got out and collected our overnight bags from the boot, telling Steve that he would have to make a quick stop at Boots in World Duty Free for a toothbrush and toothpaste! We managed to get him through security without him seeing the destination and settled into Giraffe up on the first floor of Terminal 1 for some lunch. The first thing Steve did was call Alistair at Brogan's to give him some stick for tricking him about our meeting. Little did Steve know that we had also invited Alistair on the trip, and he was literally in the bar next door, having a beer. So when Steve was on the phone with him, he just wandered over and stuck his head round the corner of the booth where we were sitting and said hello.

Next, Steve looked at the departure board, trying to whittle down the choice of destination to one of three, but it wasn't until we got to the gate that he actually knew where we were heading—Palma. The flight was on Monarch Airlines on an old wide-bodied plane, and we settled in for the trip with repeat orders of "twenty gin and tonics, please" to the very accommodating cabin crew. As soon as we landed, we all jumped into taxis to the hotel and literally just dropped our bags in our rooms, with no one bothering to change clothes. The bags were now beginning to look like unnecessary items, as we were due to be picked up the following morning at seven for an early flight back, so Steve, with only his new toothbrush from Boots stuffed in his pocket, was now the one laughing!

After nearly twelve hours of partying, with our group ending up getting splintered into several smaller ones, we all made it back to the hotel by about six in the morning. After literally only a thirty-minute lie down, we were back outside the hotel, waiting to start the trip back. Besides Steve's brother saying, "You guys know how to party," as we waited for our return taxis, one of the most memorable parts of the trip happened when we got back on the return flight. We were the last group to board, and Tom Pickles was the very last person through the plane door before they closed it. One of our group shouted out, "Shrek, sit down! You'll frighten the kids!" and the whole plane burst into laughter. After that, it was a very quiet trip back, with everyone falling asleep within a few minutes of takeoff. It was going to be difficult in the future to top that fiftieth surprise!

At home, the girls were getting bigger and had settled into The Grange School in Hartford near Northwich. With all their after-school activities and parties, the commute from Tarporley was becoming a bit of a burden, so we decided to move a little closer. We had a couple of years at a new build house on St Mary's Drive by Vale Royal Abbey Golf Club in Whitegate before finally finding a really nice older place on the edge of Delamere Forest. Summer Hill on Bag Lane near Norley needed quite a bit of work, so I began the first of what would become quite a few building projects that would start to become a bit of a new passion for me over the years ahead. We had some nice summer sailing holidays to Greece and Türkiye, combined with a few amazing safaris to Africa, which gave Lauren and Becky their first taste of animal conservation and the ever-increasing dangers animals face in the wild every day. This would be an early pointer as to the direction they would both later take with their careers. Although neither of them knew that yet, they would both end up working in the not-for-profit sector as well as setting up their own foundation to help with wildlife projects across the globe.

We continued our trips to the Lakes, where I also decided to have a full revamp of the house's interior and bring the bathrooms and kitchen a little more up-to-date. Lauren and Becky also both started to make the transition from moaning about going out on walks to really enjoying being up in the mountains, and they started to bring up friends and do bigger walks on their own, which was a nice new stage.

One further building project that I also started about this time was up in Scotland, where Gill and I had been away one weekend at a Shell customer event in Gleneagles. While walking round The Queen's Course early one morning, we came across a for-sale sign on a bit of land right next to the third fairway. It was a beautiful greenfield plot about an acre in size and was one of twelve that the hotel was selling as part of its Ryder Cup development project. We came back up a few weeks later with our builder friend from home, Bernie, to see if he was interested in building a house in Scotland for us. After a little persuasion, he said yes, and we put in an offer that week and secured the site within a month. Thus began a regular weekly trip up for him and a monthly one for Gill and me as we began to build a lovely new house that would take us just over two years to complete.

LESSON 15

NEVER BLAME THE MARKET.

The next two lessons follow on from the last one in that they talk about characteristics that I want my senior team members to adopt as they look at their teams' performance. Let's look at the first of these.

As soon as I hear one of my leaders in a sales review trying to blame the market for why they have not met their budget numbers, the alarm bells begin ringing. This is because, at the point we agree on our annual forecasts, I never try to pressure management to put forward volumes and margins that are unachievable, and I always try to put myself in their shoes and consider what I think I'd be capable of delivering. Obviously, the biggest guide to these numbers is the last twelve months' performance, especially the current run rate, overlaid with the additional sales and marketing investment we are going to make going forward.

Many leaders in other businesses I have come across over the years have obviously not had this forecasting discipline, and this getting-ahead-of-themselves phenomenon is sometimes because maybe they want to impress the external market, or they are being pressured and encouraged by advisors or bankers who actually have no idea what is realistically achievable. That usually ends badly and often fatally for the business, and there is a long list of companies that have gone this way over the last few years after some crazy early valuations. The American slang for this phenomenon is pump and dump!

For me, forecasts must be made very carefully and need to take many different factors into account if I am going to sign them off and put my reputation on the line, as ultimately, they all feed into our overall plan. These factors include the strength of our product in the market, how good our supply prices are, our local lead generation and marketing capabilities, the current sales team performance, competitor activity, technology requirements, how last year's new customers will feed through into next year's figures, etc., etc. If this is all done correctly, then even some significant market changes, such as a country moving from growth into recession and a swing of a few percent of GDP, should have little effect on our business. If there are small changes that need adjustment, the levers our management team has at its disposal can be pulled to make sure we stay on track.

A good example of this type of midyear change is our response to the several recessions I've experienced over the years, in which our bad debt numbers always increase as business insolvencies go up, especially in the SME sector. This might mean a sudden additional cost to the business of 0.10, 0.20, or even up to 0.50 ppl across a whole country's volume, which could add up to several million pounds over a year in one of our larger countries. However, I do not accept this as a reason for the underachievement of our net profit numbers, and I expect my team members to increase their margins to compensate for this shortfall. Experience has shown me that if everyone in the market feels the same pain, then this elasticity of the margin happens, and we can recover our numbers without losing market position. If we didn't operate this way, then our financial performance would fall, which would put us under pressure with bankers and suppliers as well as some unhappy shareholders!

Hence, for me, the answer to underperformance in a particular part of our operations over the years has normally been that the team there isn't good enough, and we need to make some changes. The drops tend to come hand in hand with being under-recruited, and the specific leader has failed to understand that if they don't operate on or close to the head count, then they have no chance of meeting their budget targets, however good their individual salespeople are. Good leaders always have stronger management teams under them and consequently have reduced staff churn and better overall performance. They also spend a bigger percentage of their working week on recruiting and people development as well as managing poor people out of the business. So, don't agree to budgets you don't think are achievable, and don't let your team blame the market for its poor performance!

WAR WITH A SURPRISINGLY GOOD OUTCOME

After my initial meeting with Ron at FleetCor, I did not have any more contact, and everything appeared to be settling into a new normal in which there were considerably fewer players in the marketplace. All the resellers they had hoovered up were now operating under a couple of the bigger brands that they had kept, and they appeared now to be looking more at much bigger M&A opportunities in continental Europe. Then out of the blue, I got a follow-up invite after the unsuccessful Covent Garden meeting to catch up at FleetCor's new London office near Victoria. Out of politeness, I went down to meet the FleetCor representative, but fairly quickly, the message was clear: "You need to sell to us, Bill, or things are going to get tough." The meeting didn't last long, and I was soon back on the train, heading north to Crewe from Euston.

I can't remember exactly how long it was after this meeting it happened, but one morning, I came into the office to receive a very unusual letter from one of our most important truck stops in our bunker network. The site at Rugby had written to give us a formal notice of termination, something that had never happened before, and the owner didn't even give us a reason for his decision. I was straight on the phone with him to find out that he had agreed to a new supply deal with Keyfuels at a higher handling charge but only on the condition that he stop accepting UK Fuels cards. This letter then started to repeat itself from other sites across the country, with many of the site owners who were now long-standing friends calling me and saying that they were under pressure to stop trading with us. I couldn't really understand the reasoning behind FleetCor's actions because the bunker sector was not one that we were actively trying to develop further, so we weren't being a thorn in their side. However, we did not want to lose any of the customers we currently had, and the network was a cornerstone of some of our major oil company deals, such as fastfuel, so we definitely could not afford for it to be weakened.

I got Steve, Tom, and all the team together to agree on a plan of action. The first thing we did was approach the Office of Fair Trading (OFT). We believed that after the purchase of ReD, FleetCor now had a near 85 percent share of the bunker card market and that it was using this position in such a way that was not going to be good for the customers. After furnishing the OFT with a lot of volumes and other information, we finally persuaded it to open a formal enquiry, which would at least buy us some time as we began to think about what more direct action we could take. The first thing we did was to write to all the bunker sites to let them know about the OFT enquiry so that they had easy information at hand to help them with delaying tactics if any pressure was starting to be applied.

The next thing we did was begin developing a plan for the biggest sales campaign we had ever undertaken, with the intention of trying to more than double our market share from its current level of 15 percent to 33 percent over the next twelve months. We thought that if we got to a third of the market, then the truck stop owners would definitely be able to say no to any of the new contractual arrangements that were being offered. To put it in context, it would mean trying to grow in a single year what had taken us nearly the last twenty years to achieve, so the plan was going to have to be very aggressive and ambitious. We decided its first element would be the biggest spotting campaign of all time, with a target to get the details of over ten thousand Keyfuels and ReD customers to build our initial project database. The second element would be to create two completely new, unique products on our network—one for the large bunker customers that were big enough to stock bulk diesel and one for the smaller PAYGO users. Both would have to be supercompetitive on price and maybe offer something new and unique, like Smartdiesel had. The third element would be to bring together all our best salespeople from across the UK JV offices and run a concentrated eight-week campaign so that we could attack Keyfuels everywhere at the same time with our top gun team.

So with a huge number of trucks to spot, we decided to enlist more than one hundred people from all across the business, including finance, credit, and IT, as well as sales, so that we could capture thousands of names a day. We sent them in teams of two across the country to all the busiest refueling spots with a pack of manual sheets each to collect names, addresses, phone numbers, vehicle types, etc., or any combination, depending on what was written on the side of the cab or trailer. Many of them stayed at Travel Lodges so they could be there for the two busiest refueling times of either early morning or late afternoon. These sheets were then brought back to the office and entered into the new database so we could remove duplicates and search online for any missing contact information we would need. One funny recollection was when one of the finance team members came back claiming he had broken the record for most spots in a day. His sheet was covered with "Eddie Stobart" more than one hundred and fifty times! We then pointed out that (1) we were after unique customers, and (2) Eddie Stobart was actually already an existing customer. With fifty teams collecting so many names a day, within two weeks, we were already building a pretty impressive database from the almost seventy-five thousand base of raw data. The final thing we did was to remove any names that were existing customers of ours and then order the list in terms of the number of times a truck had been seen. This gave us the perfect, condensed list of potential targets for our campaign, so we set a launch date for about a month ahead.

The new concept we came up with on PAYGO was diesel price guarantee (or DPG for short), which was effectively saying to the customer that if they bought any diesel more cheaply from anyone else during a week that we were supplying, we would refund the difference in price, hence our new slogan, "We won't be beaten on price." On the bunker card, we offered a two-year fixed rate of 1 ppl, which was a barnstormer of a deal for the bigger customers.

We also decided to do the sales process itself in a very different way from the usual one. Instead of calling the customer and immediately trying to get into sell mode, we asked the team to simply try to gather the decision-maker's name and confirm the address details, etc., and say that we were going to send a special proposal to them and call them back once they had a chance to consider it. We allocated five hundred unique records per seller and also created an internal competition as to who was going to be awarded the "Top Gun" trophy in eight weeks' time.

The launch day came round, and we were underway, slowly for the first couple of days as the guys got used to it and then faster and faster as they got into a routine. Some application forms started dribbling back in even before the follow-up sales calls, as we had included a reply-paid envelope as part of the initial packs, just in case the customers couldn't wait! It soon became a torrent, and the guys were vying every day to be the top salesperson and get the most apps on the board. We started issuing cards immediately, and there was a real buzz about the market, with our new slogan "We won't be beaten on price" repeated all the time as the battle commenced.

A more immediate problem that we needed to solve was the truck stop we had lost at Rugby, which now led us into several discussions with some big customers who said that if we couldn't find a solution, then they would have to leave us. There really were no other independent options nearby, and the only physical location capable of handling the heavy goods traffic was the motorway service area at Watford Gap. As this was a branded BP site with no chance of card acceptance for our UK Fuels card, it was really starting to feel as if we were not going to be able to find a solution. I am not sure when the penny dropped, but one morning, I came in and said to the guys, "What about giving these customers a BP card for their drivers who needed to use Rugby and then somehow merging these separate transactions into the report we give to the customers so that it would appear seamless to them from an invoice perspective?" We immediately got to work on this idea and ordered and issued some cards to three or four of the big customers that were most at risk. To our surprise, they were not bothered at all about their drivers having multiple cards, as they said that most of them already carried some as backup anyway. Then to our even greater surprise, not only did they use them at Watford Gap, where we had lost the site, but suddenly, transactions started coming in from all over the country, and our overall customer volumes with these trial customers nearly doubled. We had thought before this project that we were already getting the lion's share of the volume from these customers, but what this exercise showed us was that most of them had been using alternative suppliers for another part of their on-road diesel consumption that we weren't even aware of. Given the success of what was a defensive measure, we now saw the concept of giving customers more than one card per driver as a strategic opportunity to gain volume, and Multi-card was born. We then did the IT work to add all our card types to our single platform and identified all the customers that we thought were at risk from the truck stops we had lost. After doing this analysis, we issued extra cards to hundreds of customers, and before long, extra volume started rolling in, and the new Multi-card genie was truly out of the bottle!

Back at the head office, the campaign was proving a really big success and was already impacting our market share, which we could see from our numbers creeping up week by week. We got regular feedback from the site owners, and they were starting to see that the balance of volume was beginning to shift, although there was still a long way to go. The eight weeks were drawing to a close, and we decided to continue with a smaller project sales team to make the most of all the leads that were still in the system. As promised, we had our *Top Gun* party on a boat on the River Dee in Chester, which was a great way for everyone to let their hair down after all the hard work over the previous few months. The three winners, needless to say, had to dress up in flight uniforms and wear mirrored sunglasses!

Some months later, after many trips up and down to London, the OFT finally decided that the bunker market was not a separate part of the overall fuel card market and dropped our case. Despite this negative result, what it had done was buy us enough time for our campaign to have a real effect. Our volumes were now heading north to nearly 30 percent market share, and Multi-card meant that we had managed to defend nearly every liter.

The success of our UK spotting campaign in helping us grow our volumes quickly over a relatively short time period gave us the idea to have a go at a similar exercise in Europe to try to give our EDC business some extra momentum. At the time, the market's major players that were offering cross-border networks were DKV, UTA, Shell, ROUTEX, IDS, and AS 24. So in a similar plan to the one we hatched in the UK, we enlisted one hundred employees to go out and do some spotting. We identified all the key international border-crossing points and sent teams out over a two-week period to collect as many truck names as we could. Just as before, the names were entered into a database, with duplicates deleted, then contact details were found on the web, and a clever marketing campaign was put together to target the customers. As with all these campaigns, we needed to come up with an internal code name for planning purposes. For this one, we decided to use an acronym made up of the first letters of all of the major European market players—ROUTEX, AS 24, DKV, IDS, UTA, and Shell, hence RADIUS. Little did we know at the time, but the name of the future group had been conceived!

FIFTIETH NUMBER TWO: BIG TOM

After Steve's surprise fiftieth trip to Palma, Big Tom was on high alert as his big day approached, and some very careful planning was going to be needed if we were to catch him out with a similar sort of surprise. I decided to arrange a party at my house on the actual Saturday of his birthday, so all I needed to do was figure out a plan of how to get him there without him guessing, which was going to be easier said than done. As a first step, I started to sow the seed that I was going to be away up in Gleneagles for a few days over that weekend to put him off the scent. I then contacted his wife, Rachel, to talk her through the plan I had thought up, which was going to need a little help from her. First, I said she should book a romantic birthday night away at Soughton Hall in North Wales for the planned Saturday (not actually book one but pretend she had). Well, she did this the following week, and Tom took the bait immediately and told us at work that his wife was planning a surprise weekend away. I then got on with inviting his friends and told them to arrive well in advance, at about five in the afternoon, and make sure that none of them parked anywhere near the house. Then, for the coup de grace, at work on the Friday morning before the big day, I gave him a box with the keys to my Aston Martin wrapped inside. I told him it was a special present only to be opened the following morning on his actual birthday, and I hoped that he liked it. Inside the wrapped box, I had put the keys in a red envelope saying, "Aston for a weekend." I had also written my home gate code number, which I said I had put on the drive before I'd left with the family for Scotland, and he was free to come and pick it up when it suited him over the weekend and use it while I was away. Knowing Tom's absolute obsession with sports cars of any type, I knew he would be straight onto the hook and desperate to come and get the Aston Martin as soon as possible.

The following morning, when he opened the box at home, it almost caused an argument, as Tom wanted to literally leave after breakfast to come straight up to my place and get the car. Rachel eventually managed to point out that they had agreed to see some other family members locally in the morning and that they should swing by and pick the car up on their way to Soughton Hall in the evening. At about five in the afternoon, Rachel called to say that she and Tom were leaving their home near Telford to head up to my house in Cuddington, which should take them about an hour. The party was already well underway, with no cars parked anywhere to be seen and everyone drilled to be able to turn all the lights off and keep quiet at a moment's notice. For extra authenticity, I had even sprayed the car with water from my hosepipe after I had gotten it out of my garage and also sprayed the dry patch where my car had been parked, as it had rained that day, and I didn't want to leave even the slightest clue. As a further ploy to get him to the front door, where everyone was waiting, I put a card on the front seat, saying that I had left a bottle of champers for him by the door for both of them to enjoy at the hotel. Just before they arrived, Rachel asked Tom to stop so that she could use the toilet at the Sandiway Shell station to enable her to give me a final call as a five-minute warning to get everyone quiet. We then all crowded into the hall and front corridor and waited as quietly as we could in the dark for them to arrive, which wasn't that easy given that some people had been drinking for nearly two hours. We heard the car arrive on the gravel, and a few moments later, after a short argument with Rachel (which we later found out was Tom not even wanting to wait to pick the champagne up!), he came to the door, and we sprung the surprise. Well, he couldn't believe that we had managed to outfox him, and we had a fabulous evening, with Tom's only complaint being that he had missed out on a nice weekend driving my Aston Martin!

LESSON 16

DON'T WEAR ROSE-TINTED SPECTACLES.

I'm not sure why it took me so long to get to this particular lesson, as it's also a phrase I use fairly regularly, especially when it comes to our annual planning and forecasting sessions, and it is another critical characteristic that I want my leaders to demonstrate regularly.

I'm never sure whether it is the senior managers saying what they think Lee and I want to hear about the numbers or whether they actually believe them themselves, but either way, wearing rose-tinted spectacles is a modus operandi that isn't good for business. On a recent trip to Asia, I got an overview presentation in our Kuala Lumpur (KL) office that had all the graphs pointing upwards, with every single percentage growth figure with a green tick against it. The local manager was talking very positively about our telematics business and how much it had grown since last year. He said that we now had a record number of RGUs that were going to deliver our biggest annual gross profit, which at first sight sounded as if everything was running perfectly.

However, what was immediately obvious to me from the graphs was a rapid slowing of the growth rate in recent months, despite the fact that we now had the biggest number of salespeople we had ever had. Additionally, because we always get a decent number of new monthly sales from existing customers wanting additional trackers, the dramatic recent drop in sales to completely new customers was hidden within the numbers. So far from being the everything's-going-well message that the local leader was trying to portray, the real situation was that the performance had actually dropped off a cliff in the last four months. As I dug deeper, I began to uncover several underlying problems: We weren't generating enough digital leads from marketing, the inbound and outbound teams' daily call times had really come down, and we definitely weren't targeting the right size and type of customers, so we were only achieving an average order size of a couple of devices.

When you are trying to manage sales that operate out of fifty-six offices in twenty countries, you shouldn't need to have to visit them all in person to pick up on these types of problems, but the reality is that you, or one of your trusted inner circle, need to regularly go everywhere.

I think in the case I just described, the manager knew about these issues but just didn't want to face up to them and then take the tough decisions that were needed to address them. Most of these decisions usually involve putting pressure on people and getting rid of poor performers, which is not a trait that most rose-tinted-spectacles people have as part of their makeup, especially as they are often too friendly with their team. They are generally both too nice and too weak to make the difficult decisions, which then usually get left to a small number of us to sort out.

The main other type of person I tend to come across is the ever-optimist, who always believes that things are about to get better and that there is a great pipeline of new customers in the system just about to sign up and start delivering us revenue. These people are generally not very good at interpreting numbers. If they actually understood what the figures were telling them, they would already know that things were not looking good and were very unlikely to work out.

Either way, it is really important that you don't become a rose-tinted-spectacles person and instead become good at identifying those on your team who exhibit this trait before it's too late!

OUR BIGGEST PROJECT EVER

As I alluded to earlier, FleetCor was not the only big American fuel card company; there was also Wright Express. I also had an initial meeting and introduction with the latter in the last year, which, it's fair to say, was very different from the one I had with FleetCor in Covent Garden. Wright Express was also doing some analysis on the European market and looking at some potential acquisitions but in a far less aggressive way. Although I still wasn't interested in selling, I thought it would be sensible to have a good relationship with the company, as you never know what is coming round the corner. Its market capitalization was just over $2 billion, so it was smaller than its younger rival but still much bigger than any of the European operators in our sector.

By 2011, we had definitely overtaken FCS to become the largest UK reseller of oil company cards. Our volumes with all of the suppliers were growing fast, and for two of them, we had already become their biggest partner in the UK. This successful organic growth model, which I talk about in the next lesson, was the biggest differentiator between us and our two big American competitors and was probably the reason behind my receiving a call one day from our Esso contact, asking if we were interested in looking at a confidential project with the company. Always on the lookout for an opportunity, I signed its NDA and found out that it was tendering for a supplier to manage the whole of its European card business and had initiated a search process. The fact that we already had operations in the UK, Ireland, Belgium, the Netherlands, Germany, Italy, and France meant that there was only one country where Esso operated, Norway, where we didn't have any base or experience. This obviously put us in quite a strong position in terms of our market knowledge. However, what soon became obvious as I got further into the details of what was required was the sheer scale of its current operation and the amount of financial resources and muscle that it was going to need. Given that we were only partway through our merger and consolidation process, we definitely didn't have a single entity in our group that would be large enough or financially capable of taking on all the credit and payment commitments that we would need to give. At some point over the next month or so, it became obvious that both of our large US competitors were also in the process, but that Wright Express's lack of European assets and experience was putting them at a serious disadvantage versus FleetCor. I think Esso was keen to have two strong bids, and there was soon a suggestion that maybe we could work together and combine our different strengths. An added advantage was that Wright Express was already the major supplier to Esso in North America and already had a strong relationship and proven track record. We were obviously also interested in protecting our current reseller supply position in the UK, where our Esso Card volumes were now meaningful, so if there was some way of doing this as part of any deal, it would really suit us.

The following week, Esso's bid team came over, and we met up at my newly completed house in Gleneagles to see if we could agree on a JV structure that would work for the two of us. After a day or so of negotiation, we agreed to a 75/25 split, with ourselves being the smaller partner but retaining our ability to act as an independent reseller in the UK and any of the other countries if we wanted to. This would both protect the UK and German reseller contracts we already had in place as well as give us access to the Esso Card product in several of our other European markets. With this broad agreement in place, we went back to Esso with our JV plan and then put a joint team together to begin working on our bid. We had never tried to do anything on this scale before, and the multiple geographies, as well as the large number of existing employees we would have to TUPE—which stands for the Transfer of Undertakings (Protection of Employment) in the UK and EU—across, gave a whole new set of complexities that we would have to work through.

Over the months ahead, Steve, Malcolm, and I made many trips out to Portland, Maine, where Wright Express was based, which generally meant flying to Boston via Dublin and then driving north up the coast. Maine is a beautiful part of the world and is probably most famous for lobsters and maple syrup, so we always enjoyed good food on our trips, washed down with some locally brewed craft ale, with our favorite spots being the Portland Lobster Company down in the harbour or Peaks Island for "Reggae Sunday." We tried to do more trips in the four to five summer months, as the winters tended to be long, cold, and very snowy where huge temperature changes were possible in the space of just a few hours. Wright Express changed its name to WEX at about this time, and we set up our bid JV with the name WEX Europe Services. Being part of this tender also brought into focus how important it was going to be for our group of companies to merge. This meant that the pressure on setting a deadline for our own process began to build as we worked hard to be ready to present our bids to Esso in the best way possible. The nine months since we had shaken hands in Gleneagles went by in a flash, and suddenly, we were meeting up at a hotel near Esso's head office in Leatherhead for the final full run-through of our presentation. We had a pretty good idea that it was between ourselves and FleetCor, and given the history of our skirmish with it in the bunker business, I was keener than ever to win this prestigious contract. There were several key elements to the bid that weren't all about the headline price but also included a combination of legal conditions, sales investments, and payment terms, as well as a cohesive growth plan across all the regions.

So after a good night's sleep and a full English breakfast, we headed off for our four-hour allocated bid slot to present our plan for running and growing the Esso Card business in Europe. I remember leaving the meeting thinking it had gone well, given the types of questions they were asking, and I hoped that the good relationship both of our companies had built up over a large number of years would sway the decision in our favor. We headed off for a celebration meal even though we wouldn't know for several months whether we had been successful or not. However, it had been a marathon effort to get to this point, and the whole team was ready for some rest and a few well-deserved drinks after many months of having our heads down in figures and documents.

Back in Crewe, we had settled into our two brand-new offices, and these were really making a difference to how the teams were working together and performing. It was also the first time we had a decent number of meeting rooms as well as a proper area for employees to sit and relax at lunchtime, so it felt like a huge step up in overall feel and atmosphere.

This move from Rail House had also given us a chance to significantly improve our server and IT infrastructure. We had a new main on-premises server at the head office, with a mirrored backup server at the sales office next door. This was in addition to the growing number of cloud-based servers that we were starting to deploy to both give us additional backup as well as provide us with extra process-ing power. These new server rooms were properly air-conditioned, with fire suppression systems and physical security, so very different from the Heath Robinson–like setup we had been operating with up until then. We also had new, bigger internet connections, as there was a constantly growing demand for more bandwidth, especially at the peak invoicing periods of the month. Sending out thousands of weekly email invoices with their attached PDFs created a huge load on the system, and we were starting to run into the problem of a lot of bounce backs, as companies were employing spam filters to protect their inboxes. It wouldn't be long until we were going to have to think about customers logging on to download their bills instead of us sending them, which would both spread the peak pressure points as well as overcome the filter issues.

We had already merged quite a few of the smaller businesses, in which we had used our relatively simple gross profit model to value all the individual companies. As I explained earlier, this model took into account the average age of customers, average size of customers, credit performance, business type, etc., so that some of the smaller, older JVs with less transport sector volumes got a little more value on a like-for-like basis than the newer ones with lots of big haulage accounts. It was becoming more complicated now, as some of the larger core businesses, including UK Fuels, DCI, and EDC, had their own acceptance networks, oil company supply contracts, technology, and other infrastructure, which gave them some significant strategic value on top of just a simple gross profit multiple.

SURPRISE FIFTIETH NUMBER THREE: MALCOLM AND MARK

Malcolm was the final senior member of my team who was about to be fifty, and he had been working hard on the WEX project. He was also known as Joycey or Longshanks, as he was six foot seven and hated it whenever people commented about his height (which they did quite frequently!). For more than six months, he had been saying on an almost weekly basis that he was on the lookout for even the slightest trick that we might be up to and that we would never be able to catch him out like Genty and Big Tom. His birthday coincided with that of another of our long-term employees, Mark "Tabby" Tabb, whom you might remember from the famous Forfar site diesel rescue. I therefore had the idea to try to do a doubleheader and get them both at the same time. I decided to use a similar ploy to the one we had used with Genty and get a key customer of ours to arrange a fictitious meeting, this time one that would actually take place but that we didn't really need! Statoil in Ireland was one of our key strategic partners, and Liam Mulcahy, our main senior contact there, was only too willing to help with our plan and contact Malcolm to ask for a strategic review meeting at his office. I primed Liam with two dates (one of which I had set for the surprise), and it was only a few minutes after their initial conversation that Malcolm wandered along the corridor and popped his head round my door, asking if I was available on either the 17th or 19th of the following month to go to see Liam in Dublin. After a quick check of the diary, I said that the 17th would probably work for me. He was on the hook faster than you could say Jiminy Cricket! I gave his wife a call to tell her about our plan and that Malcolm would not actually be coming back that night, which she wasn't very happy about. I agreed as a compromise to get a flight back for him in the evening but ended up getting a couple of options, including a fallback of one the next day, just in case. We then got all the invites out, which ended up being about twenty people in total.

I then started to think about how we would try to get Tabby there unawares, which was going to be difficult, as he didn't really have any role in the Irish business. I settled on getting him to the airport for the flight we had booked for him to Dublin as the challenge instead. He was as wary as Malcolm and was constantly joking when he was in the office and not out on the road selling that no one could catch him out. I also decided to get a customer involved to deceive him and planned that they would call late in the evening before the big day to say they were really keen to see Mark urgently the following morning to talk about a new fuel contract and, as they were flying the following day, could Mark possibly meet him at the hotel next to Liverpool Airport? To make sure that Mark would have his passport with him, we created a fictitious email to all members of the senior team to please bring their passports into the office as part of a new HR process we were putting in place. We contacted everyone—except Mark—who was copied in on the mail to let them know of the ruse and not to bother with their passports. When I called Mark's wife, Jackie, to double-check, she said that he had duly obliged and packed it as soon as he'd seen the email. He'd bitten straight on the hook!

Anyway, the big day came round, and Joycey and I got on our normal early-morning Ryanair flight to Dublin after our usual coffees at Caffè Nero, with our return flight booked for four in the afternoon that day, signaling we would be straight back, so no need to have an overnight bag. I had agreed with Genty and Mike from the office to bring my stuff between them, and because Malcolm was probably going to make it home, he wouldn't need anything. I also had three additional boarding cards for Malcolm in my pocket—two for that evening at six and half past eight and one for eleven the next morning—with the rest of us as the final fallback. We hopped in a taxi and went down to our meeting with Statoil as planned, at the same time as the trap was sprung on Mark, who had arrived at Liverpool Airport only to find a load of the guys from the office instead of the customer who had apparently been desperate for a meeting! After our meeting with Liam finished, I suggested popping into Dublin for an early lunch and meeting up with Kieran from our Direct Fuels JV, as we had a bit of time to kill before our flight back. I suggested Café en Seine on Dawson Street, which was an old favorite, and so we found ourselves a table with Malcolm sitting on a chair with his back to the room. It wasn't long before we saw a few colleagues who were hiding in the room next door, and when Malcolm got up to go to the toilet, the trap was sprung! So began a big afternoon of drinking Guinness, followed by a meal at a nice little restaurant in Temple Bar, where things were already starting to get a little rowdy. Malcolm quickly realized that he wasn't going to make the flight at six and decided to go back on the later one. Next stop was the pub opposite, where the Guinness continued flowing, Sheppy started to lead the singing, and Malcolm soon forgot about his exact flight details. At about nine in the evening, he announced to everyone that he had to get back now, as he had promised his wife he would go home, and with a huge cheer from the whole pub—locals included—he left and jumped in a taxi. The party continued, and to our surprise, about an hour later, Malcolm returned to an even bigger cheer, saying that he had gotten to the airport and said he was on the eleven o'clock to Manchester but was told that the airport had closed and the boarding card he had in his hand was actually for the next day! It ended up a very long and boozy night, with Malcolm having a very difficult call to his wife to say that he wouldn't be making it home, which I think I was never forgiven for. Anyway, with Malcolm and Tabby's fiftieth done, there was only mine to go, and I was definitely not letting them catch me out.

LESSON 17
ORGANIC GROWTH IS BEST.

Our organic growth model, driven by the combination of inbound and outbound telesales operations, has been the biggest single element that has differentiated us over the years from our many competitors in the marketplace. To be successful at scale, you need to be pretty good (at least a seven out of ten) at many different elements of business, all at the same time. In our world, this means digital lead generation, data mining, fully integrated CRM, sales team management, credit vetting, invoicing, credit collection, commercial and margin management, account management, customer services, and, obviously, recruitment and performance management. Lots of companies might be good at some of these, but not very many are reasonably good at all of them, all at the same time.

When it comes to organic growth, our larger, more corporate competitors, many of which are public companies, have several disadvantages versus a private entrepreneurial business like ours, so that is definitely something we have tried to use to our advantage over the years.

First, they generally have much tighter head count controls and general personnel constraints from the top down, which makes it harder for them to make quick changes and increases in their teams. At Radius, as I talked about in lesson 5, we have always had the philosophy that, across the divisions in the sales teams, there is zero constraint on the number of people that the management can hire, even if it is well above the budgeted figure. For example, in telematics, as long as the new salespeople recruited achieve more than the group target level of, let's say, seventy-five devices per month, the local director can keep taking people on. As I explained earlier, they never actually achieve this nirvana of performance, as the more new starters they take on, the more pressure there is on the growing target number, which inevitably leads to a shortfall. It therefore becomes a constant cycle of recruitment, training, and then weeding out the poor performers to try to get as close to the seventy-five average as we can. This relentless people performance methodology is definitely not in the wheelhouse of the big PLCs and has been an important part of the Radius culture over the years.

Another advantage we have, which is intrinsically linked to the scenario I have just described, is one of longer-term financial thinking. Big public companies are driven more by their quarterly and annual financial targets and therefore struggle to make significant new overhead investments in the same way we can because of the significant impact on their short-term profitability. Our economics for most of the products we sell, especially fuel, means that getting to a breakeven point for a new salesperson can often take us more than eighteen months, with a cumulative positive position not achieved until the end of year three.

The consequence of these two advantages is that in the SME sector of the market in which we work, it is very difficult for the big corporations to compete, as they are not able to mimic our model of investing in large new sales teams that don't deliver upside bottom-line profitability for several years.

Some companies that grow very quickly through M&A alone can create enormous amounts of value if they get it right and make our thirty-five-year growth history look quite pedestrian. FleetCor (now Corpay) is a very good example of this, and despite our battle with it that I described earlier, I have great respect for the now–$26 billion business they have built in a lot less time than it has taken me to build Radius to the size it is today. Such companies are not all successful, however, as some find it impossible to then move into organic growth mode after they complete their M&A. This means that after they stop squeezing margins and cutting costs in their acquired businesses, the growth stops, and the good times stop rolling!

Doing both organic growth and M&A well is the business nirvana, but I'm afraid that my DNA is more geared to the first of these, which is what I still try to stick to today. You will read about my foray into buying businesses soon, but this was about expanding our product offering quickly rather than a change in overall philosophy, and after this brief flurry of acquisitions, we are back on the organic path now.

THE BIRTH OF RADIUS

As 2012 rolled on and London enjoyed a fabulous Olympic Games, the pressure to get on with our merger was continuing to grow. If our JV bid with WEX was successful, we would have to start work in earnest on the deal in the spring of 2013, which meant we would have to get our new group company formed before then. So, after the summer, I got all the shareholders together and talked through the timescales, saying that we now needed to bring forward our plan by six months and aim for completion of the merger by the end of the calendar year.

The pressure started to grow, with individual company valuations becoming ever more important to each of the partners as they started to think about what their final shareholding in the new merged group might be. We also had to seriously think about shareholders' agreements and articles of association for the first time because, in most cases, we never had anything legally drawn up, as nearly all of the existing JVs had operated on not much more than a handshake.

One thing I made clear from the start was that no one was going to be forced into merging their shares, and if they decided they didn't want to, then that business would end up as a part-owned subsidiary by the new entity rather than a wholly owned one. In the case of one of the original owners of UK Fuels, we agreed to buy his shares as part of the transaction, as he didn't want to be part of the group going forward.

We also needed to address the next question: what we might call the new group. We definitely couldn't use UK Fuels or Diesel Card Ireland, the names of the two biggest companies, given we were now very much a European business. We also already had longer-term aspirations to be more than just a fuel card company and hoped to start operating outside Europe, so EDC wouldn't work either.

Sticking to our tried-and-tested formula of the last twenty years, we decided that whatever name we chose, it should be made up of three words that we could later shorten to just three letters. There were lots of suggestions from the management team, and I remember us ending up with a piece of paper with probably about fifteen of our most preferred names. One of the guys suggested a word that we had used for our recent European spotting campaign project—Radius. Everyone thought it was quite amusing, given that it was actually an acronym of the main European fuel card operators rather than a geometric term. However, it started to gain universal approval, and it wasn't that long before we had added *Payment* and *Solutions* to give us a nice three-word name that we thought would ultimately get shortened to RPS. We checked Companies House and the web domain for its availability, and at some point, near the turn of the year, Radius Payment Solutions and its dot-com domain were registered. What we hadn't properly thought through was how annoying it would be to register at hotels or fill in various forms with the resulting enormous email addresses that we all ended up with. It would be more than another ten years before we managed to sort that problem out!

Now that we had the company formed, we set a deadline of the end of January for people to make their decisions. Most people could see the benefits of forming a single business and believed that not only would it allow faster growth in the future but also that the new entity would be inherently more valuable than the sum of the individual parts. Even in our fairly basic model, we calculated the valuation of the group at well over £100 million, which we thought we could significantly improve upon if it was all under one roof. However, there were some partners who didn't come to this conclusion, including those in Ireland, DCI, Direct Fuels, and Fuelwise, as well as some of our Continental businesses. After a few late, frantic calls to try to get people over the line, nearly all of which were unsuccessful, we locked the position where we were and started to get on with all the paperwork.

A few weeks later, on 21st January, after an endless session of signing hundreds of documents at our lawyers' office in Manchester, the new group was officially formed. Everyone who had chosen to merge received new Radius Payment Solutions (RPS) shares in exchange for their current ones, and we also completed the buyout of the 35 percent share of UK Fuels. Getting the deal over the line was more of a relief than a celebration, but we still managed a couple of beers at The Alchemist in Spinningfields after our marathon document signing.

This happened just in the nick of time, as within a couple of weeks of the merger, we got the fantastic news that our JV with WEX had been successful in winning the tender with Esso to buy its European fuel card portfolio, and we would now have to fulfil our 25 percent share of the financial obligations that this entailed. This was by far the biggest deal we had ever done and felt like the start of a new and exciting journey.

We also had to get on with the process of reducing the number of trading entities at the same time as forming more of a corporate structure for RPS. With lots of the partners wanting to step back or retire, we also had to begin looking around for some new people to strengthen the management team going forward.

On a personal front, the year was busy for me, with one of the highlights being the completion of the house that Bernie had been building for us up in Gleneagles. After more than two years of hard work in some very wintry Scottish weather (which Bernie continues to mention whenever we meet up!), he completed it just after Easter. Unfortunately, not long after this, Gill and I separated, although we kept the house between us for the family to use and enjoy over the next few years.

One other very sad thing happened only six months after Radius had been formed. John Atkinson, my original partner who had inspired me to start out all those years ago, died while he was away on holiday in Dubai on the 17th of November 2013. The funeral and burial took place at Preston Patrick Church in Cumbria, visible from miles around and only a stone's throw from his original bunker site at Crooklands, just off the M6. Whenever I pass with my family today on our way to the cottage, we always wave and say a fond hello to John.

LESSON 18

BIDE YOUR TIME.

Over the years, all of our successful businesses have taken us a long time to build. Whether it was developing our original bunker network, getting our telesales model to work efficiently, launching a new product, starting in a new country, or beginning a new JV with a new partner, everything has taken years rather than weeks or months to achieve real success—and in some cases, more than five years. Our expansion in Asia is a perfect example of this, and you will find out a bit more about how long that took in the next chapter.

Along the way, there have been many bumps in the road with these projects and times when it has looked as if a particular one was not going to work. This might have been because our supply price wasn't low enough, or our network wasn't large enough to attract customers, or, more commonly, our management and sales teams weren't strong enough. However, over the years, we have been good at taking our time if things aren't going well and then trying to understand the many reasons behind why this is the case before working to fix the issues. When you are in this development phase for a new entity, it is important to give yourself as much time as possible to make these changes, so we try to minimize our costs and run as efficiently as possible. Only if we have eventually exhausted pulling all the levers to try to get things profitable do we then finally consider shutting an operation down.

Sometimes, this process took us just six or twelve months to make a decision, but in most cases, the trial-and-error approach took us much longer—and in some instances, many, many years.

When I look externally at many of the new start-ups that fail, I think it is because they went too hard too quickly before they had done their proper optimization work. This means that they burn through far too much money in the initial phase before they have managed to get their key business components in the right shape, in what appears to be crazy desperation to try to be successful too quickly. The leaders of these companies are nearly always people who are breaking lesson number 1, "Care for every pound as if it's your own."

As a final takeaway, our businesses that have taken the longest to build have all ended up being stronger and more sustainable, as well as harder for our competitors to mimic. So my advice is, don't rush to stop too quickly when things aren't working well, but be prepared to make lots of changes and improvements while at the same time keeping your costs as low as possible. Then hopefully, even if it takes many years, you will ultimately reach the success you've aimed for!

STARTING IN ASIA

Over the next couple of years, some of the larger partners who had decided not to merge their shares started talking to us about the possibility of selling their equity to the newly formed RPS. Given that we had quite a bit of cash and our business model meant that we were continuing to generate more each month, it seemed sensible to begin a process of tidying up the group. So over the next couple of years, we bought the remaining half of DCI in Ireland as well as the other parts of the Belgian, Dutch, and Portuguese businesses that had not consolidated at the time of the merger. We also sold our half of the French business to Edenred while at the same time started a new 100 percent–owned French subsidiary in Lille, just near the border with Belgium.

Radius was already beginning to benefit from the centralization we had been doing, and our profits had nearly doubled from £18 million to well over £30 million per annum within the first two-year period, well beyond our original expectations.

Just as Shell had approached us a few years earlier about whether we were interested in becoming a reseller for it in Italy, it was now asking if we had any appetite for working with it in Southeast Asia. This would be a completely new geography for us, given that up to now, our furthest office from Crewe was Milan, which was only just over a two-hour flight away. The two countries Shell was particularly interested in were Singapore and Malaysia, where at least English was a common language, albeit mixed with numerous others, including Cantonese and Malay, given the very different demographics of the respective populations. Although it had definitely not been on our road map to go to Asia, I decided to visit Shell's two local teams to get a better understanding of both of the markets and whether it really was a possibility for us to begin trading there.

Singapore was my first stop, and it did feel a bit surreal landing in a country with all English road signs and where they drive on the left, but where the weather is a constant thirty degrees Celsius of humid heat. After my meeting with Shell, I headed out to have a look round and visit a few of the famous visitor spots, including Long Bar at Raffles Singapore and the Marina Bay Sands hotel. My first impression was that it was a very small market with not that much commercial traffic, so not typically suited to our type of offering.

Second stop was KL, which is more like you'd expect a big Asian city to be, with bustling traffic and not many people obeying the rules of the road! Here, there was definitely a volume opportunity, but as I found out that the market was regulated, it was going to be much harder and take much longer to get over all the hurdles of market entry. On the plus side, the cost of labor, as well as many other costs, was extremely low in comparison to Europe, and there were not really any reseller competitors in the local marketplace with a similar model. As I flew back for my connection in Dubai on the first of what became a regular fourteen-hour flight each way, I pondered whether there really was the possibility of ever being able to build a sustainable business in this very different part of the world.

After downloading my feedback to some of the team, we decided that before we could make a final decision, we needed to do some real in-country research for ourselves. Adrian, our in-house lawyer, and

Lisa, one of our experienced sales leaders, put their hands up to our offer of a six-week trip to Singapore, and within a month or so, they set off to try to find out more. We rented an apartment in Orchard Road, and they began to look at office availability, employment costs, sales and marketing opportunities, the credit environment, and much more. Although they based themselves in Singapore, most weeks they did a midweek trip to KL to carry out the same assessment there, and at the weekends, they began to explore the island and its nightlife. It was either Highlander Clarke Quay or a rooftop bar on Club Street, usually followed by a curry in Little India. They soon became best friends with the restaurant owner, who would have *pappadams* on the table as soon as he saw them coming. In KL, the usual evening itinerary started at Marini's at 57 overlooking Petronas Twin Towers for an early drink before heading off to Healy Macs, the Irish bar in the middle of Changkat.

Towards the end of the six weeks, I flew out to see them and review what they had found as well as look at a few potential office locations. We also met up with Shell in both countries and put more meat on the bones as to what a potential commercial deal might look like. The numbers still didn't look very encouraging, even with Shell offering to transfer an existing customer portfolio to us in Malaysia. However, I think the lure of the Asian Tiger market and the potential opportunity were too much, and within a few weeks, we agreed to take it on, so we started to execute the plan that Adrian and Lisa had put together. The markets were at the two extremes of cost, with Singapore being super expensive and KL being at the other end of the scale, so we ended up with very different first offices for our two new start-up businesses. In Singapore, we had a couple of small rooms in a very old part of the city, off Pickering Street, which reminded me of the early days in Holmes Chapel. In KL, we had a shiny new office on the twelfth floor of a skyscraper in the central Mid Valley area. As with all our country start-ups, recruitment and building the sales teams were extremely hard work, and it was a long, long time before we got to a position where we started to feel more settled.

The biggest of the early problems was that the customer portfolios that Shell had promised never really came to fruition as planned, and—surprise, surprise—the credit collections performance was significantly worse than we had estimated, especially in Malaysia. Therefore, it became a long, slow haul over the next years of improving our local management and optimizing costs. One thing that helped during this difficult period was sending some of our good, young UK employees over to KL on secondment, and both Becky and, later, Stuart really helped us to turn the corner from this very hard start. Today, our Asian geography is finally performing well after more than six years of hard work, with some significant financial losses in the start-up phase. We now have a strong local team in combination with several UK employees on secondment rotation that really helps with the communication of new initiatives from Crewe. Both the fuel and telematics divisions are growing nicely, and this whole project definitely benefited from the bide-your-time mentality I described in the last lesson.

On the personal front, it was now my turn to reach the key milestone of fifty, which was the age that was my original idea for retirement when I started nearly twenty-five years earlier. Well, retirement definitely wasn't on the agenda, as I was busier than ever across a growing number of geographies.

SURPRISE FIFTIETH NUMBER FOUR: MINE

Needless to say, despite my keeping a very watchful eye out over many months, the guys did manage to catch me out and surprise me on my birthday. I was with Big Tom and Malcolm for a "meeting" that they had arranged in Prague, and at some point, after we had landed and checked into a hotel, they sprang the first trap and said we were all going to jump in a taxi and head off to a secret destination. Well, we headed out in the car into the middle of nowhere, surrounded by fields and forests on a very misty gray day. After about an hour, we stopped at the roadside next to a heavily dented Lada. An old guy got out and came over and introduced himself, suggesting that we follow him. After ten minutes or so, we arrived at an old military airport with a small checkpoint, which we were quickly waved through before we finally stopped outside a 1930s aircraft hangar completely overgrown with bushes and moss. We all got out, and only then did Tom tell me that they had all chipped in at work to get me a red-letter-day flight in a MiG. As we chatted with the owner, I found out that the 1970s-built plane had been bought from Russia over ten years earlier in what sounded like a very dodgy black market deal from a former general in the military. Next, I was introduced to the pilot, who looked like an overweight version of Doc from *Back to the Future* and was dressed in an oily blue jumpsuit and couldn't speak a word of English.

After chatting outside, we went inside the building to see the plane and get a safety briefing. If I hadn't been nervous before I had seen the jet, I definitely was now. It looked all of its fifty years and had a single wire coming out of the engine manifold, connected to an old VARTA car battery. Even more worrying was the fact that the tools that were along the benches looked as if they would have been more appropriate in a garage to maintain vintage cars. After having the ejector seat mechanism explained to me and what I should do in case of an emergency, I then asked the silly question about how often the plane was serviced. The pilot's reply was the final straw in getting me extremely worried about actually going up in it when he said that there was a major one every ten years, with the next one of these due in four weeks' time! A separate concern, which eventually turned out to be a blessing in disguise, was that while all this was going on, one of their group had been chatting on the phone to the control tower that had temporarily shut the runway because of the fog, so we couldn't actually leave at the moment. I was coming to the conclusion that I really didn't fancy going up in this plane and asked if it was possible just to jump in and do a low-speed run round the block on the ground without taking off. They didn't seem to think that was fair for me and kept insisting I should go up and enjoy it and that we just needed to wait a short while for the fog to clear.

Eventually, after an hour or so, they said that the best thing to do would be for all of us to go back to the hotel and try again the following morning. Anyway, I felt a great sense of relief as we left the airfield, both trying to think of an excuse as to why I couldn't go back in the morning and praying that the foggy weather was here to stay. As we got back to the hotel bar for a well-deserved cold beer, trap number two was sprung, as I found the bar full of more than twenty friends whom the guys had organized to come out for my birthday surprise. Another long boozy night followed, which, as I remember, ended with us buying two bargain buckets of KFC at about five in the morning before eventually hitting the sack. I must have done something good that day, as my prayers were answered the following morning, and there was to be no flying again that day. My friends offered to have my money transferred to another prize of my choice, and I quickly settled on a nice weekend for two at the Monaco Grand Prix, which sounded like a much safer option.

Another thing happened that year that was definitely a first for me and something that probably brought home a little of how big the business now was. EY had approached me in January to ask if I was interested in entering its Entrepreneur Of The Year program. Our local EY manager agreed to do most of the entry paperwork and said it wouldn't involve too much time, so after a bit of cajoling, I agreed. The key interview day was over in Leeds, where all the entries from the north were judged by either previous winners or prominent local businesspeople. The awards ceremony was held at The Lowry Hotel Manchester just before the summer, when I was really happy to find out I was the overall winner for the northern region that year. This meant it was then down to London in October for the national finals, where I ended up being a category winner for business products and services and was just pipped to the post by Rosemary Squire of the Ambassador Theatre Group, who was awarded the overall winner. Tim Morris from EY led the after-party celebrations with a trip to Mahiki on Dover Street, near Piccadilly. Here, he introduced everyone to the famous "The Treasure Chest," which, as the name suggests, is an old pirate's chest full of ice, various spirits, and champagne rather than gold coins! Numerous long straws are stuck into the mixture, and about eight people at once can consume the extremely strong concoction! A great night ensued, even though we all looked a bit out of place with our dinner suits on.

During the process, I had met some really interesting people among both the judges and other competitors, and it had been quite a nice change for me to be talking to people who weren't involved in the diesel business. It was also the first time in my working life that I started to understand the word *entrepreneur* a little better and realize that maybe I did fit into that category in a few ways, even if it had not been part of my initial career plan. One of the judges from the regional round in Leeds recommended a very good CFO who had helped him run one of his businesses, and given that I was always on the lookout to strengthen my team, I asked him to set up an introduction for me. Within a couple of months, Simon Oldfield joined and set about strengthening and professionalizing our finance group, which had to evolve to manage the increasing scale and complexity of the company.

Another side effect of being involved with this particular EY event was that it started to raise the profile of Radius in the outside world. It wasn't long before I started to get emails from both investment bankers and private equity (PE) companies wanting to come up to visit us and see if we were interested in looking at a deal. This was a new world that I really knew very little about, having just had my head down in the narrow vertical of diesel cards for the last twenty years. We had already been talking internally about what might be the next stage for Radius, and we were definitely interested in considering a process that would allow some of the partners to release some of the capital value. With this in mind, we began to engage with some of these new contacts to learn a little more.

As 2014 drew to a close, we were rapidly approaching our twenty-fifth anniversary. Over the years, our annual parties had become bigger and better events that everyone looked forward to as a chance to let their hair down before the Christmas break. We had moved on from the early ones at Warmingham Grange and had now visited Alvaston Hall, Crewe Hall, The Moat House, and the football ground in Stoke as our numbers got bigger each year. At some point, we had moved to "no partners" to reduce the numbers, but even after this change, we were now struggling to find locations that could squeeze everyone in. As Emma, our HR director, and I sat down to think about the twenty-fifth, we decided that, because it was a special anniversary, we would also invite all our European teams to fly across to join us. We set a date for the party in early January and made the decision to use an external planner for the first time, as it was becoming just too big a job to manage all the logistics internally.

We eventually chose Holly Moore from Make Events as our partner and settled on The Mere Golf Resort & Spa near Knutsford as our venue. Genty, Tom, Malcolm, Mike, Angela, Sheppy, Karen, me, and a few other colleagues decided to put on a fun game show as part of the night, and we also had a couple of bands, Schwing and The RPJ Band, to provide the music. It ended up being a fantastic night and a really great way to mark the success of the first twenty-five years of the business. The Europeans also appreciated the chance to come across for the celebration, even if a couple of the planes were delayed, and some of them arrived at the black-tie evening in jeans and hoodies, as their luggage hadn't made it!

Funnily enough, just as I'm writing this section during a Sunday lunchtime at home, Emma (now our CPO) has just emailed me to say that Craig Charles has confirmed that he can come to DJ at our thirty-fifth party. So the good news for you is that now, you have only ten years of the story to go until I get to the present day!

My eldest daughter, Lauren, had also graduated with a first from Leeds in Spanish and geography, making me a very proud father. She was now set on following her mum into the teaching profession and definitely didn't want to be selling diesel. One more thing happened around this time: I met Eleanor, who was hosting a Prince's Trust charity event at a dinner I had been invited to. It wasn't long before I bought her a pair of walking boots and waterproofs, and she always recalls that on our second date, I took her over Striding Edge on the way up Helvellyn!

LESSON 19

OWN YOUR OWN CUSTOMERS.

If you are trying to build long-term value in a business and create something that you might want to sell in the future, then the issue of customer ownership needs to be very high up your agenda.

Our fundamental business model since the early days of telesales has been a sell-direct-to-the-customer approach, in which we find the customers, do the selling, contract directly with the end customers, invoice them, take the credit risk, and then collect the money. Not only does owning this complete life cycle give you a higher margin opportunity, but you are also then free to market additional products and services to your customers and build on this direct relationship. This cross-sell opportunity is becoming increasingly important to Radius as we diversify away from fuel.

The downside of this model, though, is that it is a high-cost, high operational management one, which means it inevitably takes quite a long time to both build the business as well as get a financial payback. For us, as the overall business transitions from one that was fuel card only for the first twenty-five years to one in which we are now a wider mobility and connectivity supplier, this direct-to-customer access is proving a critical differentiator and helping us add enormous value. Not only are we able to create very low-cost leads from our base of four hundred thousand existing customers (mostly in the fuel division), but we have also found that we get a double benefit of them becoming more sticky, helping us to dramatically reduce our churn rate.

This doesn't mean that we don't do any indirect or white label business, only that we see this channel as one that helps to give us scale and capabilities rather than as our core source of income. Today, across all the divisions, we are about 75 percent direct to customer in terms of volume and over 90 percent with respect to gross profit, which we believe is a good balance and one that we want to maintain going forward.

In some ways, having a direct-to-customer model has slowed our growth versus some of our competitors, many of whom operate on a purely indirect basis. This is especially true in telematics, where companies such as Geotab, the world's largest company in this sector, have seen exponential growth through their global reseller relationships. However, for us, by operating in the direct-to-SME space, we think this approach gives us a unique position with higher margins and greater overall sustainability in the longer term. As I said earlier, we believe it is also helpful when it comes to business valuation, as having lots of direct customers can make a material difference to the EBITDA multiple someone is willing to pay for your company.

As you build this base of valuable customer data, you also have to continually improve the way you protect it. This might be from either external cyberattacks (which are now almost a daily occurrence) or something much more old-school, such as when a devious employee leaves you to join a competitor, with a list of your customers. This particular issue has been a constant challenge since the early days, and I thought it might be useful to give you a taste of just one incident that happened over twenty years ago, when one of our employees left and then sought to profit from selling our data to a competitor.

For a little background, one of the advantages of our original JV structure in the UK was that customers often moved between our different brands without necessarily realizing that the companies were part of our wider group. As we operated these JVs in a very hands-off way, even most of the sales employees were sometimes unaware of our group structure, and we just let them compete freely with each other in the marketplace.

Well, one morning I received a call from the MD of our JV in Burnley, saying he had been contacted by a salesperson who had recently left our UK Fuels team in Crewe. The guy was offering to sell a spread-sheet containing the full contact data of several thousand customers that he had downloaded onto his laptop just before he left. He said he was offering it to them first, and if they weren't interested in it, to just let him know so that he could then try one of the other fuel card companies in the area. Once I heard about it, I definitely didn't want the risk of this happening and was desperate to try to get our data back as fast as possible. I immediately contacted the local police in Burnley to tell them about the theft and said that if they thought it was useful, I could arrange for someone to meet this person and pretend to be from our JV so that they could potentially arrest him and retrieve his laptop. This was definitely out of the ordinary for the local constabulary; however, I eventually persuaded the station chief to take me seriously and said I would drive up there immediately and meet him to agree on an exact plan for the sting! At the same time, I contacted an old friend of mine who lived locally, who agreed to play the part of the willing buyer, given that we did not want any chance of anyone he knew being recognized.

The MD from Burnley got back in touch with the fraudster and agreed to a meet at two in the afternoon at Banny's, a famous fish and chip restaurant at the end of the M65. After I explained my plan to the police chief, he agreed to send a van with three officers to wait round the corner until the guy arrived and showed my friend the data on his laptop. I waited in the car park to watch from a distance as the trap was sprung. At about a quarter to two, the officers stormed into the restaurant, and the fraudster was arrested, read his rights, cuffed, and put in the back of the van.

I then went inside and met up with my mate for some well-deserved fish and chips to thank him for helping before heading home after what had been a pretty tiring day. After a night in the cells, the guy was eventually released, and although he only ended up receiving a caution for his crime, we got our data back and knew that he wouldn't be doing anything like that again anytime soon!

The moral of the story is to own your customers and protect this very valuable data with your life!

THIRD-TIME LUCKY ...
WITH TELEMATICS

Back over in Ireland, Kieran, our JV partner just south of Dublin, had mentioned to me several times at our recent meetings that he was looking at starting to offer vehicle tracking to his customers. He had decided to use a local partner, Transpoco, and wanted to know if I was interested in a discussion about the opportunity across the wider group. It wasn't a subject I knew too much about, but it was one that had started to come up in conversations more frequently over the last year, as FleetCor had made a couple of large acquisitions in this space with Masternaut in the UK and NexTraq in the US. I also knew from all my interactions with WEX that it had several existing partnerships in which it was cross-selling third-party telematics products to its customer base, so there was obviously some linkage with fuel cards.

One other thing that prompted me to decide to look into the opportunity further was that we were starting to get fairly regular approaches from our customers to supply fuel card data electronically to various telematics suppliers. This particular issue gave me the most concern because if telematics companies started to come into our space, they could potentially become powerful new competitors for us. As Kieran got going with Transpoco, I took him up on his offer and had a couple of meetings with it to start understanding how we could potentially work together. As part of our discussions, we also talked about a possible investment opportunity in which we would actually take a significant equity stake in its business. However, after a couple of months of talking, we eventually couldn't get a deal over the line, so I started to think about other options for us.

My first thought was that we should become a reseller for one of the leading global suppliers in a similar way to our contracts with the major oil companies. We spoke to several potential ones who all came to Crewe to show us their user software and talk through the commercials. We finally got down to what we thought was the best option, which was Fleetmatics, a company that had grown really quickly in the US and now had a huge customer base across many international markets, including the UK.

However, it soon became evident when they started talking about the business model, they were suggesting that we weren't going to be able to get to an agreement. Fleetmatics was proposing that it wanted to contract directly with the customers, thereby relegating us to being effectively just a commission agent rather than a reseller. This would mean breaking one of our golden rules that I just described in the previous lesson, "Own your own customers." Therefore, it didn't take us long to say no to this proposal before we then had to go back to the drawing board to look at what other options we had.

One thing that had become clear during the various software demos was that the products were not that complex, and in many ways, we thought the look and feel of our new Velocity portal was actually nicer. With this in mind, within a few weeks, we made the decision that we would build our own platform as an extension of our system and immediately got down to deciding what functionality we would need to create a minimal viable product. Within just three months, we had it up and running with an initial dashboard of Live Map, Trip History, and Driver Performance, with most of the work having been done by a single developer. We used exactly the same look and feel as Velocity, which was a very easy-to-use tile-based interface we knew the customers liked using for their fuel reports, but we gave it a nice new brand—Kinesis.

One bit of expertise we didn't have to complete our solution was any knowledge about tracker hardware, and we decided to get over this issue by using a local company called Matrix for the supply of the black boxes themselves along with the SIM connectivity and supply of the raw positional data. The initial launch used a plug-in onboard diagnostic device made by CalAmp, which, according to the market, our customers should simply be able to just plug into the port in their vehicle. This original concept of the customers self-fitting the boxes soon proved flawed, as not many customers actually plugged them without a lot of phone calls, and quite a few never did it at all. We soon moved to an install model using a wired device that needed an engineer's visit to fit it in the engine bay. This quickly improved the conversion rate but had the downside of adding a significant cost in both the engineers' time as well as our own internal operational resources to schedule all the appointments.

Our initial view on sales was that the existing teams could now also sell vehicle tracking alongside fuel, and it wasn't long before we had our first customers using Kinesis. It soon gathered pace, and within six months or so, we began to realize that this project was going to be a long-term success, so unlike tires and vehicle leasing, it was going to be third-time lucky with telematics!

We also realized quite quickly that our plan of using the existing fuel sales teams wasn't going to work, as the sales process was very different and the product much more complex. We therefore set up a new dedicated team and started calling into our customer base to build the business. Over the next year, we rolled Kinesis out across our other markets, first to Ireland, followed quickly by our Continental markets. Big Tom got moved across to head up the sales operations. We also continued to develop the functionality of the platform and started to release new updates and tiles on a quarterly basis. Additionally, we built a backend server that could communicate directly with the devices, which allowed us to stop using the third-party arrangement we had started with.

For the first time, we had a good second product at a competitive price to sell to our fuel customers, so we started to put our attention on how we could optimize this cross-selling process. The word *referral* started to be used in our vocabulary more and more as we asked all our customer-facing people in fuel to talk about telematics during every one of their voice-based customer interactions. Salespeople, account managers, customer services agents, credit collectors, and operational employees could now all put the interested customer information they had gathered during these calls into the simple new web portal we had built. This would then feed directly into the telematics teams. Sometimes, if the customer wanted to speak to a person straightaway, these calls would literally be passed across as "hot referrals" with a really good chance of conversion. We paid a £5/€5 commission to all the individuals who gave the referrals, and it wasn't long before this new concept became our biggest driver of growth for new sales.

We also started to target customers from our database in a more scientific way by looking at where we were selling most successfully in terms of customer size and type, and then started to build some first simple propensity models to concentrate our efforts on these verticals.

Our two main offices in Crewe on Macon Way were starting to feel very congested, and it was about this time that we first started to think about what we were going to do next. Not far away, in Crewe Business Park, we could see from the building that we had rented for our JV with WEX that there was a large green field of land that looked as if it would make a perfect plot for an office. We approached the owners, Pochins, a local building company, about the possibility of developing the site with a building to potentially fit more than five hundred people. After a positive first meeting, we got AEW Architects from Manchester on board to sketch out some ideas to create a real state-of-the-art, modern facility. This time round, I wanted to create some really nice communal spaces for the employees, and top of my agenda were a big, well-fitted gym and a large café and kitchen area. The project progressed over the next few months, and after many back-and-forth iterations between me and Phil from AEW Architects, the new £14 million Radius Campus design came into being. In addition to the gym and café, there was a big central atrium with lots of new collaboration spaces, as well as our more traditional floor plate that we would need to house the different teams.

After a couple of rounds with the local planners, who didn't make life easy for us, we finally got our planning permission through, and Pochins cut the first bit of earth to kick the building phase off. The team and I were really excited about the move, as we knew what a lift it would give to all the employees, given how cramped we now were. To really get the final touches right, we took on an interior design company called SpaceInvader from Manchester to help with all the furniture and soft finishes. I also thought it would be fun to have a theme for the building and decided to have a few *Doctor Who* figures scattered about the floors to create some interest. During the building phase, I spotted a spare bit of balcony overlooking the front of the atrium and thought we could create our own TARDIS there, which we could use as a small meeting room. True to form, this new space was going to actually be bigger on the inside than you thought it was going to be from the outside, as well as looking like an old blue telephone box. Now all we had to do was wait just over a year for the builders to do their work and turn these plans into our new home.

LESSON 20

REWARD OVER THE LONG TERM.

Rewarding key partners and employees has always been an important part of the ethos and culture of Radius and has definitely helped contribute to the fantastic growth and success we have achieved over the last thirty-five years. John Atkinson, one of my original partners, was definitely the greatest influence for me with respect to rewards, as he was probably the most generous person I have ever met. He got much of his enjoyment from helping and watching other people succeed, as well as seeing them enjoy the benefits from the generous incentives that he put in place. Looking back, it wasn't purely a philanthropic act, as these people normally then worked tirelessly for the success of the business, which obviously ultimately benefited the shareholders (including John)!

At the center of his reward mechanism, and one that I have continued from the early days of UK Fuels, is quite a unique LTIP, very different from those often found in large PLCs. Although the scheme has had to change and evolve over the years, especially after we merged all the businesses together in 2013, we have still managed to keep its essential components working in a similar way to the one that John originally gave me when I started.

The primary concept is that the person receives growth shares instead of ordinary shares and that they have zero value at the point when they are given. In the early days, it was quite easy for me to replicate this for my management team, as in the mid-1990s, we were creating new JVs every few months, and I was able to give a 5 percent allocation of new shares to each of my senior directors at the time. For example, I would hold 35 percent of the new JV equity and give my finance director 5 percent, my IT director 5 percent, and my sales director 5 percent, with the other 50 percent going to my new partner (who also sometimes gave 5 percent blocks of their shares to people who joined with them).

As we set up more and more of these companies, my management team would end up with multiple lots of 5 percent, which in some cases gave them as much incentive as one of the main JV partners, as they would maybe accumulate 40 percent in eight different companies. These awards were obviously then fully aligned with the success of the business and had a big potential upside. It also meant that we all accepted lower salaries and overall packages than would normally be the case. This created a real risk-reward environ- ment in which everyone put the company's success first, with growth and profitability while keeping costs low as top priorities. When we merged the businesses together in 2013, some of these older-serving members of my management team were among the largest share- holders in the new Radius entity.

It isn't quite all give and no take with our scheme, however, as there is a vesting period of four years, whereby if the employee leaves before this time has elapsed, they have to relinquish their shares with no benefit. This helps us to retain our best people, especially if they receive several different allocations of shares over a ten-year period or more.

Over the years, we have had several significant events that have enabled people to sell these shares, the largest of which is the PE deal that I am going to talk about in the next chapter. This transaction alone allowed us to release over £350 million in cash to the shareholders, which added a further twenty new millionaires to those who had already passed this mark before the deal. The total number of millionaires created by our LTIP scheme since the inception of Radius back in 1990 now stands at more than sixty, which is a wealth distribution unlike anything else I have seen in the private sector over my forty years in business. These people have a lot to thank my original partner, John Atkinson, for!

INFLEXION POINT

When we merged all the businesses back in 2012, the number one aim was to create more value for all the partners by having a single, strong, central company. We had definitely now achieved this since doing the deal, with our profits more than tripling from £16 million to well over £50 million. During this period, we began to talk about the longer term and what we should ultimately do with the business, as well as think about how we could release some or all of this value for the shareholders. The most obvious route we had thought about, and also the easiest to understand, was a trade sale to one of the major market players, such as FleetCor, WEX, or Edenred. However, many of us thought that there was an exciting future ahead and weren't ready to stop working and didn't feel we wanted to sell up completely. The investment bankers who were now making frequent visits to Crewe began talking to us about other options, including a potential flotation or IPO, a PE deal, a merger with a competitor, or, more simply, just gearing up the business by borrowing money from the banks and having a superdividend.

After getting all the partners together to talk through these various options, the consensus was to look at some form of partial sale, which could hopefully be treated as a capital gain to take advantage of the 20 percent tax rate that was currently in place. The most likely choice, given the quantum of money we were thinking of releasing, was some form of PE deal. As none of us, especially me, had previous experience in this area, we were going to need some outside help. So it was finally time to appoint an advisor from among the many who had visited over the last eighteen months. Over the next six weeks, we saw four or five banking teams, including our main corporate partners, Barclays and HSBC, as well as some other firms that were strong in our sector. Eventually, we settled on Deutsche Bank (DB), which had advised on the minority sale of Eurowag (one of our European competitors) to TA Associates, a leading global PE company. This bank had also been the most bullish about our valuation during the advisor presentations—a trait we would see many more times in the future from numerous bankers! It had suggested that Radius could be worth as much as £1 billion, which would be an incredible uplift on our original merger value of just over £100 million only five years ago. DB was also confident that there would be lots of players interested in our 25 percent minority stake, despite the fact that most of the medium to larger deals in the market were for a controlling interest of 50 percent or more.

The launch of this process was the start of my learning about the whole new world of PE companies and investment banking. We began working on our teaser to present to potential interested parties as well as started to pull together a much more detailed commercial and financial analysis of our business. We employed separate companies to produce commercial due diligence (Boston Consulting Group), financial due diligence (EY), and technical due diligence, as well as to start to populate a huge new data room. This would be used later by a final small selection of buyers to enable them to do their own diligence. We also ran separate selection processes to pick whom we would use from a legal perspective, as well as one to appoint a specific debt advisor to manage the interactions with the banks. With the final two advisors from Clifford Chance and GCA Altium on board, we were pretty much ready, and when I sat back and looked at our potential total cost for all our bankers' and advisors' fees if the transaction was successful, it was now an eye-watering £13 million. One final piece of the jigsaw was to give the project a name, and I think it was DB that came up with the fairly unexciting choice of Herald, after the name of the road where our head office was situated in Crewe.

With the teaser now ready, DB started to make appointments in my diary to meet some of the PE companies for what they termed "fireside chats." These introductions involved me talking through the teaser document for about thirty minutes and then answering a myriad of questions fired at me by sometimes four to five people at a time. I think DB's plan was for me to see nearly every single PE company, as by the end, the total list added up to more than forty different investors. I saw GIC in Singapore, Khazanah Nasional Berhad in KL, Ares and GTCR in Las Vegas, Silver Lake, Welsh Carson, and Warburg Pincus and Blackstone in New York, as well as General Atlantic, Francisco Partners, CVC Capital Partners, TA Associates, Advent International, KKR, TCV, Hellman & Friedman, Apax, Permira, Ontario Teachers' Pension Plan, and Ardian, among a host of others in London. This meant that I got to know the streets and coffee shops of St James, Mayfair, and Marylebone pretty well as I trooped about between meetings, with sometimes up to four in a single day. Most of them made positive noises about being interested in Radius, and the DB team agreed to put them on the list to contact once the full pack was ready.

DB planned a two-stage process in which there would probably be eight to ten bidders in round one, which would then be whittled down to the three or four that were most keen for round two. So the first eight were chosen and given the full pack of information, with the promise of receiving full access to the data room and all our vendor due diligence if they made it into the second round. Our bankers then began to put pressure on the bidders to put in a high price, and they were told they had to be at the £900 million mark if they were going to make it to round two. Eventually, after a couple of weeks, four of them got to that level, although it would later become clear that none of them were actually thinking that they would ever be prepared to pay that much!

General Atlantic, Welsh Carson, Francisco Partners, and TCV (all from the US) then signed NDAs and started to work through all the documents and data that DB began opening up for them in the now very large data room. It was then all quiet for ten days or so until we started to get feedback and questions on some of their initial analyses. This immediately began to ring warning bells with me that this second stage was going to be more about trying to find holes in our figures and forecasts to give them a reason to come down from their initial bids.

We then had meetings with each of them to discuss the terms of the deal and their exit rights, etc., which also started to take a different turn than planned. Far from being a straight equity investment and share purchase in which everyone ended up with equal rights, they all wanted much more downside protection, and the structures were beginning to look more like a debt transaction in which they were second in line after the lending banks, with the rest of the shareholders, including me, relegated to third place. This combination of both value and term changes meant that the deal was starting to look very different from the one we thought was achievable just a few weeks earlier. The discussions became ever more negative, and the group soon reduced from four to three, and then from three to two, until we were finally left with just one company standing: Francisco Partners.

After one final push with it to try to get a deal done at £800 million, we decided to call it a day and asked DB to stop the process. We were going to need to have a rethink alongside a well-earned rest, as the senior team and I were completely exhausted after more than nine months of effort.

On reflection, I think probably the two biggest reasons we failed to get a deal done were that there really weren't that many PE players that regularly did minority deals on the scale we were looking at, and the high-pressure approach taken by our bankers to try to create a bidding war and push people really hard was not the type of environment that a genuinely interested investor was going to engage in. Although it wasn't an ideal ending to almost a year's work, we definitely learned a lot about the sort of metrics that PE companies wanted to look at, and we decided to improve some of our regular reporting to include more details on customer churn, which had been top of their agenda.

Only a few weeks later, I received an email out of the blue from a UK-based PE company called Inflexion that would go on to lead to a very different conclusion. My first question to Inflexion was, "Why did we not get to meet the first time round?" given that I thought I had been introduced to every possible alternative already! Well, it transpired that it had approached DB, but it had been considered too small at the time to do a deal of the size we were looking for, so it hadn't been asked to participate in our process. In fairness, that was probably true at the time, but Inflexion had recently launched a new, larger partnership capital fund and was now looking for a significant investment opportunity to cornerstone this new tranche of money.

After a brief conversation over the phone, I agreed to meet one of its partners, David Whileman, and his right-hand director, Josh Kaufman. They came up on the train to Crewe the following week, and over the course of the day, we ran through some of the key financials and current performance statistics, and I also gave them an insight into the reasoning behind the failure of our deal process and what key items we hadn't been able to get agreed on. That evening, we went out for Italian at Piccolino in Alderley Edge, and during the course of the dinner, we gradually ticked off the key contractual items that had been the sticking points. By the end of the meal, we had pretty much gotten to an agreement and shook hands, with both sides feeling positive about working together going forward. On price, we had said at the outset of the day that we would not accept a value below £800 million and that if they didn't think they could get to that number, then we shouldn't waste too much time. They could see that this was a red line for us, and although they would obviously need to do their diligence, they thought the figure was a fair number given our profitability, growth rate, and the multiples of our main comparables in the market.

Over the next few weeks, we got our legal and banking teams up and running again and opened up the data room to let Inflexion do its diligence. The most difficult part of the discussions was the details around its exit rights and how Inflexion could realize its stake once its normal four- to five-year investment period came to an end. This finally got agreed upon at one of our many Clifford Chance sessions, and a date was set for signing in late November. As we operated a Mastercard product within our portfolio, it meant that we would have split signing and completion dates, as we would have to wait for up to eight weeks for the Financial Conduct Authority (FCA) to approve the transaction before the deal could finally be done. So on 23rd November, we all headed to the offices of Addleshaw Goddard in Manchester, the lawyers acting for Inflexion, to sign the final bits of paperwork and then wait for our group of six banks to get all their documents signed and exchanged. Addleshaw Goddard's representatives had brought a good selection of beers and wines into the meeting room, and as we arrived at four in the afternoon, it looked as if we were going to be settling in for a long night. We weren't shy in asking to have a beer, and after an hour or so, our group of about fifteen was in a relaxed mood, with not much moving on the transaction side. By seven, we realized we were definitely going to be there for a longer evening and decided to pop out to Wagamama downstairs to have something to eat and give us a break from the waiting. After an hour or so break, it was back to the meeting room, where the drink supply that had been running low had been fully replenished, and so it was back to the beer. We were starting to think that we would have a nice evening even if we didn't actually get the deal over the line!

We didn't have to wait too long, as at about ten at night, we got the final call that all the documents were signed, and we were free to go out and celebrate if we wanted to. Everyone was in a good mood, and we headed down to one of our usual haunts, Revolución de Cuba, and ordered a few buckets of iced beer. I don't remember it being a particularly late night, as we were all pretty tired, but it was the end of quite a long and arduous process, and everyone was definitely ready for a break. I also wanted to mark the deal with a wider group of work colleagues, advisors, and family, so the next day, I had a look at places in London where we could potentially book a midweek night before Christmas. After looking at a few options, I settled on reserving a floor at Mahiki, the scene of the EY Entrepreneur Of The Year event afterparty. So just a couple of weeks later, on the 6th of December, about eighty of us descended on Mayfair for a few celebratory "Treasure Chests" and drank shots on surfboards brought over to us from the bar to the theme music from *Hawaii Five-O*!

With the deal signed off, it was good to get back to work, with everyone able to concentrate on trying to deliver our plan rather than preparing the endless reports and analyses demanded by the PE companies. The FCA kept within its timescales, and towards the end of January, the approval for our transaction came through, so we could then get on with completion. It was the morning of 30th January when people started popping their heads round my office door to thank me, as money from the deal began to hit personal accounts, giving them the real rewards over the long term I talked about in the last lesson. We hadn't known exactly which day this would happen, so with nothing planned for lunch, I ordered two bargain buckets from KFC as we celebrated in the boardroom! That evening, I organized an impromptu party for the management team at my house, with a jazz band and takeaway curry. Everyone was in a good mood, given the new, improved state of their bank accounts, and we had a great evening before we had to get back to work to start delivering our new five-year plan.

The transaction had enabled me, the other shareholders, and the management team to take out approximately £350 million in cash between us. About £200 million of that came from the new debt we had taken on as part of the deal, and the other £150 million from Inflexion for the purchase of its 24 percent shareholding. We now had to try to more than double the value of Radius over the next four to five years to enable Inflexion to get the return it was looking for on its new investment, so there was obviously a lot of work ahead.

In the middle of the deal process, I had also been lucky enough to win the Entrepreneur of the Year category at the Lloyds Bank National Business Awards, which was a nice accolade for how far the business had come since those original days above the hairdresser in Holmes Chapel.

At home, my younger daughter, Becky, and my nephew, Andrew, decided to take on Mount Kilimanjaro. With Lauren and Gill already having conquered the peak a few years earlier, we didn't want to be the only ones in the family to be the odd ones out. We all made it after a tough final day, and it definitely gave us the taste to try a few more bigger treks in the future. Later that year, I also took my first proper sabbatical from work, having never had more than two weeks off at a time since I started out with Esso back in 1985. Roy kindly agreed to stand in for me while I was away for this six-week period, so Eleanor and I began planning our itinerary.

We started with a quick stop at the Abu Dhabi Grand Prix before heading south to Cape Town with a first stop in the city at the Cape Grace Hotel followed by a beautiful few days at Richard Branson's Mont Rochelle vineyard in Franschhoek. While we were there, I decided to mark the special trip by bleaching my hair blond for the duration of our travels to see if blonds really do have more fun! From South Africa, we flew across to Australia, where we headed up to Hamilton Island for a week's sailing around the Whitsunday Islands. Then it was over to New Zealand to visit Queenstown before setting off on the Milford Trek, where after climbing over the McKinnon Pass we finished at the awesome Milford Sound, home to hordes of sandflies that swirled round us in black clouds! A quick stop in Brisbane followed, before we made the flight out to the town of Alice Springs, where we had a nice early-morning ten-kilometer walk round the base of Uluru. Then it was up to the Blue Mountains, where we stayed at Wolgan Valley for what was probably the most relaxing part of the trip before heading back to Sydney for Christmas. We watched the start of the famous Sydney Hobart Yacht Race on Boxing Day morning before continuing our eastward circumnavigation round the world. We finished the trip at a New Year's block party in Honolulu, Hawaii, and finally got back to Manchester in early January. I decided while I was away that blonds definitely do have more fun, as two different couples that we got chatting to thought I was in the music business!

In July of 2017, Becky graduated with a 2:1 from Leeds in graphic design, so now, both daughters were in the world of work and trying to find their way with their own careers. After renting in Bowden near Manchester for the previous few years, I had also embarked on building a new house, so along with the Radius Campus office, I now had two big projects to manage, with endless amounts of things to be agreed on every week. I also decided to give myself a treat from the deal proceeds and headed off villa hunting in Majorca, where I think the combination of mountains and sea makes a perfect destination to relax and spend time in the sun. At first, we looked around some places that needed quite a bit of work, but we instead opted for a newly renovated place where the sellers agreed to leave all the new furniture they had put in to help sell their villa. It would be nice to go and relax there and not have to think about having to do any renovations round the house.

On a final note, my father passed away at Easter on the 31st of March 2018. He had been such a strong influence in my life, both with his drive and determination at work as well as his passion for walking on our many holiday trips to the Lake District. I am pleased that he managed to see the deal with Inflexion happen, as he had shown a never-ending interest in the evolution of Radius, even if he had been a bit skeptical when I first left Esso to start on my own! We scattered his ashes on the slopes of our favorite mountain Helvellyn not far from the original cottage he and mum had bought all those years ago and a place we regularly visit on our many trips to the Lakes.

LESSON 21

DON'T LET SOFTWARE PROJECTS GROW LEGS.

Over the years, not keeping proper controls in this area will definitely have cost us in the millions of pounds rather than the thousands, and if what I read in the papers is anything to go by, we are not the only business to have suffered this way. This lesson sits a little on its own, but because it is something I have to think about more often now as our telematics business begins to scale, I thought I would put it here.

Let me give you a recent example. Today, I had a meeting on a Salesforce development project in which we are urgently trying to complete our rollout in this division to replace our now aging CRM system, which should help us improve the speed and quality of the sales journey. Two months in, and the team is already coming back to me saying that the project is going to take significantly longer than expected. Apparently, the building of the new authority matrix to make sure that the salespeople don't give too much margin away is proving much more complex than they had originally planned. Second, a new automated look-up to bring existing customer information through from another database took an additional month versus the plan. This type of project creep is like a virus that seems to exist everywhere in the IT world.

First, the software teams start to build bits of functionality that were never originally asked for because they think it will make the system look better or work better. In this case, the auto look-up was not even discussed or authorized as part of the original plan. Second, while they are building and come across something significantly more complicated that the project team hadn't considered, such as in this case, the authority matrix, they start doing a huge amount of extra work without communicating back to the management team or even thinking that they need to seek approval. They simply don't understand that they are meant to be working towards a release deadline as their number one aim, but instead, in their eyes, they try to chase the perfect bit of software, even if it's going to add months to the delivery date. In most cases of the two issues I described above, if they had come back immediately after identifying them in the first couple of weeks, then we would have either scrapped that piece of functionality altogether or agreed to do it in a later release.

It is fair to say that the more software guys we have taken on, the less efficient we seem to have become, which I think is a globally recognized scientific equation! I wish sometimes that I could turn back the clock to when we only had a couple of good developers and before I had heard the titles project manager, business analyst, solution architect, or UX/UI testers.

Even if you don't enjoy software, as we transition into the world of AI, you will have to make sure you keep a close eye on all your projects, or you could make some very expensive mistakes, similar to some we have made over the years.

BUILDING THE NEW DIVISIONS WITH M&A

With the deal complete and all our financing in place, we started to talk more seriously about making some acquisitions to help develop the business faster. Although our five-year plan did not include M&A, we had always assumed that we would begin to look out for opportunities that could further develop our existing divisions of fuel and telematics as well as potentially help us move into new sectors. Now that Radius had a higher profile after the transaction with Inflexion, we began to get approaches from advisors selling a plethora of types and sizes of companies. Among these were several vehicle-tracking businesses, and in October 2016, we made our first acquisition with the purchase of Track You. It was based in Wrexham and had a particular strength in the utilities and police blue light sectors—a part of the market we knew very little about. Over the next few years, many more acquisitions followed in which we looked to strengthen our technical know-how, widen our range of products, as well as help us enter into some new geographies. In the UK alone, we bought Plant I, Sure Track, Can Track, and Vue, which gave us a whole raft of new customers in the dashcam, stolen vehicle recovery, ambulance, and plant and machinery verticals.

With the telematics business starting to gain good momentum and our cross-selling model really helping with this speed of growth, we started to think about whether there was another product that we could add and develop in a similar way. Given our M&A activity, we were now being pitched to by bankers on an almost weekly basis, and one sector that started to come up regularly was telecoms, which I decided was worth a closer look. One big advantage here was the obvious fact that every single customer we had would be a user, so we would never get a response to a sales call of "Sorry, we don't have a need for phones in our business!"

So after going to see several potential opportunities over a six-month period, we settled on taking the plunge into this new sector in October 2018 with the acquisition of Adam Phones in Chiswick. One of its unique advantages versus many of the other companies I had seen was that it had supply relationships with nearly all the major mobile providers, including Vodafone, O2, and EE. Over the next couple of years, many more telecoms companies followed as we worked hard to build some critical volume as well as start developing our technical knowledge. In 2019, we bought Trinity Maxwell, Reliance Networks, and Pure Telecom and rebranded this whole new division as Radius Connect. After each acquisition, we began to integrate the operations as well as grow the individual sales teams so we could implement our model across our wider customer base.

All these acquisitions were progressing, and so was the development of our new campus office on Emperor Way. After a few last-minute teething problems, including ceramic floor tiles that wouldn't clean and large glass windows that kept shattering, we officially opened our shiny new sixty-six-thousand-square-foot facility on 11th December 2018, just over eighteen months after we had first broken ground. We had the amazing Olympic Gold Medal rower "Katherine Copeland" (my cousin's daughter) to officially cut the ribbon alongside Andy Sherwood (our first customer), Elaine Palmer (our first employee), and the local mayor of Crewe. It really felt like the beginning of a new phase for

Radius, in which we now had a much nicer environment for people to work in as well as somewhere we were proud to bring our partners and suppliers. It wasn't long before the gym started getting busy in the morning, with people enjoying the free breakfast we started providing as extra encouragement for an early workout. The café also quickly became a busy hub, with people racing down to enjoy Natalie's katsu chicken and filled baked potatoes. Not that long after we had moved in, we realized that our Eurocard and Eurosales buildings by the station were actually looking quite tired, even though they were only ten years old, so we decided to do a full refit of both of them using the same designers and contractors we had used for our campus. Within twelve months, this was completed, and now these buildings also have a great new look and feel, including a new gym and café.

With the telematics and telecoms businesses both growing, we started to think about more products that would also fit well with our vehicle-related customer base. We had considered insurance several times over the previous years, but I think we had been put off by the regulated requirements of the industry. However, on 4th November 2019, we decided to take the plunge and bought The Burley Group, a small broker in Sheffield. It specialized in the transport sector, which we hoped would fit well with our growing customer bases across both fuel and telematics.

This final acquisition of the year meant that, as Christmas approached, we now had four distinct divisions within the business, so a very different proposition from the fuel card–only company we had been for our first twenty-five years. With the three new divisions and their growing sales teams hungry for leads, we began to improve and further professionalize our cross-sell operations. One of the most important things we did was to completely overhaul the commission structure for the referrals. Rather than just give a flat rate amount of

£5 per device per lead, we decided to share a percentage of the full value of the sales commission. By giving the referrer a 33 percent share, we significantly increased the total amount they could earn each month as well as raised the profile of these people and groups, so they felt as important and valuable as the sales team members. In some large cases, the referrer could now receive up to several hundred pounds for a single customer rather than the £30 or £40 they were getting before. This had the effect of rapidly growing the monthly numbers, and we were now heading towards ten thousand referrals per month across the group. This was a huge benefit for our new divisions and gave us a unique advantage versus our competitors, especially as the conversion rates for these leads were significantly better than those we were getting through our paid digital channels.

Having made big steps forward in this voice-driven referral process, I started to look more closely at the digital journey for our existing customers and how we could potentially tap into that. Up till then, we had not really created many leads from this area, and the first thing I decided was that we needed a new "shop window," where customers using any of our services could easily see what other products we sold. We registered radiuscompare.com and started building a new web portal where existing customers could see all our solutions in a single place and then follow a simple process that would create a lead, which would then be forwarded on to our relevant sales teams. We created links to the new site from every single digital touchpoint we had with our customers, including our login screens, our Velocity portal main menu, our price notification emails, our electronic invoices, and many more. It wasn't long before this new lead source started gathering momentum, and because these customers were proactively looking for new products, they started converting at over 15 percent, well ahead of what we were achieving across our other channels. We also introduced banner advertising to show our special offers and continually worked on improving our journey optimization to strive for even better results. Within a few months, we were on a clear trajectory towards a thousand new leads per month, which today has more than doubled to over two thousand. This nicely added to all the leads we were gaining from the voice referral operations and accounts for more than three hundred new customers per month across the divisions.

One final thing happened before we moved into 2020—we opened up in another new country. This time, the office was pretty much as far away from Crewe as you can get—Melbourne! We had been approached by two experienced guys from the industry who had seen what we had been doing in the telematics space and were interested in setting up a local JV, much in a similar way to the original JVs we had started in the early days. After a few virtual meetings and a face-to-face visit to Crewe, we started Radius Australia in a small start-up office just south of the city.

Nine months earlier, we had decided that we couldn't go past our thirtieth anniversary without having a good party to mark the occasion, so we were going to have to try to top the fabulous twenty-fifth that we had had at The Mere Golf Resort & Spa. Once again, we asked Holly Moore from Make Events to help plan it for us, and we soon realized that there were not many venues in the Manchester area capable of catering to the over one thousand people we wanted to invite. After visiting a couple of options, we soon settled on Manchester Central, formerly the G-Mex, which had been Manchester's primary music venue before the Arena opened in 1995. Holly came up with a huge list of possible options for hosts and bands, as well as the overall theme, and once we saw Dermot O'Leary (famous for hosting *The X-Factor*) as one of the choices for MC, we immediately jumped to book him. For the bands, we chose Schwing to start, followed by

Jamie Cullum as the headline, and finally The Earth Lights to close the night. We settled for a simple, smart, black-tie theme and then started to work on all the travel and accommodation logistics to get everyone there from across Europe, as well as a few of the senior management from even farther afield.

As the party date of 20th January approached, I decided that for a bit of fun, I would make a singing cameo appearance on stage and chose a mash-up of "Ain't No Sunshine" and "Mustang Sally." To help me and to significantly improve the quality of the performance, my daughter Lauren agreed to a duet in which she took the bigger role and all the high notes! A couple of weeks before the big day, I met up with Dermot in London to agree on a script and some games for the night, which included "Beat the Boss," where the employees could roll a giant foam dice on stage against me and win some big cash prizes of up to £5,000 per throw!

The evening went off perfectly and Dermot did a fantastic job, with several country teams having practiced some group dances as well as everyone having a laugh at Lauren and me in our cowboy disguises singing on stage. Quite a few people took a while to recognize us, and some even thought we were a proper group, which I took as quite a positive on my singing performance, or maybe they had just had a lot to drink already!

Little did we all know, as we finished the night at our traditional venue of Mojos (shabby New York dive bar style) for late drinks, that the world was about to change, and Manchester Central's next role would be as a hospital rather than a party venue. It would be only eleven days until the first case of COVID-19 would be registered in the UK, and then just a few weeks more before the pandemic would rapidly spread across the world.

LESSON 22

WORK FROM THE OFFICE.

Almost every week, there are articles in the news extolling the virtues of home working. These are generally written by people working from home or representing groups of people who work from home, who love saying how much extra time is saved by removing the daily commute and therefore how efficient it is (are turkeys about to start voting for Christmas, as we say in the UK!). Then there are equally as many business leaders with the complete opposite view to this— that actually, home workers do less than 50 percent of the work of someone in the office, as well as not contribute to the drive, culture, and entire fabric of the company.

To some extent, in the UK, I blame the political leaders who rushed during the COVID-19 pandemic to say that home working should be the new normal and that everyone could now use Teams and other technologies to communicate, so there was now no need for people to waste time going into the office. The reality, however, of running and building a business and all the associated performance management, which most politicians know absolutely nothing about, is very different.

Employees need managing, and as soon as you remove that daily and often hourly interaction between supervisor and team member, efficiency slips. From our systems data, we could see very early in lockdown that the call times of our telesales, account management, and credit teams dropped by more than 50 percent within weeks of the forced move to work from home during COVID-19. In IT, in which keystrokes are a good measure of activity, we also saw dramatic reductions, which was a view shared by many other local senior business leaders I knew.

People are now walking the dog, going to the gym, meeting friends, having their haircut, going shopping, playing padel, waiting for an Amazon delivery, doing the school run, and carrying out countless other things that they do not normally do during work hours. The savings in time from the commute have now completely evaporated, and there are now big chunks of the working day when people are literally unavailable. Home working has even created new products such as mouse jigglers, aimed at trying to stop bosses from understanding how little employees are really doing!

Also, you can't manage and develop teams properly when they are remote, as the communication and interactions you get online are completely different from the ones that you get when you are face-to-face. Our new, and especially our young, people need to sit next to experienced employees to help them build the knowledge and way of working required to develop them into our managers for the future. This is really highlighted by our graduate program, which has shown us just how much effort is needed, but also just how important this face-to-face time is, as these young people join the working world.

Needless to say, we don't have a flexible-desk policy either, and we believe that the relatively small extra part of a person's full-up cost of having a specific desk for them added to our overheads is massively outweighed by the disadvantage of not having them close to their supervisor and team.

Having said the above, I also understand the importance of a good work-life balance. I soon realized, after working nearly twelve hours a day, seven days a week in my first two years, that I didn't actually achieve more than if I had worked a more normal five-day week. I ended up so tired on a Monday morning and much less efficient than if I had properly rested over the weekend. Luckily, I did learn that lesson quite early on at UK Fuels and, in year three, got into a much better routine of work and life. Today, I want people to go home at night on time and forget about everything Radius, so hopefully, they can look forward to the challenge of working hard and helping the business develop when they arrive the following morning. Work has always been an important anchor and constant in my life, and I believe the in-office version has been hugely positive in helping me to enjoy my downtime more.

In the last six to seven years, as Radius has reached a new stage in its life cycle, it has been good that we have been able to invest in improving the overall look and feel of our facilities that now span more than twenty countries. In Crewe, which is our biggest base, we now have gyms, cafés, a yoga area, a music room, a bar, a coffee shop, and many different collaboration spaces. We also put on a free breakfast, which has proved very popular for every employee who wants to try to beat some of the local commuter traffic. We do want to be flexible with our employees and try to accommodate specific requests, but I'm afraid I won't be changing my mind on the fact that I believe it is best for the business if people work in the office.

On the good news side, we believe we have had an unexpected boost since COVID-19, as many of our competitors followed a very different approach from ours, with many of them going to a hybrid model and some even moving completely remote. We have definitely felt a benefit from this over the past couple of years in the form of their reduced competitiveness in the marketplace, which has helped us accelerate customer and volume growth in several of our key geographies. I'm not sure how long this will continue, as there are now regular press articles about these companies returning to a full five-day-a-week-in-the-office operation after eventually waking up to the fact that the tail was beginning to wag the dog!

COVID-19

Following our thirtieth anniversary party, events seemed to move incredibly quickly from the first bits of news about a new virus in Asia to the complete lockdown in the UK announced by Boris Johnson on 23rd March. Our volumes in Malaysia and Italy, where we felt the impact first, lost almost 70 percent of business pretty much overnight. We therefore knew we were going to see some huge drops, especially in the UK, and none of us had any idea just how low things would go and for how long they were going to last.

As soon as the seriousness of the situation started to become obvious, we began convening daily management meetings to discuss strategy and actions and immediately started to reduce head count, starting with the most recently recruited employees. After the new furlough scheme was announced and we understood how the rules worked, we went through all our teams with a fine-tooth comb to decide what was possible and started a daily routine of reviewing every list and increasing the numbers on the scheme. Within four weeks, we had reduced the full-time head count by 200 people and furloughed our first 150, which brought down overall numbers from 1,585 at the time of the party to just over 1,200 at the end of April. By August, we had made further cuts of 150 and increased the total number on the furlough scheme to over 300. Hence, in only three months, we had reduced our global head count by over 650 to a little over 900. This action might seem dramatic, but it felt like we were fighting for the survival of the business and absolutely had to put the company's health above everything else, including the shareholders and employees. We also had our banking covenants to consider, including our critical ratio of debt to income, and therefore, if our gross profit was going to drop dramatically, as was very likely to be the case, we absolutely needed to cut costs quickly and hard.

Within a few days of the lockdown announcement, we managed to get the nonessential workers set up at home but kept some of the key operational staff members who couldn't be moved set up in the office under the new separation restrictions. The senior team and I all stayed at home for a couple of weeks, but as soon as it was legally possible for us to be in the office, we were back in Crewe every day trying to manage the business in this very new set of circumstances. It soon became obvious from the telephone call times and PC usage that home working was not proving very efficient for us, so as soon as we could start getting our teams back into the offices (within the new rules), we did. The "work from the office" lesson is a key part of the Radius culture and what helps us to be successful, and hopefully, the more detailed explanation I gave in the last lesson gives a little insight into our reasoning behind this conclusion.

Luckily for us, the new divisions of telematics, telecoms, and insurance had income that was nearly all subscription-based rather than usage dependent, so they did not have anywhere near the downward spike that fuel was experiencing. Across the fuel business territories, the picture was not the same in every country, and in Germany and the Netherlands, it was a much smaller blip down versus Malaysia and Italy, which were hardest hit. To our relief, the UK and Ireland, our two biggest markets, both of which had dropped off significantly, started on a slow upward trajectory from their low points of about minus 40 percent.

What we started to realize was that although personal trips in cars and vans had almost come to a complete standstill, most businesses, especially those in the food industry, had to keep going, albeit under a set of new restrictions. In some cases, we saw certain verticals, including taxis, buses, and coaches, come to a dead stop, while others, such as takeaways, go into exponential growth. Some of the taxi drivers just swapped jobs overnight and were now busier than ever delivering food in the evenings.

There was also one positive side effect of the big drop in retail fuel volumes at the average petrol station—they all decided to sell what small amounts they were pumping at a higher margin. This had the knock-on effect of improving margins across most of our regions and helped to partly compensate for our reduced volumes. As the months ticked by, we reached certain milestones, and once we got back to 80 percent of our pre-COVID-19 volumes, we felt we were now over the worst and that we could begin to plot a course for the future, even if it was going to take many more months before we would get back to normal. When the end of our financial year in lockdown finally arrived in March 2021 and we could properly see all the effects of the actions we had taken, we found that despite the incredible headwinds we had experienced in the business, we had still managed to grow our overall gross profit, so our unbroken trend since 1990 remained intact. The fast cuts we had made to our overheads in those first couple of months also meant that, against the trend across nearly the entire marketplace, we had also managed to grow our bottom-line profitability during the COVID-19 years.

We did also find some upsides in our inability to travel during this extended period. The biggest of these was that it gave Lee and me time to look more closely at some of our central operations, including IT, credit, and finance, which had definitely been swelling in people numbers too fast over the previous five years. The cost cutting we had been forced to make in lockdown had shown us that we could manage perfectly well with a significantly smaller team, so we set about reorganizing some of the structures. We also looked into some of our longer-term investment decisions on key IT projects that had been bogging us down. As a result of this deeper dive into projects, we cancelled a move to a new financial system that had been sucking up an increasing amount of money and people resources, as well as pressed the button on migrating our divisions onto Salesforce. Our in-house CRM system, Cruise, had begun to look very outdated, as the marketing world was becoming increasingly digital, so moving to a new, modern system was now essential to help us continue to maximize our cross-selling model.

We had also undertaken a grassroots review of our customer data after finding how badly it had deteriorated and cleaned every single address, contact name, contact number, number of vehicles, type of vehicles, and, most importantly, business type field. This cleansing process would prove increasingly important as we built our ever more sophisticated propensity models and began to look at the first use cases of AI to improve customer targeting and conversion.

We didn't let COVID-19 stop our train of acquisitions either, and during the lockdown period, we completed a record number of deals. These included many across the new telecoms, insurance, and telematics sectors, which helped us continue to strengthen these new divisions.

In telecoms, we bought Connect Total Communications and Amelix Telecom in 2020. This was followed by The Frontier Group, Rainbow Communications, Tariffcom, and a majority stake in a

Dublin-based business, Telcom, in 2021, and finally, Air Telecom from Birmingham in February 2022. This took the total number of acquisitions in this division to ten in just over two years.

In telematics, we bought CyntrX in Green Bay just before the lockdown in November 2019 and Modus in California in May 2021, which opened up the huge new market of North America for us as well as gave us some big enterprise customers in the truck and vehicle leasing space. Modus also had a unique app-only solution that was used by a large insurance company for new driver assessment, which added a new vertical for us in a fast-growing part of the market. It was quite an eerie diligence process as we all met up in Las Vegas during lockdown and wandered around the quiet streets and bars, where all the shows and concerts were temporarily cancelled. This did, however, have the benefit of some easier rules regarding drinking in small groups, which meant that we really enjoyed having a few cocktails at Baccarat Bar at the Bellagio on the two nights we were there. This made a very welcome change for us after over a year of isolation back home. We also bought a 50 percent stake in Key Telematics at the end of 2019, a business that had a pure white label model with a very advanced platform that complemented our own home-built Kinesis solution. A few years later, we would complete the purchase of the other half of Key and position its solution, which we renamed Kinesis Pro, as one of our core products alongside Kinesis.

Finally, in the insurance division, we bought Milestone in September 2021—a specialist in the taxi and courier sector—followed by Keystone Insurance, a small Dundalk-based broker in April 2022.

Lee, Simon, and I also took the opportunity to think more about the longer-term strategy for Radius, as the lockdown gave us much more time together without the usual operational disturbances. One thing we knew we needed to begin considering seriously was the global energy transition and how it was going to impact the business. Our first thought was that we needed to learn more about electric vehicles (EVs) and how their gradual increase in numbers would, over time, start to reduce growth in our fuel division. With this in mind, when we got approached about potentially investing in Chargepoint Europe, a small Dutch manufacturer and reseller of commercial EV chargers, we decided this was a good opportunity to start our journey into the new world of electricity. The company was based in Arnhem in the center of the country, and there were definitely a few jokes at the time about the deal being potentially *"A Bridge Too Far"*! As I talked about earlier, I was brought up on old 1970s war films, so for any of you that have never seen or heard of it, it's a classic starring Michael Caine, Sean Connery, Gene Hackman, Anthony Hopkins, Ryan O'Neal, Robert Redford, and Dirk Bogarde among many more.

We followed this acquisition in June 2022 with a complementary one in the associated charger software space with a company called EVBackOffice, a South Africa–based platform for managing the EV units remotely. Its system could not only collect the transactions from the chargers but also present them to the customers in a really easy-to-use web- and app-based interface. These platforms are going to become an increasingly important part of the overall solution, especially once they include payment capabilities and access to on-road charging networks. We eventually added a third small piece to this jigsaw with the purchase of a majority stake in EV charging solutions, a small Nottingham-based unit installer. Finally, when we were approached by an Irish company looking to divest its small energy broker business, we decided that selling electricity would also fit well with our overall product set and would be the perfect final piece to complete the foundations of our fledgling EV and energy division, and this deal was completed in December 2022. Powerhouse

Energy Management, as it was called, started to feel the immediate benefit of our cross-sell model as we began to feed it with leads from our UK and Irish customer bases.

There would be one more final division that we would establish during this period of acquisitions and one with a very different cash requirement. One of our largest telematics customers, which we had acquired, was a company called Global Go, a van and car rental business based near Loughborough. It approached us directly to see if we were interested in buying the shares of the existing majority owner, who had decided to sell. This was quite a divergence from our relatively low capital requirement models that we operated in the other divisions, but with the majority of our customers using vans, it seemed quite a logical product to add. Our strategic view was that if we became a vehicle supplier, then we would be in a strong position to retain business as the customers moved from internal combustion engine vehicles to the new EVs. Within a few months of the approach, we completed this deal in October 2021. This was followed by a second similar one in Ireland with Traction Finance, a Belfast-based leasing company, in July 2022.

The COVID-19 period had therefore proved to be a very strategic time for Radius, when we had made nearly twenty acquisitions, including a "Magnificent Dozen" in 2021 alone. With these six clear divisions now established, all we had to do was understand the new ones, integrate them, and make them all work well! This was going to prove a much longer and harder job than we probably thought at the time and would really stretch the management team members, most of whom had spent all their working lives in the diesel business.

One final thing I have to mention before I leave the subject of M&A is this: Don't believe everything that the shareholders you are buying from tell you about their plans for retirement after they have gotten their money and come to the end of their noncompete period. In over a third of our deals we have done, far from going off to play golf, travel the world, take up a new hobby, or spend more time with the family or one of numerous stories we have been told, the previous owners have just started again and tried to do as much damage as possible by stealing employees, customers, and intellectual property. Not everyone is as they seem, so buyer beware!

Karen and Bill's Big Radius World Trip
Ten years had now passed since the famous fiftieth birthday party in Dublin for Malcolm and Mark, and given the ongoing COVID-19 restrictions, there could be no repeat of the last trip. However, at a small gathering to mark this occasion, I joked with Karen Shone, our second employee, who was about to retire, that when lockdown was fully over, I would take her on a round-the-world trip of our offices to celebrate this event properly. So, as her retirement date loomed and the international travel bans imposed by most countries looked as if they would start to be lifted, I decided to make good on my promise.

So on the 2nd of April 2022, after getting the first of our many, many COVID-19 tests of the trip, Karen and I set off from Manchester to our first stop, Singapore. With only one full day there, we went to see our main local partner in the morning, quickly followed by our second COVID-19 test and a quick trip to the beach on Sentosa Island. In the evening, it was off to Sky Bar at Marina Bay Sands, followed by the Long Bar at Raffles for a Singapore Sling before finishing off the night at the lively Highlander on Clarke Quay.

The following morning, after a negative test result, we were straight off to Australia, where we had planned a visit to our new Melbourne office. Alan, our partner and MD, was there to meet us at the airport and take us to a nice downtown hotel, where we needed yet another test before we were even allowed to check in! With no rest allowed on our whistle-stop tour, we were straight out for a nice Chinese meal in which sweet and sour crocodile and kangaroo with cashew nuts were both options on the menu! I think we opted for something a little more traditional, like crispy duck and Singapore noodles. We finished the night off at a nice speakeasy bar, Eau De Vie, which Alan was very impressed by, given that it was a recommendation from one of my friend's daughters, who had recently been working in the city. The next day, with our bodies now definitely out of sync with jet lag, we enjoyed a gentle jog along the Yarra River, which gave us a little flavor of the fabulous city life that locals enjoy here.

A visit to our new office followed, and in the afternoon, we went out to see one of our larger telematics customers, who uses our asset trackers on their construction and rock-breaking equipment. Then it was back to a local testing pharmacy on our final day in Oz before Alan took us south out of the city to have lunch and a walk round the beautiful Pt. Leo Estate on the Mornington Peninsula. It was at breakfast the next day when we first started to worry about our COVID-19 test, as we still didn't have the result that had been promised to us the previous night. We decided to go early to the airport and try to check in without the results and see what would happen. After queuing for an hour or so, we arrived at the desk and were told that we absolutely could not board without our certificates. Starting to get very worried with the minutes ticking by, we went to a rapid test facility in the terminal that promised a ninety-minute turnaround, which would still just about leave us enough time to get through security. It was just as well that we decided to do this, as our original tests didn't finally arrive before the next day, which obviously would have ruined our very tight schedule. Next, we dashed back to the check-in desk, pushing to the front of a very long line to see the original guy who had turned us away, and we were finally checked in for our flight to Honolulu via Sydney. As soon as we got through security, we quickly downed several glasses of champagne in the lounge to celebrate our negative results and try to relax after a very stressful couple of hours. Once on board, we quaffed a few more to celebrate "no more tests," as these would be the last we would need before getting home.

The Hawaii stop was the only location where we didn't have a work event, but it was handily located exactly halfway across the Pacific to our next destination, which was the US and the bright lights of Las Vegas. When I had originally planned the flight itinerary, I had done a quick search to see if there were any events on that night and noticed that an old band from my younger days, Kool & the Gang, was playing at Blue Note Hawaii in Waikiki. So when we landed, after a very quick check-in, it was straight down to the beach for a piña colada before heading to the gig, where we definitely had a few too many Long Island iced teas. It was pretty much a completely new lineup apart from one old original bass player, but the band did a great job of performing all the old favorites, including "Celebration" and "Ladies Night"! The following morning brought an early start for a quick trip round Pearl Harbor and the Battleship Missouri (Mighty Mo) before heading back to the airport and our onward flight to Vegas, having spent less than twenty-four hours on the island. The jet lag was really starting to kick in now, and we were either wide awake or falling asleep at different times of the day. We had a morning meeting with the Modus telematics team, followed by a nice Italian meal at LAGO at the Bellagio. Then in the evening, we watched the "O" version of Cirque de Soleil before a late dinner at Rivea at the Delano hotel, which felt very different from my last visit there during lockdown.

So after an epic nonstop journey round the world that had started in Manchester just eleven days earlier, Karen and I finally boarded a flight for Heathrow to complete our circumnavigation and the end of our adventure. We had an amazing time and one that neither of us will ever forget. However, we both also came back feeling that we would not want to repeat that trip anytime soon, as it took us nearly two weeks to fully recover and get our body clocks back on normal time.

A couple of other major changes happened for me personally during the lockdown period. The first of these was the launch of a family charity, The Helvellyn Foundation. Over the years, the business had supported many local good causes, mainly focused on helping young or disadvantaged people. However, I had always wanted to do something personally, and with both my daughters keen to pursue careers in the not-for-profit sector, COVID-19 gave us more time together to talk about what we could potentially do as a family. Let me start by saying that without Lauren and Becky, the new foundation would not have gotten off the ground, as they provided most of the drive and effort to get it going when we set it up over three years ago. Since then, we have helped more than twenty-five causes across the social and conservation sectors, ranging from the Bumblebee Conservation Trust in the UK to the African Wildlife Foundation and the global The Shark Trust. We have had some great feedback from the charities we support, and I have also tried to provide some business mentoring when requested to complement the financial support we give.

As I said earlier, there were two personal changes that happened in lockdown, with the other being the birth of my third child. This was definitely not in my original life plan, but I have really enjoyed bringing Finn into the world, and I'm hoping that the saying "a new baby keeps you young" comes true.

LESSON 23
KEEP MOVING YOUR PEOPLE.

All of the strongest managers and directors we have had over the years moved many times during their careers with us and therefore gained a wide range of experience across many different parts of the company. They also had jobs during these rotations that involved traveling, as attempting to properly learn about how Radius works without visiting some of our fifty-plus offices is absolutely impossible. Hence, as we now work to regenerate the business and its management for our next period of growth, it is essential to continue with this movement ethos with both our graduates and the rising stars coming up through the structure.

One of the problems we have encountered is that not enough of the senior management we have brought in from outside have understood this particular aspect of people development. I think it's a mentality that you only really learn if you have had to bootstrap a company from its very early beginnings. These managers are often just too used to being spoon-fed in a more corporate environment, in which the people/HR departments make most of the development decisions for them, so they haven't been given the opportunity to build the experience they need.

It is only in the last few years, as our overall people numbers have grown rapidly from just over a thousand before COVID-19 to nearly three thousand today, that this issue has become more pressing and one we have had to take deliberate action to fix. The first thing we did was to specifically identify our group of top talent and not rely on the usually over-positive annual performance nine-box grid scores that many of our management fill out (we have a lot of nines that should have been sixes!). I now trust only a very small group of my team to put this list together, and Lee and I have the ultimate sign-off as to whether individuals finally make it on or not. Once we make sure that they are currently in an appropriate role under a good role model, we then fix a date that is the deadline for their next development rotation. By doing it this way, the clock is always ticking with the divisional leaders, so they know well in advance that they are going to lose one of their good people and can start to work more constructively with their colleagues to get a replacement. We now have the pressure on to change the culture of people who hide and hold on to their good talent just because it makes their life easier!

This way of thinking is really starting to make a difference within all the populations of talent that we have, and it is probably most notice-able within the telematics graduate group, where, hopefully, we are establishing a young team that will help us to become a world-beater in this sector in the next few years.

REGENERATION

With Radius in its new multidivisional form after our intense period of M&A, we now had the job of trying to get all these new businesses to work properly and adopt our core model of organic growth. In every division, we accelerated the taking on of new sales staff as well as driving our overall referral and cross-sell methodology even harder. In addition, we also began to think more about overall branding, as we now had a very large assortment of different trading styles and entities that had been inherited from all these acquisitions.

I remember one day in late 2021 when our head of digital, Colin Peters, came into my office and said that he thought there was a chance for us to buy the domain name radius.com. At that time, it was owned by a major credit card company, which I think had acquired it through a banking business it had bought and then decided not to use. To cut a long story short, after a period of more than a year of negotiation, with much discussion about price, we finally became the proud owner of radius.com on 7th December 2022. This would go on to prove a very pivotal point in our brand consolidation, which today makes us feel a little better about the substantial price we paid at the time. We also got an added bonus, as after the domain had been transferred to our servers, we realized that it had actually been used before and had thousands of existing links, which meant that it immediately got very high organic search rankings in many of our markets.

Following the deal, the first thing we did was to change every employee's email address to our new name and thus introduce all our customers across the world to the Radius brand. We then began the slower process of shutting down many of our smaller websites and migrating them to the new group one, thus hugely simplifying our web presence. We also changed many of our registered company names in each country away from their current mix to the more relevant Radius Business Solutions. In the UK, we made an even better change, as we managed to secure Radius Limited, which was owned by someone who had stopped using it and was willing to sell it for quite a modest £20,000. Today, in just over two years since we launched the new website and branding, we already have more than one hundred and seventy thousand visitors per month from twenty different countries. These visitors already bring us over one thousand and seven hundred converted new customers monthly, and as we continue to build out content and connections, we expect this to keep rising and be one of our strong central pillars for new business generation going forward.

Hopefully, you will have picked up from reading the lessons before each chapter that many of the topics I cover specifically involve people issues. Having good people is the single most important thing a business needs to succeed. This means more than just finding and recruiting good people but also caring for them and giving them the experience they need so that they can develop into future leaders of the business. In the early years, when we were relatively small, it was much easier for me to be close to most of the employees and make all the key people decisions. As we've scaled faster, especially in the last ten years, this has become much harder, which then makes it very important that your senior team and their direct reports learn these skills—otherwise, things can soon get out of control. The cost cutting we did during COVID-19 really showed Lee and me how some departments had become fat and inefficient and how senior managers, as well as some of the leadership team, had lost all grip on doing the people part of their role properly. As we began the work of restructuring and rebuilding these groups, we realized that we needed to invest a lot more time and effort into developing our younger people. If we were going to be able to build this much larger business and meet our longer-term growth aspirations, we couldn't simply recruit our way to success but needed to have a much better balance of homegrown talent.

One of the most significant changes we made was to completely overhaul our fledgling graduate program. Rather than taking just five or six new students on per year, we increased this to more than twenty and widened the number of departments we put them into. We also spent more time and care in our assessment of candidates, as well as giving them the chance to interact with our existing grad group during the process. Finally, the people team focused more on the Russell Group universities and raised the bar on the class of degree we would accept, with the overall effect of improving the quality of the new cohorts as well as the quantity that would now join each September.

We also completely rethought both the job roles we put the new grads into and how our rotation program worked. Instead of them doing short-term project work before moving on to a different group every three months, we now put them straight into a proper full-time role in which they would stay for a minimum period of at least twelve months. This had the effect of us getting much better value out of them as well as giving them enough time to learn their role and feel a real sense of contribution before moving on. We also made sure that we only put them under our best managers so that they had good role models to learn from. One final thing we encourage on our grad program is to have a rotation away from Crewe either within the UK like Sheffield or Leeds or further afield in one of our overseas offices. Today we have four grads in KL, one in Melbourne, one in Essen, and two in Atlanta, with plans to move many more over the year ahead, which is really helping accelerate their development. We are now over two years into this new way of working, and can see that it has energized the whole program and is creating a growing pool of experienced talent that is starting to materially improve the performance of the business.

The second and much larger cohort of people we then turned our attention to was our existing population of talent within the business. Up until now, these people's development had been quite haphazard and very much dependent on the quality of the senior management that was overseeing their particular areas. Given that we hadn't been happy with much of the leadership team, this meant a root and branch review of nearly everyone in the company. This not only showed that many of our top performers had been stuck in their roles for three or four years but also identified a whole new group of talent that we had been completely unaware of. Similar to the graduate program, we then began to move these people into new roles and give them a wider experience of the groups to prepare them for the future so that they could also take on more senior roles in the business.

The "keep moving your people" philosophy I just described has really helped us speed up the development of our graduate population as well as many of our more long-standing people, which should hopefully be of mutual benefit for both the company and them over the long term.

As I alluded to a little earlier in the book, when Lee Everett joined the company over ten years previously, little did I know that, eventually, he would become my successor and take over as CEO of Radius. Following his role as MD of EDC, he slowly took on more responsibility within the fuel division before eventually taking over nearly all its day-to-day running activities. As the new verticals were set up during our acquisition spree, he also picked up most of these, as I started to concentrate a larger proportion of my time specifically within the software and operational parts of the telematics division. Finally, in October 2023, after a handover that had actually been going on for more than two years, he took over as group CEO, another critical milestone in our regeneration process.

So now, at the time of writing this, Lee and I are already starting to see the fruits of all the people development changes that we have been making, as our younger employees are able to take on more responsibility because of the experience they have gained as part of the program. We are therefore hoping that within another two to three more years, we will have an even stronger group of energetic and excited people who can begin to take over from Lee and me, the last of the oldies still standing!

Before I leave the subject of regeneration, I want to touch on one more topic that has really helped us to galvanize our ambitious plans in the telematics space. Following the completion of our new campus head office in 2018, a local developer that had helped us with the project got into financial difficulties, and we got the opportunity to buy the last remaining undeveloped plot of land on our business park. Although at the time we had only just opened a big new building and weren't really in the market for more property, it was at a relatively low price, so we decided to buy it as extra security for the future. It wasn't that long before this move proved right, as within three years, we were already starting to worry about our overall office capacity in Crewe, especially with all the new growth we were now seeing in telematics. With the campus having had such a positive impact on the employees and the overall feeling at Radius, I wanted to try to make this new office (Arden Square) even more modern and different from anything else we had done before.

The first thing I did was sit down with Phil, my architect friend from AEW, and talk through all the different ideas and requirements we had for this new space, and get him to draw up some designs that would fit within the planning permissions that already existed for the plot. For the central atrium area, I had quite an ambitious plan to try to recreate something I had seen in Terminal 3 at Manchester Airport. There, you can look down into the departures area from the business lounge through a glass cylinder that runs up through the center of the building. This has the effect of bringing in light but without the normal noise you get in a central core, thus creating a lot of quiet spaces in a unique visual setting. We agreed on a cone shape that would rise and become narrower on the upper floors, ending with a large glass cap on the roof.

Second, to give the building a real wow factor, I decided that we would have a rooftop bar and outside terrace that we could use as an entertaining space as well as for training and other functions. As this building was going to be for telematics, we also needed a warehouse and packing area for the growing operational demands of storing and sending out all our cameras and tracking devices. This obviously had to be in one of the ground floor wings, where we could also create a delivery area for pallets and larger consignments. For the café concept, I wanted to choose something very different from the campus and settled on a pizzeria with ovens and a serving area laid out exactly like those found in one of my favorite High Street chains. As a final touch on the catering side, I wanted to put a proper coffee shop in the entrance so people could enjoy their favorite coffee in the morning as they came in through the door to work. The final thing that was needed was a theme, similar to the Doctor Who one that definitely causes a bit of discussion and fun on the campus. For this, I chose another one of my childhood TV favorites, *Star Wars*, so I asked Phil to put some different colored lighting into the central core and sky bar areas. We also had a bit of unused office space in the roof area, where I suggested to Phil and the interior designers that we create a special meeting room along the theme of the Millennium Falcon. As a final touch, I ordered a life-size C-3PO for the entrance hall, a carbon freeze of Han Solo for the new training area, and a smaller Yoda model to sit on the bar! With everything agreed, we went to tender and, within six months or so, cut the first bit of ground and started building.

In January 2024, about eighteen months later, we took possession of our shiny new Arden Square office and started to move the first group of our telematics employees in as we fired up the pizza ovens for the first time. On 4th April (we couldn't manage to schedule May the Fourth!), we were very lucky to get Martin Johnson, England's Rugby World Cup–winning captain, to make a short speech and cut the ribbon on our roof terrace. We did have a few of our team dressed as stormtroopers, and I think Martin would have made a great Darth Vader if we had asked him. With the opening completed success-fully, it was now down to the hard work of using this fabulous new facility to help kick-start this division into its next phase of growth, which was going to be critical if Radius was to deliver on its overall long-term plans.

Across the globe, many other office improvement projects had been completed. In the previous two years, we had opened new offices in Milan and Essen; moved to new, bigger, and more modern locations in Sheffield, Ipswich, Leeds, Dundalk, Lille, and Caldas da Rainha; taken a second floor in Ronse; and even started in a new country with an Auckland location. It is a never-ending task of growing and improving facilities to try to make them as modern and friendly as possible to help us continue to attract and keep the best talent. It definitely feels a long way away from those early years above the hairdresser's in Holmes Chapel!

LESSON 24

GET YOUR REPORTING STRUCTURE RIGHT.

Another regular problem we encounter when we take on a new manager or director who has worked at a large corporation is that they often have little idea or concept of good reporting lines. Lee, now the CEO, and I are constantly fighting to keep order and control in the business against these people who have grown up in their previous jobs with either matrix reporting or very long, stringy structures. Most of them are simply oblivious to the deficiencies this brings, as they have always worked in that type of environment and just accept it as the norm. When I am trying to fix things that aren't working in the business, this is one of the first places I look to make changes that will hopefully then improve the operations and performance of the teams.

This lesson comes near the end of the book, as it is an issue that has gradually crept up on us over the last few years as our head count has grown into the thousands. It is also one that is made significantly more complex when you have made twenty-five acquisitions over a fairly short period of time.

So let us start with matrix reporting. As I hope you have picked up from the previous chapters, the beating heart of our business is telesales. For this area to operate well, you have to have very defined targets that disseminate from the divisional owner, right down through the organization, and finally to each individual salesperson on the front line. The ownership of these targets has to be crystal clear so that you always have a neck to wring if performance is not where it needs to be. Away from sales, whether it's developing a new piece of software, monitoring credit limits, sending out weekly invoices, paying suppliers, or developing a new digital marketing brochure, you still have to follow the same principle and have a very clear hierarchy of responsibility. Matrix reporting does not give you this clear definition and leads to an environment in which people do not take individual ownership for particular tasks, which is a critical part of good business performance.

So, how many direct reports should a person be able to manage in a good structure? Well, my view after thirty years is that it should be a minimum of four and probably a maximum of eight. This isn't always possible, especially when you are down at the lower part of an organization, but it still needs to be a guiding principle that you think about as you add people to any structure. This type of hierarchy allows you to spread the load of responsibilities across several shoulders, which should also then give you time to be able to take a more strategic view as well as regularly dig down into the details of each of the areas to keep checking for problems and fixing them.

Normally, the central functions, such as finance, credit, IT, marketing, and people, are where poor structure warning bells first begin to ring. They either can't answer the question of who a particular person's boss is or draw out a structure that is so long and stringy, in which there is even sometimes one-on-one reporting with ten people still sitting below this single person in the structure. My simple comment to the director of that function is that they need to get rid of one of these two people, as they must be doing the same job! I sometimes think that if I left some of the worst culprits to themselves, we would end up with a structure of over twenty people deep, making that division extremely inefficient as well as making effective communication of problems almost impossible.

One final factor that also makes us very different from a large corporation is the speed and regularity with which we change our reporting lines. Optimizing our people to make sure we are utilizing our best resources in the most important areas of the business is critical when you are scaling quickly. What is right one day is not necessarily right the next, and you always need to be trying to do the best thing for the business while at the same time developing your talent. Your managers need to understand the very important principle of "the business comes first," even if they think they are sometimes losing some responsibility as you try to optimize reporting lines. Once the good ones understand why you are making the changes and hopefully see the positive effects after you have made them, they will get onside and start making these decisions for themselves in the future.

So, for those technologists among you, I thought I would ask ChatGPT the same question, given that I am trying to learn a little about how

AI can start to help improve Radius. I decided to ask a very open question with virtually no prompts, so it was a proper test!

> **Question:** What is the best reporting structure for a company with 3,000 people?
>
> **ChatGPT response:** Determining the best reporting structure for a company with 3,000 people depends on various factors, including the nature of the business, management efficiency, and communication effectiveness. However, a balanced approach typically involves a reporting structure that maintains manageability and operational efficiency.
>
> One common method is to use a hierarchical structure with a reasonable span of control, often between 5–10 direct reports per manager. Let's explore an optimal span of control and calculate the number of layers required.
>
> **Assume an average span of control of 6.**
>
> Layer 1   (Group CEO!) 1 person
> Layer 2   6 People
> Layer 3   36 People
> Layer 4   216 People
> Layer 5   1,296 People
> Layer 6   7,776 People
>
> Given the above calculation, a span of control of 6 results in 7,776 people at the 6th layer, which exceeds the 3,000 people company size. Therefore, a span of control slightly smaller or different structuring might be more appropriate.

Iterative calculation with a slightly adjusted span.

Let's try an average span of control of 5.

Layer 1   (Group CEO) 1 Person

Layer 2   5 People

Layer 3   25 People

Layer 4   125 People

Layer 5   625 People

Layer 6   3125 People

A span of control of 5 results in 3125 people at the 6th layer, which is close to 3000.

Recommended Span of Control and Layers

Considering practical management and communication efficiency:

Span of control   5

Layers of management   6

This structure ensures: Manageable direct reports each and efficient communication.

So there we are! Maybe I should have asked ChatGPT to write the entire book to complete it in an afternoon in a much more eloquent way! I daren't ask it another question, or I will feel redundant, so I will leave that to you. Anyway, my minimum of four and maximum of eight that I suggested at the beginning of this section wasn't too far off the mark.

THE FUTURE

It was at a board meeting in late 2020 when David from Inflexion first mentioned that it was coming to the point in its investment cycle at which we should begin the process for finding an exit for Inflexion. PE normally invests for a period of three to five years, and we were fast approaching the third anniversary of our time together. It would probably take us at least twelve months to run a full process, so we needed to begin work now. The first thing we did was appoint a banker, and after several presentations from potential parties, we settled on Goldman Sachs (GS), which showed some very high valuations for Radius at the top end of its projections.

We started to prepare a new five-year plan as well as pull together everything we would need for our presentations and diligence work, and we targeted the summer of 2021 as the time to begin talking to potential new investors. Once that date arrived, it was back to the streets of Mayfair and Marylebone, seeing multiple PE companies per day for fireside chats before facing the familiar questions about the future of fossil fuels and what the energy transition would mean for our fuel business. It felt a little like déjà vu when, in 2016, the US funds, many of which were based out in the high-tech but sometimes sheltered environment of California, were questioning whether we would still exist in five years' time. Well, they definitely got that one wrong, as we had almost doubled our volumes since then, and our fuel business was in good health, with many good years still ahead of us before the transition will really begin to kick in. The feedback from the meetings also felt very much like before, as I think our bankers started to push a little too hard, especially given the size and minority element of our proposed transaction.

A few potential buyers emerged, and we began to have some more positive discussions at that point, before suddenly, on 24th February 2022, everything changed. Russia invaded Ukraine, and the world was suddenly in turmoil. The energy markets spiked enormously as the crisis grew, and PE investors everywhere took a backward step on deals, preferring to wait and see how this new, unprecedented situation would unfold before committing their capital. The UK political crisis ensued with the appointment of Liz Truss on 5th September, quickly followed by a budget that sent the financial markets into turmoil, too, which effectively moved PE from its current speed of very slow to one of complete stop.

As the year began to draw to a close, all this news meant that we were not going to get the deal we had planned done anytime soon, despite the fact that our own performance was on track and our banks were still fully supportive of financing a new deal. At some point in early November, we officially called a halt to Project Rainbow with GS and decided to take a step back to think about what alternatives we had. One thing that came to mind quite quickly was whether it was possible for the company to buy the shares back and utilize the additional debt that our core set of banks had agreed on. We were obviously not going to be able to finance buying all the shares, as it would be too big a number, but we thought it was probably possible to go partway and buy half of Inflexion's 24 percent stake. Just before Christmas, I met up with David and put forward our proposal, and he agreed to come back early in the new year once they had a chance to think it through. So in early January, after plenty of wrangling over price and terms, we shook hands on a deal and got the teams working on making sure everything was in place. We eventually signed this new deal on 1st June, and after a period of just over ten weeks while we waited for FCA clearance, we completed it on 10th August 2023. Similar to six years previously, I got plenty of thank-you calls that day from many of the LTIP shareholders who had shared in the £24 million we had paid out to the management team. This deal added quite a few new names to the number of millionaires created since the start of UK Fuels back in 1990.

Although we had agreed as part of Project Rainbow to move many of our remaining committed contractual dates with Inflexion out by a further year, it would be less than twelve months before we would start thinking about how we would try to finance the purchase of Inflexion's remaining stake. So at the point of writing these final couple of chapters, the first discussions about "Project Falcon" are underway, so hopefully, by the time you read this, we will have come to the end of our period of partnership with Inflexion and started a new phase in the history of Radius. If I ever put pen to paper again, the whole PE experience would make a book on its own, and I have already had a few ideas for a working title. However, it's been an immense effort to do this one, so I will not be rushing to start again soon!

Just over a year after my handover to Lee, I am starting to feel a little less pressure in my day-to-day workload, which is probably why, after nearly four years, I have finally been able to put pen to paper and push on with finishing this book. Lee also reached a big milestone in his life this year—his fiftieth birthday. A little like me for my fiftieth, he was planning a mini seven-week sabbatical and round-the-world trip and had kindly asked me to step in while he was away, which I'm not sure the rest of the team was looking forward to. Anyway, given that it was now a long time since one of our famous fiftieth surprises, I thought it important to give him an old-style UK Fuels birthday trip, so I started to put my thinking cap on to come up with a new idea to catch him out!

LEE'S FIFTIETH

After considering three or four alternatives, I settled on something that I had also never done before: an Ibiza Closing Party. Now all we needed to do was to find a slot in Lee's diary that would work and a very cunning plan to make sure he didn't suspect what we were up to. For the plan, I settled on the tried-and-tested technique we had used with Malcolm and Steve of asking a very important supplier or customer to suggest a meeting on the day we were planning for the trip. Nick and Kathryn from Vodafone kindly agreed to help and sent an appropriate email to Lee, suggesting we get together for a strategy session on 2nd October, so the trap was set. Fiona Lee's EA then booked lunch at Beso Beach for the afternoon, followed by some VIP tickets for Dimitri Vegas, who was playing at Ushuaïa in the evening. I then organized a private plane with NetJets so that we could leave very early in the morning and give ourselves plenty of time to check in to the hotel and have a few drinks before heading off for lunch.

Next, I drew up a list of a few of Lee's closest and oldest work friends to invite and ended up with a small group of eight people whom I then let into the secret so that everyone could organize their travel plans. We also all agreed to buy a set of beach co-ords to wear (which most of us had to Google to understand what they were!) so that we would hopefully blend in with the younger clubbers.

So as Lee sat down for dinner in Manchester with Kathryn from Vodafone and Chris, the CRO of our emerging businesses division,

Kathryn suddenly pulled out a card I had written, which she gave to Lee while Chris filmed on his iPhone to catch his reaction. The card said, "Happy Birthday from Bill and Eleanor, you need to be at my house tomorrow morning for 5:45 am!" So after the meal, Lee headed back to the hotel for a relatively early night, having called his wife and found out that we hadn't even trusted her with the secret of what we were going to do.

The following morning, when Lee arrived, Frank, Paddy, Jonathan, Saul, and I were all waiting at the house, eating fresh sausage baps, and he was still none the wiser about the day ahead. When a black minibus turned up in the drive, the penny dropped that we would be flying somewhere. This also explained why Fiona had called him a couple of days earlier, saying he needed to bring his passport into the office that day so we could get some important documents legally witnessed. Even at the airport, we managed to keep the destination secret, as I asked the two pilots to join in with the deception. So as we took off from Manchester at quarter to seven in the morning, already sipping our first glasses of champagne, and one of the pilots gave a forecast for the weather in Shannon, Lee still didn't know that we would be heading south for sunnier climes. It was only when we were finally settled onto our flight path and he could see the inboard monitor that Lee knew we weren't going to Ireland but much more likely Spain, as we were now heading due south. So, over the next two hours, as we drank through the stock of chilled champagne and beer, Lee had several attempts at guessing where we would be landing. All these proved wrong, and it was only as we were on our final approach to Majorca, far out on our left-hand side, that the destination became clear, and we got out his present of a co-ord for him to unwrap. While we all had cheap ones from ASOS, Fiona had treated Lee to a much nicer quality one from Reiss, but it wasn't even matching, which we all thought was a bit of a cheat!

Anyway, we had a fabulous day at Beso Beach, followed by a trip to Ushuaïa, where Matt and Nick, who had traveled separately, joined us as a further part of the surprise to make up the eight. The night finished relatively early for some of the team that had overindulged; however, a few of us, including me and Saul, managed to make a late-night stop at KFC before eventually heading to bed. Needless to say, it was a very quiet journey home the next day, with everyone sleeping all the way and not a drop of alcohol drunk. Lee's birthday trip will definitely be remembered as one of the best ever and up there with the famous Majorca and Dublin ones for Steve, Malcolm, and Tabby.

LESSON 25

NEVER STOP LEARNING.

So you made it through to the final lesson, and as I said at the beginning, I hope that some of them have struck a chord with you, even if you haven't agreed with them all. This feels like a good place to end, as it's probably one of the main reasons I am still as excited about the business today as I was when I first started building the original fourteen-site bunker network back in 1990. Let me try to explain in a few paragraphs why I think continuous learning is so important, as well as why it has helped keep me so invigorated.

Probably the biggest benefit I have had from all the traveling I have done and all the different businesses I have been to see across the world is all the new things that I have learned from all of the different people I've met. What you begin to understand is that there are so many different verticals and opportunities in every industry, and in many cases, individual people and companies might special-ize in only one or two of these. They become experts in their own areas, in which they have often found unique ways of adding value to a particular product or solution. Therefore, by visiting all these different businesses across a vast array of sectors, I have built up a unique set of knowledge that I can then apply across Radius. These small incremental changes (remember kaizen) have given us a material advantage and helped us grow faster in often very competitive markets.

For example, in telecoms, it might be a way of maximizing the sale of security software with each handset, or in telematics, how to best associate Bluetooth tags with vehicle trackers, or in fuel, how to use futures pricing to increase margins and cash flow from the bunker network. To give you an idea of the amount of traveling I have done to build this experience since we started our telematics division in 2016, I have visited over twenty industry competitors in five different countries and six camera and tracker hardware manufacturers across the USA, China, Lithuania, South Korea, and Denmark and had meetings with five global network SIM suppliers, as well as numerous installation companies that help fit the equipment into the customers' vehicles. It is this accumulated knowledge and experience that are central to driving our hardware and software strategy as we aim to become one of the world's leading players over the next five to ten years. Evolving technology, especially AI in the telematics camera business, means that new ideas and concepts are constantly appearing, so you can never sit back and think that you have the perfect product or solution, as there are always new things to learn.

Individuals who don't travel and don't have a learning mindset do not realize how little they actually know about their own industry because they work in quite a narrow area and have not had much exposure to the outside world.

It is therefore very important to always think you're closer to the bottom of the learning ladder (a three out of ten) rather than the top (a nine out of ten) so you're always listening to new concepts and new ideas, even if you don't believe that they all hold water!

CONCLUSION

So more than four years after I woke up on that morning in January 2021 thinking about chapters for a book, I've finally come to the end. I have learned so many lessons over the years and tried in this book to bring out the ones that have been most important to me. I hope you have found that some of them have prompted you to think a little differently about these topics and maybe give them more importance as you plot your own exciting journey in the world of business. I also hope you have enjoyed some of the Radius story and got a bit of a feeling for some of the fun we have had, as well as all the hard work we have had to put in.

The order of the lessons in the book is based on how the story of Radius unfolded from the first days back in 1990 up to the present day. But as you apply any or all of these to your own leadership or entrepreneurship, it might help to think of them under two broad groupings: communication and culture, and business strategy.

The first of the two groupings revolves around people and people management and represents where I am spending the biggest amount of my time today as we take the next steps to try to scale the business from having three thousand people to five thousand, and potentially ten thousand.

COMMUNICATION AND CULTURE

- Lesson 1: Care for every pound as if it's your own.
- Lesson 8: Relentless performance management.
- Lesson 10: Tell your boss.
- Lesson 11: Ask your boss.
- Lesson 12: Don't believe anyone; test everything.
- Lesson 14: Think everything's going badly.
- Lesson 15: Never blame the market.
- Lesson 16: Don't wear rose-tinted spectacles.
- Lesson 20: Reward over the long term.
- Lesson 22: Work from the office.
- Lesson 23: Keep moving your people.
- Lesson 24: Get your reporting structure right.
- Lesson 25: Never stop learning.

This second grouping is more specific business lessons I have learned over the years that cover operations, sales, growth, and other aspects of strategy.

BUSINESS STRATEGY

- Lesson 2: Start before you're ready.
- Lesson 3: Sell what you've got.
- Lesson 4: Compartmentalize.
- Lesson 5: Do more of what's going well and stop when it isn't.
- Lesson 6: Don't spend too much time and effort hunting whales.
- Lesson 7: Make lots of small improvements.
- Lesson 9: Do things in the right order.
- Lesson 13: You can have volume and margin.
- Lesson 17: Organic growth is best.
- Lesson 18: Bide your time.
- Lesson 19: Own your own customers.
- Lesson 21: Don't let software projects grow legs.

Thank You

My career, especially all these years building Radius, has been an interesting and exciting journey for me, especially seeing the transition from an analogue world with printed materials and post to the incredibly fast and boundless digital world of today. AI is going to change this even more over the coming years, so we are living in very exciting times.

I really wish you the best of luck with your career and hope that you are lucky enough to find something you can be as passionate about at work as I have been about Radius.

Thank you for reading.

—Bill